DATE DUE

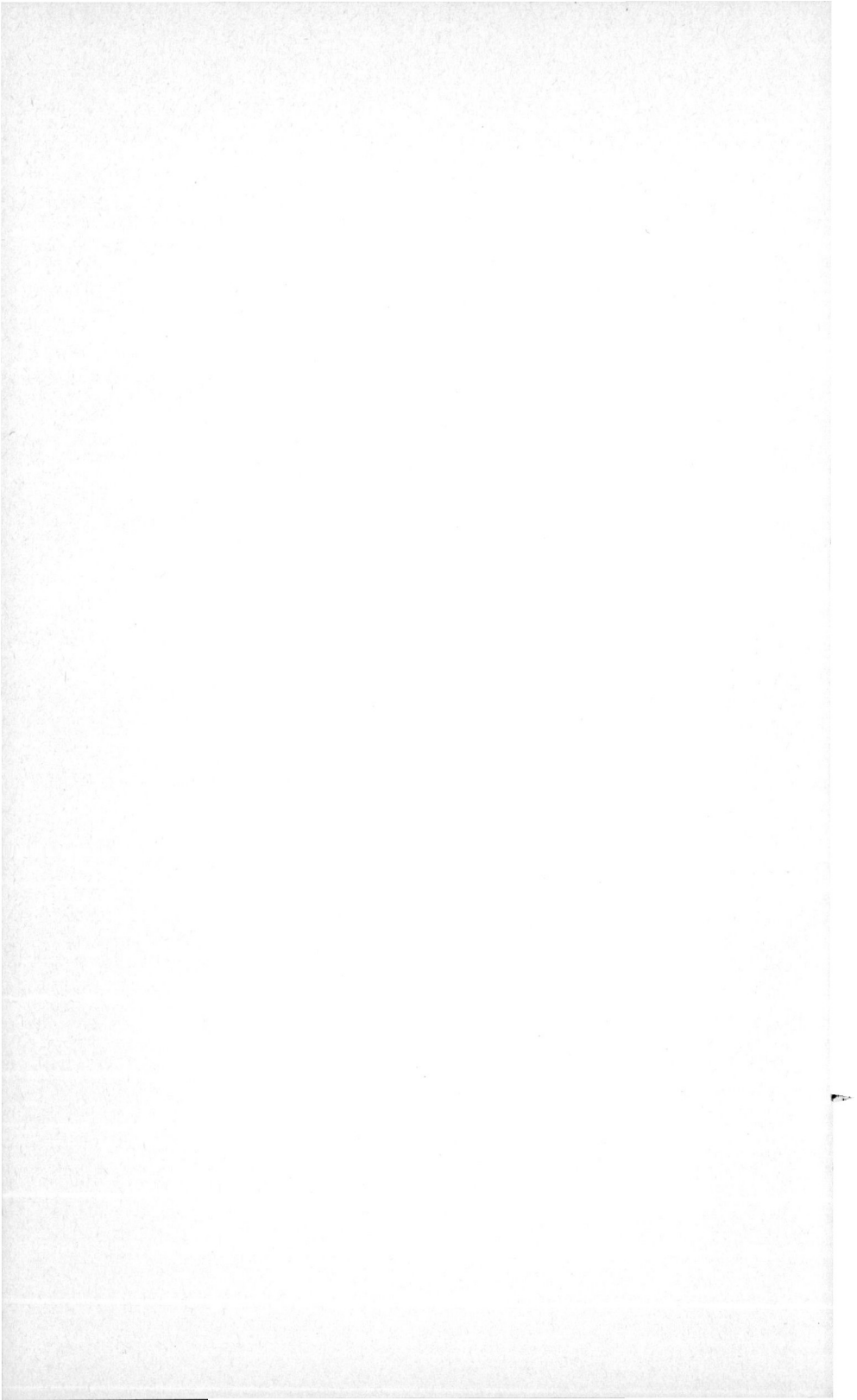

MUIRHEAD LIBRARY OF PHILOSOPHY

An admirable statement of the aims of the Library of Philosophy was provided by the first editor, the late Professor J. H. Muirhead, in his description of the original programme printed in Erdmann's *History of Philosophy* under the date 1890. This was slightly modified in subsequent volumes to take the form of the following statement:

'The Muirhead Library of Philosophy was designed as a contribution to the History of Modern Philosophy under the heads: first of Different Schools of Thought—Sensationalist, Realist, Idealist, Intuitivist; secondly of different Subjects—Psychology, Ethics, Political Philosophy, Theology. While much had been done in England in tracing the course of evolution in nature, history, economics, morals and religion, little had been done in tracing the development of thought on these subjects. Yet "the evolution of opinion is part of the whole evolution".

'By the co-operation of different writers in carrying out this plan it was hoped that a thoroughness and completeness of treatment, otherwise unattainable, might be secured. It was believed also that from writers mainly British and American fuller consideration of English Philosophy than it had hitherto received might be looked for. In the earlier series of books containing, among others, Bosanquet's *History of Aesthetic*, Pfleiderer's *Rational Theology since Kant*, Albee's *History of English Utilitarianism*, Bonar's *Philosophy and Political Economy*, Brett's *History of Psychology*, Ritchie's *Natural Rights*, these objects were to a large extent effected.

'In the meantime original work of a high order was being produced both in England and America by such writers as Bradley, Stout, Bertrand Russell, Baldwin, Urban, Montague, and others, and a new interest in foreign works, German, French and Italian, which had either become classical or were attracting public attention, had developed. The scope of the Library thus became extended into something more international, and it is entering on the fifth decade of its existence in the hope that it may contribute to that mutual understanding between countries which is so pressing a need of the present time.'

The need which Professor Muirhead stressed is no less pressing today, and few will deny that philosophy has much to do with enabling us to meet it, although no one, least of all Muirhead himself, would regard that as the sole, or even the main, object of philosophy. As Professor Muirhead continues to lend the distinction of his name to the

Library of Philosophy it seemed not inappropriate to allow him to recall us to these aims in his own words. The emphasis on the history of thought also seemed to me very timely; and the number of important works promised for the Library in the very near future augur well for the continued fulfilment, in this and other ways, of the expectations of the original editor.

H. D. LEWIS

MUIRHEAD LIBRARY OF PHILOSOPHY

General Editor: H. D. Lewis
Professor of History and Philosophy of Religion in the University of London

Action by SIR MALCOLM KNOX
The Analysis of Mind BERTRAND RUSSELL 8th impression
Clarity is Not Enough by H. D. LEWIS
Coleridge as Philosopher by J. H. MUIRHEAD 3rd impression
The Commonplace Book of G. E. Moore edited by C. LEWY
Contemporary American Philosophy edited by G. P. ADAMS and W. P. MONTAGUE 2nd impression
Contemporary British Philosophy First and second series edited by J. H. MUIRHEAD 2nd impression
Contemporary British Philosophy Third series edited by H. D. LEWIS 2nd impression
Contemporary Indian Philosophy edited by RADHAKRISHNAN and J. H. MUIRHEAD 2nd edition
The Discipline of the Cave by J. N. FINDLAY
Doctrine and Argument in Indian Philosophy by NINIAN SMART
Essays in Analysis by ALICE AMBROSE
Ethics by NICOLAI HARTMANN translated by STANTON COIT 3 vols
The Foundations of Metaphysics in Science by ERROL E. HARRIS
Freedom and History by H. D. LEWIS
The Good Will: A Study in the Coherence Theory of Goodness by H. J. PATON
Hegel: A Re-Examination by J. N. FINDLAY
Hegel's Science of Logic translated by W. H. JOHNSTON and L. G. STRUTHERS 2 vols 3rd impression
History of Æsthetic by B. BOSANQUET 2nd edition 5th impression
History of English Utilitarianism by E. ALBEE 2nd impression
History of Psychology by G. S. BRETT edited by R. S. PETERS abridged one-volume edition 2nd edition
Human Knowledge by BERTRAND RUSSELL 4th impression
A Hundred Years of British Philosophy by RODOLF METZ translated by J. H. HARVEY, T. E. JESSOP, HENRY STURT 2nd impression
Ideas: A General Introduction to Pure Phenomenology by EDMUND HUSSERL translated by W. R. BOYCE GIBSON 3rd impression
Imagination by E. J. FURLONG
Indian Philosophy by RADHAKRISHNAN 2 vols revised 2nd edition
Introduction to Mathematical Philosophy by BERTRAND RUSSELL 2nd edition 10th impression

Muirhead Library of Philosophy

EDITED BY H. D. LEWIS

ACTION

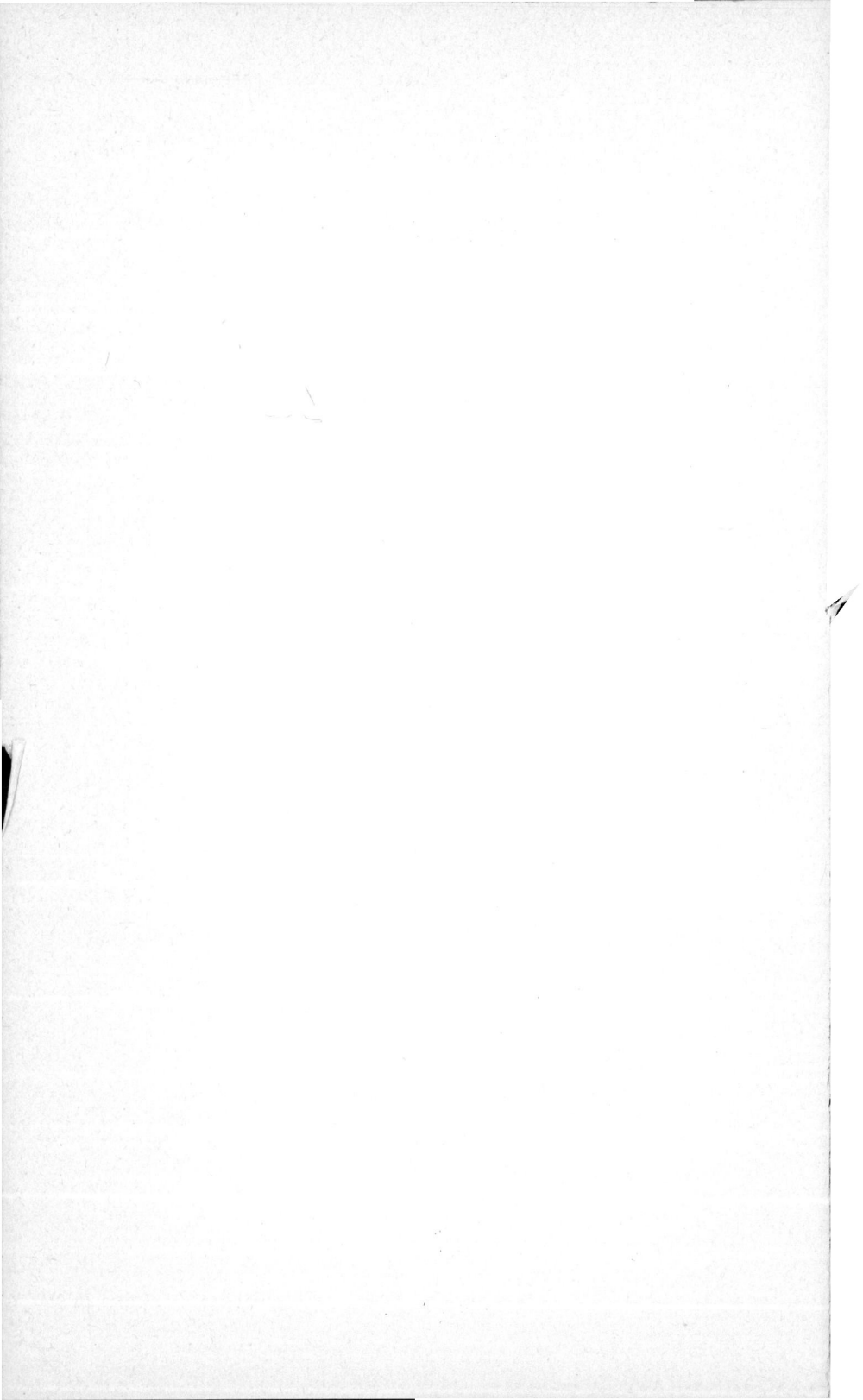

ACTION

BY

SIR MALCOLM KNOX

LONDON . GEORGE ALLEN & UNWIN LTD
NEW YORK . HUMANITIES PRESS

FIRST PUBLISHED IN 1968

PRINTED IN GREAT BRITAIN
in 11 point Imprint type, 1 point leaded
BY UNWIN BROTHERS LIMITED
WOKING AND LONDON

TO MY BROTHER
ANDREW MARSHALL KNOX

PREFACE

This book is a revised version of Gifford Lectures delivered in the University of Aberdeen. The general subject was *Action and Belief*. This volume contains what I had to say on the first of these nouns. From various quarters I have received the criticism that the order of exposition ought to have been reversed. I could have replied that *Belief and Action* was the title of a well-known book by the late Lord Samuel, but I prefer to justify my choice by appealing to certain quotations: 'If any man will do his will, he shall know of the doctrine'; 'Action will furnish belief' (A. H. Clough); 'Action will take you a step higher, and belief will thereby be strengthened' (John Oman).

Perhaps I ought to have substituted 'Faith' for 'Belief', because it was religious belief which I had in mind. I have nothing to say about a belief, e.g. that it will rain tomorrow. This book ends with some questions about the connection between action, as the kernel of ethics, and religious belief. The further question of what faith can reasonably be accepted by a man who has heard the call of duty and who has been brought up in the western world and therefore in a Christian civilization is faced in the second course of lectures which is to be delivered in 1968 and which I hope to publish separately in due course.

A few years ago, when I was introducing a Gifford Lecturer to a St Andrews audience, I said that appointment to a Gifford Lectureship was one of the two highest honours which a scholar could receive. I was therefore astonished when, a few months later, I received an invitation to a Gifford Lectureship in the University of Aberdeen. For this invitation I am most profoundly grateful, and to those responsible for issuing it I tender my heartiest thanks. Recognition of the fact that while I was engaged in administrative duties I tried not to desert scholarship was something which touched me deeply and in which I still take great pride.

Nowadays a man called to a Gifford Lectureship must humble himself before his predecessors. He cannot have failed to read their lectures in published form or to compare the poverty of his achievement with the riches which they have showered on their listeners and their readers. I am aware that I cannot draw the bow of the many distinguished men who have lectured on this foundation in the four Scottish Universities. But I accepted appointment because I thought I could expound the convictions resulting from the reading and reflections of a lifetime and so comply with what Lord Gifford intended. His will prescribed *first* that the subject was to be Natural Theology, interpreted in the widest sense, and including, in particular, the study of ethics, *secondly* that the lectures were to be 'popular', and *thirdly*, that the subject was to be treated, as astronomy or chemistry are, without reliance on revelation.

I will say something about each of these prescriptions. First, my subject was not so much chosen as forced on me by my own interests and studies over the past forty-five years. For seventeen years I professed moral philosophy, and one of my major interests outside my professional work has been the ecclesiastical history and theology of the last 150 years. It was natural therefore that I should take advantage of Lord Gifford's specific mention of morals and begin there, and then proceed to religion within the bounds of reason alone; and it is part of my thesis that this second topic is by no means unconnected with the first.

Secondly, what Lord Gifford meant by saying that he wished the lectures on his foundation to be 'popular' is to be discovered from the public lectures which he himself gave on topics allied to Natural Theology. These privately printed lectures are 'popular' in the sense that they were prepared not for specialists but for the intelligent general reader with an interest in the great problems of human life, its nature and destiny. This example I have attempted to follow. I hope to interest those general readers who retain an interest in the traditional problems of philosophy and in the fundamentals of religious belief, but who are not satisfied either by the modern reduction of philosophy to linguistic analysis or by the confident assertions of orthodox dogmatics. Many of my own assertions will appear to be no less confident, and I accept this forthcoming criticism, but I think that the need of the hour is for the assertion of positive beliefs. To voice all the necessary qualifications and reservations would be incompatible with my desire to interest the non-specialists for whom my lectures were primarily prepared.

Thirdly, there is a ban on revelation. This, in the sense that Lord Gifford imposed it, I accept. In this I am at the opposite end of the spectrum from a former Gifford Lecturer in Aberdeen, Karl Barth. When Archimedes, seated in his bath, solved his problem and shouted εὕρηκα, he would have been equally well understood if he had said that the solution had been revealed to him. All discovery is a revelation, and this is no less true if the discovery is preceded by an effort to discover, just as after climbing a hill the view is revealed to our eyes. There is, however, another sense of revelation, as when, gazing at a sunset, we say with the Psalmist, 'the heavens declare the glory of God', or re-echo the words of the poet, 'dull would he be of soul to pass by a sight so touching in its majesty'. (It passes my comprehension how this could be said of that sight by one who lived amongst the hills.) The colours of the sunset, and the musical instruments and the sounds issuing from them as we listen to great music, are natural in the sense that they are part of a material world. But they are not merely natural phenomena. As a young man, Hegel wrote a diary of his journey in the Bernese Oberland, in which he speaks of the mountains as unimpressive. They are just *there*, he says. They had no meaning for him and revealed nothing beyond themselves. Others think differently: the glory of the sunset, the sublimity of the symphony, the majesty of the everlasting hills are in the world, but not of it. They are, to those who discern it, a revelation of something beyond themselves. No merely scientific or naturalistic account of these phenomena can satisfy anyone who has had the experience of the glory, the sublimity, the majesty, and reflected on what that experience is and implies. Discovery is revelation: and the beauty of the sky and the hills, the beauty of art, reveals something beyond itself. So interpreted I can understand revelation. But the notion of a *special* revelation of religious truth I have no difficulty in renouncing. I am afraid that I am in sympathy with Francis Newman when he says that 'it is assumed by believers in a special revelation that God speaks from without and that what we call reason and conscience are not his mode of commanding and revealing his will'.[1] This assumption seems to me to be incompatible with a doctrine of the Holy Spirit. Perhaps I can claim support from another former Gifford Lecturer in Aberdeen, Dr Clement Webb, who writes: 'Reason apprehends what is revealed, but what is revealed is what reason can apprehend.'[2]

[1] *Phases of Faith*, p. 93, 1874 edn.
[2] *Problems in the Relations of God and Man* (London, 1911), p. 27. Cf. also: 'The language of . . . reason and conscience which speaks in God's creatures is the only universal language in which he can reveal himself to all men.' H. S. Reimarus in Lessing's *Werke* (Berlin, 1956), vol. vii, p. 710.

My theme—a study of moral experience, its development and manifestations, and then of what is to many a contradiction in terms, a reasonable religion which I think it implies—had of course already been treated by former Gifford Lecturers, and indeed my scientific colleagues have sometimes suggested that all that can be said on these topics, and perhaps more than all, has been said already. In defence, I can but appeal to the French writer who said that: 'It has all been said before. But no-one remembers. So it must be said all over again.' Since I make no claim to originality, I must acknowledge at the start whence my views have been mainly derived.

The Gifford Lecturer who, so far as I know, came nearest my own topic, was W. G. de Burgh whose lectures in St Andrews on *From Morality to Religion* I heard and have always valued. But his approach to the subject was different from mine. He knew and believed more. While I would not wish to minimize my debt to him, not only for the lectures but for many friendly discussions, my debt, so far as this book is concerned, is far greater, first to Hegel, to whom I was first introduced by my father, a pupil of Edward Caird, and to whose works and their translation I have devoted so much of my energy in the last twenty-five years. Secondly there is my debt to John Oman, whose *Natural and Supernatural* is one of the very few philosophical masterpieces in English (or should I say Scottish?) philosophy in this century, and thirdly to my own tutor in Oxford, R. G. Collingwood, to whom indeed I owe more than I could ever express, even were I Chrysostom himself. My debt to him is owed for all he taught me as my tutor, for his lectures, for his publications, for our conversations, for his letters during the nearly twenty years of our friendship, and for his *reliquiae* which I was privileged to read but which his instructions forbade me to publish. Much of his teaching I have adopted; some of his phraseology has become second nature to me. Although these lectures may owe more to Hegel than to him, they could never have been written at all if it had not been for the stimulus of his teaching and the wealth of ideas to which he opened my mind.

These three mentors have taught me most of my philosophy; their influence is discernible on nearly every page that I have written. If my reflections on what I have learnt from them have led me to depart in certain respects from their teaching, I think that this is what they would have wished and indeed expected. I infer this, so far as Hegel is concerned, for no one taught more clearly than he did, despite what histories of philosophy say, that a philosophy is a child of its time, comprehending what spirit has achieved up to now, and that a new form of life and therefore a new philosophy must emerge later. My friend Collingwood always thanked me for criticism and held that a pupil was unfaithful to his master if he merely re-echoed him.

No one is more conscious than I am of the imperfections of what I have written. Often what has been dealt with in a paragraph ought to have taken pages. Many is the topic that should have been discussed, though it goes unmentioned. But I have decided to publish instead of spending time on a further revision which might go on indefinitely. To be a perfectionist is to fear criticism and to be reluctant to acknowledge error.

That what I have written is old-fashioned is incontestable. It belongs to the pre-Wittgenstein era, and indeed smacks of the nineteenth century. This is not surprising. Not only is my mind steeped in Hegel, but I read and re-read Scott and Trollope, Balzac and Stendhal, and cannot find my feet in modern novelists; and I never tire of Chopin, Schumann, Brahms, and Liszt, whereas the music of the twentieth century is above my head.

I am indebted to The Clarendon Press for permission to quote from N. Tinbergen's *Study of Instinct* and from R. Robinson's *An Atheist's Values*; and to Messrs G. Allen and Unwin for permission to quote from B. Blanshard: *Reason and Goodness*, J. Laird: *An Enquiry into Moral Notions*, W. G. Maclagan: *Theological Frontier of Ethics*, H. J. Paton: *The Modern Predicament*, and C. H. Waddington: *Science and Ethics*.

Finally I record my special gratitude, first to my wife, without whose encouragement and aid for more than half my lifetime my work could never have been done; secondly to many friends in Aberdeen, for their cordial hospitality; thirdly to Mrs G. R. McKie, who in three summers welcomed my wife and me to her charming house at Mellon Udrigill, where these chapters were first written and twice revised; and fourthly to our friend Miss J. S. M. Allan, who typed the lectures twice.

T. M. KNOX

Crieff
September 1967

B

Postscript

A few days before the final proofs had to be returned, Professor H. J. Paton did me the great kindness of reading them, in spite of his difficult journey back from America. He saved me from many errors and would have saved me from more if he had read the book at an earlier stage. In recording my gratitude to him now, I would also record my gratitude for all the help which he has given to me for the last forty-five years.

T. M. KNOX

Crieff

March 1968

CONTENTS

page

CHAPTER 1

FROM NATURE TO MIND

1. LEVELS OF MORAL EXPERIENCE

In the days before I became a teacher of philosophy, I was in business and for a time was responsible in London for the management of a group of plantations which I occasionally visited in West Africa. In that capacity I became convinced that the financial loss on one of the plantations was due to inefficient management. I recalled the manager to London and dismissed him. This experience forced me to rethink much that I had read and learnt about moral philosophy.

My difficulty did not arise from a conflict between reason and inclination; it was that of choosing between two duties, when to fulfil one was to fail in the other. What struck me most powerfully, however, was that the two duties were not on the same level, like those examples given in many text books on ethics, when the duty of keeping a promise to a friend conflicts with the duty of giving immediate aid to another. My problem was a conflict between two different levels of experience, the level of economic life and the level of personal relationships.

To become acutely conscious of different levels of moral experience was to realize that the conditions of human life are such that men simply cannot help doing wrong; circumstances force them to adopt, to act on, and, paradoxical though it may seem, to act conscientiously on, a moral standard lower than that of the ideal. I was quite clear that it was my duty, as a salaried employee whose job it was to make my plantations pay, to discharge the manager. And yet, I asked myself, can it be a duty to reduce a married man with a family to penury—for his chances of alternative suitable employment were slender at that date? The duty of loving my neighbour could not be fulfilled; involved in a large business organization, I had to act on its standards and, in this instance, impersonally. Only in the Kingdom of Heaven could the moral ideal be universally applicable. In the kingdoms of this world lower standards have to be accepted and this seems to be a moral failure. But the curious thing is that a failure to accept them is a moral failure too. To plunge a nation into the horrors of war must be wrong; and yet not to have gone to war with Hitler's Germany would have been wrong too. The conscientious objector forgets that he is living in this world, and not in Heaven. Young people are apt to see the whole realm of action in terms of black and white, evil and good; and the choice of the good seems simple and obvious. Unfortunately the choice is more often between evils, and in a moral conflict both parties may have right on their side. It is so easy to condemn another if you have not his responsibilities to carry.

It would not be difficult to proceed from these trite reflections to a sort of moral nihilism. If men cannot help doing wrong, and if different standards are applicable in different departments of life, perhaps the best thing to do would be to act conventionally and without reflection, or in any way that pleased ourselves. This would only be a sensible line to take if the varieties of moral experience were simply unrelated, a mere jumble of different standards, or if, for example, the pleasant, the useful, the right, and the dutiful were just different themes and not variations on the single theme of goodness.

I have spoken of levels of moral experience. The word 'experience' is important. Those who have not read Hegel accuse him of trying to deduce the world from pure thought alone; I have learnt from him more than from any other philosopher to base my philosophy on the solid rock of experience. By 'experience' here, I mean experience of life as it is lived and not experience of how men talk. 'The logical study of the language of morals' is Professor Hare's conception of ethics, not mine.

Experience is always compact of subject and object, and these both vary together. The sort of experiencing corresponds to the varying nature of the object. What are the hills? The answer depends on the subject's level of experiencing. To one man they are beautiful; to another (or to the same man at another time) they declare the glory of God; to another they are material for geological or botanical study.

Much the same is true of levels of moral experience. The moral consciousness does not come on the scene adult, as Athene did from the brain of Zeus. It develops from a primitive or childish level to its culmination in the notion of duty. It develops *pari passu* with the growth of self-consciousness and reflection. There is consciousness before there is self-consciousness, and reflection on a self-conscious experience is the means whereby the potentialities of self-consciousness are further developed. Reflection alters what was there before. A trivial example may illustrate the point. A child's frequent exhibition of bad temper may well be a conscious experience, but it is not yet the consciousness that '*I* am bad tempered'. Reflection on this self-consciousness when it is achieved discloses the possibility of choosing either to be bad-tempered or to cure this failing.

This advance in reflection, which at the same time is an advance in moral experience, is the beginning of self-transcendence, and this too I learnt from Hegel. It is perhaps unfortunate that his *Phenomenology of Spirit* has been less studied in this country than some of his later writings and that it is less difficult to understand in German than it is in the English translation.[1]

We begin our life as babies on the natural level but we are possessed of a capacity to transcend this level and to rise to the supra-natural or spiritual level. This is possible only because at the start we are more than natural. This is what those people forget who, having risen far above the natural level, still try to erect a moral system on a natural basis. They forget that *any* moral system is non-natural. Only if they fall below the moral level can human beings live the ordered life of ants or bees. There are those who would urge that our conduct is dictated by our physical frames or by heredity or by environment, or by some or all of these; and to these scientists we must come in due course. Instead of studying conduct they reduce it to behaviour, and so to something just as natural as the behaviour of the rats and cockroaches that enter so frequently into their experiments.

2. NATURE

As I shall have to make frequent use of the distinction between the natural or material and the mental or spiritual, I must try to explain it at the outset. 'Nature', says John Stuart Mill at the start of his *Three Essays on Religion*,[2] 'is all that is. We all live according to nature, whether we do good or bad.' This is materialism, but

---

[1] There is a valuable account of some of its more important sections in A. MacIntyre: *Short History of Ethics*, London, 1967, ch. 15.

[2] London, 1874.

Mill's argument has not advanced far before we find him saying that man must strive to amend the course of nature and bring what he can control into accord with a high standard of justice and goodness (p. 65). There is then a standard of goodness by which nature, or what is, is to be judged, and so Mill joins hands with Plato whose form of good lies ἐπέκεινα τῆς οὐσίας, beyond being.

It may be a pity that we cannot avoid speaking of the 'natural' altogether. The different senses of the word may become clear if we consider with what it is contrasted. The natural which is the opposite of the artificial is not the same natural which is contrasted with the moral or the supernatural or the realm of grace. Natural philosophy means a theoretical, as distinct from an experimental, study of nature, although the meaning of nature in this context still evades definition. Natural religion is philosophical, as distinct from revealed, religion.

Further confusion arises from our meaning by 'nature' either the starting point of human development or its culmination. For example, the development of mind from babyhood to maturity may be called natural; but nothing could be more misleading. The development is possible only by rejecting the natural or animal level at which we start, by putting away childish things; much harm has been done by those psychologists who have ignored this essential negative moment in any process of mental development.

On the other hand, some will speak of the *spiritual* nature of man, but this obscures the truth. There is a sense in which man's true nature is what he can and ought to become, not what he is at the start. It would be less misleading to regard spirit as man's destiny rather than as his nature. 'Live according to nature' is a commonplace of Stoicism, but it could equally well (though in a different sense) be a slogan of Epicureans. The Stoic thinks of reason as man's true nature, while the Epicurean begins, wherever he ends, with the satisfaction of natural appetites.

It may be tempting to say that nature is the object of scientific study, i.e. that abstraction from the world of our experiences which can be measured or observed or inferred from measurements and observations. And this would be a useful definition if we did not also speak, for instance, of a sunset as a 'natural' phenomenon, though the scientist's account of it has to omit just what gives the sunset its value and significance for us, its glory or its beauty. There may be a place for a philosophy of nature, as well as for scientific study, but if so, the object of the philosophical study will be nature as *experienced*, as therefore a moment *in* experience, not any abstraction from it. For the philosopher, therefore, nature will be the matrix of mind, and questions will then arise about how far back in the evolutionary process we can discern the seeds which later are to burgeon into life, consciousness, and spirit. Nature exists *for* mind, in other words, it is mind which describes nature as nature, and it is only for mind, therefore, that nature exists as nature, i.e. nature is something that exists for mind alone.

To survey the evolutionary process is beyond my competence, but I am starting from the view that an evolutionary process has culminated in man's mind, for which alone indeed this process exists. It will be said that it is absurd to suppose that the whole process, with the immensities of intergalactic space, exists for the sake of producing mind on one tiny planet; but nature is prodigal— 'consider frog spawn' as Collingwood once said. Let us remember our Hegel: 'Man because he is mind should and must deem himself worthy of the highest; he cannot think too highly of the greatness and the power of his mind.'[1] Let us not be bludgeoned by astronomical figures or persuaded to draw comparisons between the size of the universe and the littleness of man. The mind which explores the universe, and which, by probing the mysteries of nature, enables us to dominate it and subdue it to the purposes of human life, outsoars in worth the nature out of which it has arisen.

My fundamental distinction is between the natural level on which our life begins and the mental or spiritual level which it is possible for us to attain. Another way of putting the same distinction is that we begin life as animals but can rise above animalism to a moral life. I have said that these clear distinctions can be blurred by talking of morality as natural or of spirit as our true nature. But philosophy is a form of literature and it can never do justice to its subject matter if it substitutes symbols and mathematical formulae for the suppleness of language. I am not to be expected to use 'natural' in always the same sense; I expect the sense in which the word is used to be clear from the context, and if it is not, so much the poorer thinker I am, so much the more

[1] Heidelberg inaugural address, October 28, 1816.

inadequate is my command of language. The same is true of my attitude to terminology generally.

3. DEVELOPMENT FROM NATURE TO MIND

I have referred to a development from nature to mind. Some may interpret this as implying a distinction between mind and body and as demanding, what other Gifford Lecturers have provided, an exposition of the relation between body and mind. This, however, is a misunderstanding of what I wish to maintain.

At birth, I have said, we are at the animal level. But that is not the whole truth. We are animals possessed with the potentiality of becoming moral beings and rising to the spiritual life. If nature is the matrix of mind, and if man emerges from an evolutionary process, it would be reasonable to expect to find in the animal kingdom some germs of the moral life, and these there may be in some animals domesticated by man. But so far as we know, the mental and moral development possible for man exceeds that of all other animals.

Furthermore, I have said that we rise above the natural or animal level to mind, morality, and spirit. But this is not the whole truth either. We can never leave nature or the animal completely behind. This is the truth which has been seized upon by behaviouristic psychologists. It is the glory of human life that mind and spirit can dominate it; the shame and shortcoming of human life that that domination can never be complete. We are therefore concerned not with a body and a mind and a relation between them, but with a human being, a synthesis of opposites, one of which, the animal, can be recessive and the other, the mental and moral or spiritual, can be progressive. It is a mistake to forget or to ignore the feet of clay. In this life we are not disembodied spirits. We should never forget, for example, the effect of drugs on the personality.

If this account of the rise from nature to mind is correct, then it follows that what is important for human beings is an understanding of their life and its goal. There can be no comprehension of it in terms of its origins. The study of nature is *necessary* in order that we may be enabled to change our natural environment to make it subserve the purposes of human life. But it lacks the *importance* of a study of human conduct. The scientist will insist that he pursues his investigations regardless of their utility, and there is no reason why he should not, although it is interesting to find that those psychologists who reject psychoanalysis on the ground that it is *unscientific* are themselves most interested in the cure of neurotics. When Bradshaw's Guide existed, there were enthusiastic students of that fascinating volume who could give you the times of trains on which they would never travel. They pursued the truth for its own sake, and there are those who pursue scientific investigation in the same spirit as that of those who try to solve a crossword puzzle. To identify the 135 species of midge or to study a collection of 10,000 snails, as a research worker supported by the Carnegie Trust did, is a harmless occupation, like that of the pure mathematician, described by G. H. Hardy, whose elegant proofs have a quality and an appeal similar to those of works of fine art. Let every man pursue his own intellectual interest, but in the last resort we must apply the test of utility, utility to human life. Scientific discovery is necessary for human life; that is its justification; but if it is argued that its justification is that it discovers truth about nature, then we have some reservations to make, because the *truth* of nature is mind. We are constantly told that research, pursued regardless of utility, may eventually produce something with a practical application. Rutherford is said to have regarded the splitting of the atom as a scientific achievement, but of no practical use to anyone. And others since his day have used this example as a justification for pursuing research disinterestedly, i.e. in order to discover the truth about nature. No doubt they discover many facts about nature, but if they forget the possibility of practical application, their work has no more justification than the activity of the man who satisfies curiosity by studying the railway time table without wishing to travel, or the salary lists in *Whitaker's Almanack* without being or intending to become a civil servant.

In any event, either science is necessary in order that life may be lived or it is a harmless gratification of curiosity. It is admitted that we can never know in advance into which of these categories a given piece of scientific research will fall. In neither case is this research of the *first importance*. What is important is a consideration of how we are to attain not life but the good life. What sort of life is worth living for a human being, as distinct from an animal, and how can we attain it? It is to a solution of this question that philosophy and religion have a contribution to make. Science can make none. Science cannot get further than what is. It cannot say what ought to be. Good and evil elude the telescope, let alone the microscope or the spectrophotometer.

Many problems of conduct arise for us, however, only because there flows in us a stream of biological life. Impulse, instinct, and appetite all arise from our animal nature; we may control them consciously or by drugs or by behaviour therapy and we may modify them; we may re-orientate them or sublimate them; but we cannot get rid of them. In the evolutionary process, the human mind is second to nature; a product of nature and not its pre-condition; to that extent even Marxists are right. But the product modifies not only our conception of its producer but the producer itself. Mind transforms our life from the natural life of plants into the spiritual life which it enables us to attain. This is what Marxists and some psychologists forget. They also forget that nature is the sphere of the finite; everything in nature is bounded by something else. The finite, however, implies its opposite; to describe something as finite is to presuppose an infinite, and it is against the background of the infinite alone that the finite is intelligible. Although mind develops through and out of nature, it is not itself natural. To the range and power of mind no limit can be set; its thoughts are not external to one another as the table and the chair are. In this sense mind is the infinite for which alone the finite sphere of nature becomes an intelligible whole.[1]

This demands some further explanation. As I have already hinted, speculation on the relation between body and mind is vain. Theories of interaction between body and mind or of psycho-physical parallelism all make mind external to body; they therefore apply to mind the category of externality; and this means reducing it to nature. Other theories make body the determinant of conduct and regard mind as irrelevant. This failure of a theorist to grant importance and independence to mind is odd, to say the least. So far from being external to mind, body is a name for an elementary stage in what we call mind. Mind is body becoming conscious of itself. We know from the history of modern medicine how dangerous it is to attempt a cure of physical

---

[1] These last four sentences are so obviously Hegelian and so fundamental to his thought that I need not multiply references, *Hegel–Studien Bd.1*, Bonn, 1961, p. 28, may serve as one.

symptoms without considering the mentality of the patient. When the patient thanks the surgeon for his skill after a very difficult operation which has been successful, and the surgeon replies: 'You were a very good patient', he is simply stating as a fact that the patient's mental attitude had contributed in an appreciable measure to the success of what the knife had done to the physical frame. Nevertheless if mind is body becoming conscious of itself, it never leaves body, or its past, behind.

Nature is intelligible and is mastered only in so far as it is known, i.e. in so far as we can discover its laws. But these are not themselves natural. To understand nature means seeing it as dependent on universals, on laws which are the expression of thought. These laws cannot be conceived as *external* to nature, or they become natural all over again and therefore unknowable because unobservable. It is useless to try to understand what nature is in itself apart from mind or before the emergence of mind; because to make the effort is of necessity to import mind into it. In fact we cannot keep mind out of it. If nature is intelligible by mind, this can only be because mind in some form is there already, namely as the universals or laws which unite what is otherwise dispersed in space and time. It is the emergence of mind from nature, and mind's reflection on nature, that makes nature intelligible for the first time. Nature is the matrix of mind, because underlying or penetrating the self-externality of nature the universals were present originally. If matter existed before mind, that was in the past; and the past does not exist; it exists only for the mind that reconstructs it by historical enquiry. And there is no understanding nature unless it be admitted that there is in it the potentiality of mind which in the fullness of time has been actualised.

Just as the inorganic world is a place for organisms to live in, so nature as a whole is a place which is to be known.[1] The universals or laws of its being are not put into it by mind. We cannot say that man makes nature, for the evidence is that man arises from nature and can never wholly surmount his natural constituents. But if man did not impose universals on nature, but found them there, whence did they come? They are not there for observation;

[1] Or as St Augustine said of plants: 'they cannot know, but they seem to wish to be known'. (*De Civ. Dei*, xi. 27. I owe the reference to Schopenhauer, *World as Will and Representation*, Eng. tr., Indian Hills, 1958, i, p. 201.)

they are the object of thought and not of sight; if then they are there, the sole means of understanding nature and finding its dispersion in the self-externality of space and time intelligible, they must have been there at the creation, implicit therein and awaiting for their discovery the emergence of mind, their counterpart and knower. This is an argument from cosmology to deity, but my concern is with a moral argument based on a consideration of the forms of action, and to these I now turn.

4. MIND AS NATURE'S CHILD

If we accept a theory of evolutionary development, and consider its stages up to the emergence of man, we may begin with a space-time continuum, see developing within it electrons moving in rhythms, patterns, or clusters, and then, developing within these, chemical qualities, and, arising from all of them, *life*. Corresponding to these stages are the sciences that study them, beginning with mathematics, the most abstract of all, and proceeding by stages of increasing concreteness to physics, chemistry, and biology. Notice that the lower stages in this series still survive, in however modified a form, in the higher. Life as we know it is in space and time, and it has physical as well as chemical constituents. Biology cannot dispense with mathematics, or with physics and chemistry either. The higher, however, is always the truth of the lower; to take the reverse view is to substitute the abstract for the concrete and to ignore the negative moment intrinsic in any development, as distinct from any succession.

The stages in the development of life from the most primitive organisms up to man I need not describe; for if, as I have said, men are animals with minds, the possession of mind modifies their animalism. The lower stage is not present in the higher as a sort of unaltered kernel; nature, as Goethe said, has no shell or kernel—it is just externality. There is no getting to its heart, because there is no heart to get at. It is only by modification of a lower stage that the higher emerges. Nevertheless, the lower stage is not absent or abandoned; it is present, though modified.

Human beings, as the products of an evolutionary process, carry with them, however modified, the preceding stages from which they have emerged. We are bodies occupying space and time; we can be counted and our shape can be geometrically described;

we have mass; the movements of our limbs are physical movements, highly complex, and bio-physics is a progressing science of increasing importance. We are also chemical; the processes of digestion, secretion, and so forth are subjects for bio-chemical investigation. Like plants or insects we are also organisms, and this fact provides more of the truth about us than any spatio-temporal coefficient can.

5. ELEMENTARY FORMS OF ACTION

These facts all have their place in a comprehensive study of human action. But I propose to mention here only two primitive levels of action to which they are relevant. The first is the most rudimentary type of action,[1] that of bodies in space; the second is the reflex action which occurs only at the level of organism.

As bodies, our first and most primitive form of action is passivity. This may appear to be something that a logician must reject because it is a contradiction in terms. We must, however, always keep in view the fact that when we are confronted with opposites or contradictions, each takes its meaning from the other and has no existence without the other. This confrontation is like the sun which makes indispensable to one another the original and its shadow. Passivity is to self-conscious decision or activity what body is to mind, the lowest and most primitive instantiation of the concrete and fully developed reality.

The body, as passive, occupies space; but it is *doing* something. No doubt the body must be of a certain size, and so far it is *being* something. But by occupying space it is keeping others out of it and therefore is *doing* something, however passive we could describe it as being. A body occupying a vantage point in a football crowd at a cup-final is keeping others out of it; the crowd may be so great that this body cannot move; it cannot help being where it is, and to that extent it is passive. But nevertheless it is doing something by keeping others out.

This doing is the most rudimentary form of action and therefore it involves the most rudimentary kind of freedom. To occupy space is something which no one can compel one to do or prevent one from doing, and to that slender extent occupancy of space is

[1] My account of this type of action is based on conversation with R. G. Collingwood.

C

free. But it is also not free at all but determined because although bodies have the power to occupy space they have no power to refrain from doing so.

I pass over mechanical action which would involve time as well as space, in order to make brief mention of reflex action. I am not concerned here with the mechanical movements which occur when a doctor tests 'your reflexes', e.g. when he taps your knee and your leg rises; but rather with experiences like blinking, if a fly seems to be going to settle on your eye, or sneezing or yawning or warding off a blow. These are not mechanical actions, because what prompts them is not equal in energy to that behind the action itself. But they are actions; they do not happen to us, as when we are thrown off our balance by the lurching of the train. The energy comes from within, even if we do not release the energy consciously or deliberately. We may afterwards realize why we blinked or sneezed or yawned or resisted an assault, but at the time it was an unconscious and unpremeditated reflex. Such reflex action is the action of an organism; it cannot be ascribed to any lower evolutionary level.

I have tried to show how the preceding stages of evolution are recapitulated in the human being as the background to human conduct. These stages cannot explain that conduct, but it may well be that human conduct itself may cast some light on the significance or character of the earlier stages. In particular the germ or at least the presage of human conduct is found in animals, to go no further back; and this helps us to explain animal, not human conduct, despite what some investigators have supposed. Animals move from place to place and their movement is of a different kind from that of the planets or that of the iron filings irresistibly attracted to the magnet. The forces of attraction and repulsion which move the planets in their orbits operate *ab extra*. We no longer suppose that their motive force is their love of God. But the animal moves *in quest* of its food. Even if it receives some impulse *ab extra*, it is nevertheless self-moved on a quest of its own.

CHAPTER 2

INSTINCT

If we ask for a scientific explanation of animal movements such as the migration of birds, we may be referred to instinct. As this concept is often used to explain some human actions too, or at least one level of human conduct, it deserves examination.

From scientific works on the subject I have gleaned the following:

1. TANSLEY

It is characteristic of organisms, no matter how primitive in the scale of evolutionary development, to react to the world round about them. Their reactions all tend to preserve the life of the individual organism and to perpetuate the species to which it belongs. Some bring the organism into contact with food and into media favourable for its life; others withdraw it from harmful or dangerous surroundings; others again ensure the mating of the two sexes. What happens is that some stimulus from without impinges on the chemically unstable substances of which protoplasm is composed, and breaks them down, thus releasing the energy with which they are stored. This liberation of energy proceeds in definite ways according to differences in the stimulus received, so that the organism does not just explode but responds in specific ways to the environment. The differential character of the response depends on the elaboration of the nervous system and it is said to be man's more complex nervous system which enables him to react in so many more ways than a jellyfish can.[1]

These reactions, thus described by A. G. Tansley are what some psychologists call instincts, whether in animals or man.

2. JAMES AND MCDOUGALL

I quote two psychological definitions of an instinct. The first is William James's:

'An instinct is acting in such a way as to produce certain ends

[1] *The New Psychology*, London, 1922, ch. 3.

without foresight of the ends and without previous education in the performance. A rattlesnake knows how to use his grooved tooth and poison gland against his enemies: he bites them instinctively. The infant supports its life by sucking—instinctively.'[1]

Secondly, McDougall describes instincts as 'certain innate tendencies of the mind that are common to all members of one species . . . They supply the driving power by which all mental activities are sustained . . . An instinct determines its possessor to perceive and attend to objects of a certain class, e.g. food, to experience an emotional excitement of a special quality on perceiving such an object, and to act in regard to it in a particular manner or at least to experience an impulse to such action (e.g. eating').[2] This cycle of reactions is something which, if followed through, subserves the life of the organism. McDougall wrote thirty years after James, but in this matter at least did not improve on him. Later psychologists seem to have become less interested in human instincts. For example, Professor and Mrs Knight devote the bulk of the short chapter on instincts in their *Modern Introduction to Psychology* (London, 1948) to instinct in animals.

3. TINBERGEN

Therefore, what may be more important than either of these psychological definitions is the work of a neuro-physiologist, Tinbergen, who wrote thirty years after McDougall and some years after the Knights. Tinbergen shows, in particular, the inadequacy of McDougall's description of instinct as a tendency of the *mind*. 'The purposiveness of any instinct', he writes,' is safeguarded by the fact that all the activities forming part of a purposive behaviour pattern aimed at the attainment of a certain goal depend on a common neuro-physiological mechanism . . . Any definition of an "instinct" should include not only an indication of the objective aim or purpose it is serving, but also an indication of the neuro-physiological mechanisms . . . An instinct [is] a hierarchically ordered nervous mechanism which is susceptible to certain priming, releasing and directing impulses of internal as well as external origin, and which responds to these impulses by co-ordinated movements that contribute to the maintenance of the

[1] *Principles*, London, 1890, ii, p 383.
[2] *Introduction to Social Psychology*, London, 1920, p. 20.

individual and the species.'[1] Tinbergen goes on to argue that neuro-physiology is relevant to the study of all behaviour, human as well as animal. Man, he says, truly enough, 'is an animal'[2] but in man there is a subjective side which is not amenable to objective study (i.e. study by scientific methods). 'When the food-seeking drive is around, the subject experiences hunger; meanwhile his neural mechanisms are at work. Discovering those neural mechanisms is not discovering that subjective phenomena do not occur.' *Awareness* of need, a need that eating will satisfy whether the subject knows that or not, is a fact; that 'the enteroceptors in the muscles of my stomach will cause impulses to run to my hypothalamus' is also a fact, and both facts must be taken into account in any full treatment of the phenomenon of hunger. Thus far Tinbergen.

4. HOW FAR THE NOTION OF INSTINCT IS APPLICABLE TO HUMAN CONDUCT

If the concept of instinct is to have any value in the study of human conduct, it must be given precision. Thus I have here to part company with Professor and Mrs Knight because although they regard instinct in man as different from instinct in animals, man's instincts being far more under control,[3] they do not draw out the implications of this. They do refer to the misuse of the term 'instinct', and therefore to its ambiguity, but they add to the ambiguity by calling fear an instinct. It is not easy to maintain precision in the analysis of mind, but we can try by avoiding a confusion of instinct with feeling or appetite or passion or desire. It seems to me to be unfortunate that O. L. Zangwill blurs so many distinctions by insisting[4] that use of the terms 'reflex' and 'instinct' is only a matter of personal preference; that 'appetite', 'instinct', and 'emotion' are entirely arbitrary terms; that fear is an emotion; and that a tendency to don or doff clothing according to the prevailing weather might properly be called an 'instinctive propensity'.

If instinct in man is essentially the same sort of thing as instinct in animals, then it can be characteristic only of human conduct at a very low level. This is the great strength of William James's

---

[1] *A Study of Instinct*, Oxford, 1951, p. 112. [2] *Op. cit.*, p 205.
[3] *Op. cit.*, p 177. [4] In his *Introduction to Modern Psychology*, London, 1950.

definition. It focuses attention on the *ignorance* of the organism in instinctive action. If sucking is instinctive in the infant, then the same notion of instinct cannot be used to explain a child's eating, still less an adult's. In infancy man begins with responses and impulses of the same neuro-physiological, and thus of the same unconscious, kind as those of the lower animals and organisms. Instinct, so far as man is concerned, is a description of *infantile* or immature behaviour. The inner impulse or reaction is not a conscious desire but a feeling of dissatisfaction. The tired child does not know that sleep is what it wants: the hungry infant does not know that the sucking of nourishment is what it wants or needs or, indeed, that it is hungry. This infantilism is what Tinbergen neglects. When I am conscious that it is hunger that I feel, I have already risen above the level of instinct to appetite. Instinct is purposive for *us*, who know what is going on; but not for the infant. It is unconsciously purposive, as James so clearly saw. The rhythms of the organism's life have indeed a direction, but of this direction the organism is not conscious. The rhythms may well be said to proceed instinctively, that is unconsciously, and at that stage without any mental control. Consequently the satisfaction of the instinctive drive is innocent, and it is also a form of freedom. The wants which are instinctively satisfied are not chosen, and therefore the satisfying of them is only an elementary freedom, though a freedom a stage higher than the freedom of body which has already been mentioned. From a higher point of view, and once body has developed into a higher stage of mind, what at a lower level is freedom of satisfying instinct is slavery to appetite.

Any attempt to give the notion of instinct an intelligible sense by confining it to infantile behaviour, as James does, is at odds with McDougall, not only because he talks of instinct as a tendency of mind, but also because his list of instincts darkens counsel. He regards them as the basis of adult conduct and, though his lists vary, here is one: 'Fear, pugnacity or anger, repulsion or disgust, curiosity, self-assertion, self-abasement, parental instinct, reproduction or sex instinct, hunger, gregariousness, acquisition, construction.'[1] In reading this list we realize at once how far away we are from the scientific precision of James, let alone Tinbergen. In this list McDougall departs from any scientific concept of

[1] *Op. cit.*, p 203.

instinct as a response to environment, serving biological ends. A
child may play with bricks and so make a 'construction', but play,
a child's mental reaction to its environment, is in a different class
altogether from the infant's sucking. McDougall has begun to
widen the concept of instinct in such a way as to make it meaningless, and he does this, one presumes, in an endeavour to explain
higher levels of human behaviour. But I have said already that
any attempt to explain the higher by the lower is doomed to
failure. It is guilty of C. D. Broad's 'genetic fallacy.'[1]

We cannot enter into the consciousness of the infant and we have
to describe its life in very much the same way and by the same
methods as we would describe an animal's. We may therefore be
justified in describing its activity as instinctive in the sense that
can be given to that word by combining William James with
Tinbergen. We may go further: we may describe as an operation
of the sex instinct certain vague feelings and urges of late childhood and early adolescence. But these may be called the working
of instinct only because their rhythm and direction are not understood by their subject. Instinctive drives are those with a
biological foundation, impelling to action in a subject who
understands them *not*, and who is conscious of them only as
needs, not needs for some specific object. Instincts are neither
appetites nor desires.

5. MISAPPLICATIONS OF INSTINCT TO HUMAN CONDUCT

This is so important for the understanding of human conduct and
especially for morality, which some would wish to *reduce* to
instinct, that I must mention some contexts in which 'instinct'
commonly appears, though without justification.

(i) When Huckleberry Finn was dressed up as a girl, he was
detected when something was thrown on his lap and he brought
his knees together, instead of parting them as a girl would have
done (Chapter 11). It would be a commonplace to say that he
acted 'instinctively'. But this is a mistake. If his action was not a
reflex action, it was something learnt.

(ii) Asked to describe how I tie my tie, I may say that I do it
instinctively, because if I start to wonder how I do it I may fail
to do it properly. But this is certainly not instinct. It is habit.

[1] C. D. Broad, *Mind and its Place in Nature*, London, 1937, Introduction.

There is no analogy here with biological rhythms. Just as in the preceding instance, the activity is learnt and then repeated often enough until a habit is formed. I tie my tie not instinctively but habitually.

(iii) A motorist may say: 'I was driving my car and when a child suddenly ran in front of me, I swerved instinctively.' This too is a misdescription. What the speaker has forgotten is that thought is quick. An 'instinctive' swerve might well land the motorist in the ditch. In fact he realizes the child's danger and acts quickly, and his action is so judged as to enable him to avoid the child, and the ditch, and the oncoming car. He may misjudge the situation, and there may be an accident, but his action so far from being instinctive is judged; and a misjudgment is still a judgment.

(iv) 'He knew instinctively that the man was an enemy.' This is a gross misuse of language, yet how often it is perpetrated! Knowledge and instinct are contradictions. For 'knew instinctively' read 'sensed' or 'felt'. Even these words, however, may provide further ambiguities, and I would prefer to say, even if it be an Americanism, 'he had a hunch that the man was an enemy'. This describes the situation precisely and it has the advantage of avoiding all those expressions which have been the mainstay of so much philosophical discussion.

(v) Sometimes it is even said that duty is done 'instinctively'. A man plunges into the canal to save a drowning child. A man rushes into a burning house to save a work of art which he knows to be there, and in the room where it is he finds a baby crying in its cot. He saves the baby and forgets about the work of art. Now in these instances there is the saving of a life, and to that extent the notion of instinct as serving a biological purpose is relevant. But the action is not instinctive. Plunging into canals or rushing into burning houses, at the risk of one's life, is an activity which instinct, if it operated at all, would inhibit. The instinct of self-preservation, if it exists, would block both of these rescues. But why should the man who risks his life to save a work of art save the baby instead? Is this not instinct? Perhaps it could be if fear had inhibited reflection. But if so, the man was not dutiful, even if his act, in someone who acted with full consciousness, would have been a duty.

(vi) Sometimes there is talk of 'instinctive feelings', e.g. pity for others in misfortune. Here once more 'instinctive' is robbed of all clear sense. If we do pity others, it is because we have been taught to sympathize with them. The torturer does not pity his victims. Pity was not prominent in the spectators of Roman gladiatorial combats or in the supervisors of horrors at Belsen. If instinct is to be used as an explanation of why some people feel pity, it cannot also be used to explain why all infants suck.

(vii) In an Andrew Lang lecture at St Andrews, that eminent lawyer, Lord Macmillan, permitted himself to speak of an 'instinct for justice'. Justice, however, is a moral idea on a relatively high plane. It would be more reasonable to speak of an instinct for injustice, since injustice is far more prevalent, or should I say more natural, than justice.

(viii) The native finds his way through the forest 'instinctively'. Here 'instinct' is simply a cloak for ignorance. Its use may go along with the belief that the native does not think as we do, but has a 'primitive mentality'. If we do not see or recognize the signs of which the native makes use, we fly to 'instinct' as an *asylum ignorantiae*. A similar stricture must be passed on some psychologists who speak of an instinct for shelter or clothing. Shelter would seem to have been devised for an obvious reason and continually used for the same reason. There is no analogy with the infant's sucking or with neuro-physiological mechanisms. To regard clothing oneself as an instinct is once more to depart from the insight of William James and the scientific investigations of Tinbergen. I have seen natives in the plateau of Northern Nigeria shivering with cold in the early morning and yet completely naked. The Book of Genesis knows better than the psychologists, or if they repudiate that text they can think of adornment.

This philological excursus may have seemed tedious; and it may seem that I labour the obvious. But it would have been discourteous in writing on moral philosophy in 1967 not to pay occasional lip service to the linguistic analysis which for so many years has passed as philosophy in most universities in these islands.

6. IF INSTINCT EXPLAINS INFANTILE BEHAVIOUR, IT CANNOT EXPLAIN ADULT BEHAVIOUR

I have argued that if the concept of instinct is to function effectively as an explanation of behaviour of any kind, it must be given

precision, and this can be done. I have also argued, by accepting
William James's concept, modified by what Tinbergen has found
in relation to neuro-physiological mechanisms, that if we ask why
the infant sucks, an answer in terms of instinct is intelligible; but
if that be true, the same sort of answer cannot provide any
rational explanation of the behaviour of a man who is conscious of
wants and of the means whereby they can be satisfied. It is a
mistake to argue that, because both men and infants must assimilate nourishment if they are to live, men eat 'instinctively' and not
because they desire to do so or because they do so deliberately—
in the absence of desire—in order to continue to exist. It is not
intelligent but perverse to say that the instinct which drives the
infant to suck is present and operative in the hunger-striker also,
although he refuses to allow it to drive him to act. This is perverse,
because the concept of instinct is introduced in order to explain
conduct, and if it explains why the infant sucks it cannot also
explain why the hunger striker refuses to eat. It is true some
psychologists would retort that in order to understand what the
hunger striker does we must take account not of one instinct alone,
but of all of them; and other instincts which might be relevant to
the hunger striker's case are masochism and self-abasement. But
this is no explanation of what the hunger striker actually does,
because it does not tell us why one instinct should be operative in
him to the exclusion of the rest. In McDougall's list of instincts
we encounter 'gregariousness' and 'combativeness'. It is true that
men sometimes choose crowded beaches for a holiday and that
sometimes they do not associate together in a common enterprise
but vie with one another or fight one another instead. But
McDougall's 'instincts' cannot answer the crucial question of why
on a given occasion men are gregarious and on another occasion
combative. To refer to instinct to explain war and peace, society or
civil strife, is not to illuminate these phenomena in the slightest.
The same fundamental concept cannot explain *both* the regularities
of insect life *and* the diversification of human life.

The final evasion of the psychologist is to speak of propensities
rather than instincts. This change in terminology may be a
recognition of the fact that adult conduct differs in some way from
the conduct of infants or insects, but it does nothing to explain
adult conduct or what men actually do. We want to understand
what men do, not what they are, or might be, prone to do. It may

be that men would be prone to domination by instinct if they were not men but just animals; but men have to struggle against propensities in order to become and remain men. Let us therefore confine the concept of instinct to its proper place, to the behaviour of bees or rattlesnakes, and to the behaviour of infants, but abandon this conception in relation to adult conduct at its maturity, except when we are concerned to explain the conduct not of an individual but of a crowd. In a crowd, emotion may run so high that reason is suspended and the members of the crowd may act like infants, instinctively, quite unconscious of what they are doing or why.

7. DIFFERENCE BETWEEN ANIMAL AND INFANTILE BEHAVIOUR

While it is convenient to speak of the infant's behaviour as instinctive, the difference between infantile and animal behaviour must not go unobserved. The infant is potentially a self and a mind in a way in which the rattlesnake is not. The infant's instincts are those of an embryo rational being. Into the degrees of mentality in animals we do not need to enter, but whatever their mental level, and however high, it is a level permanently lower than the level of human mentality. For evidence of this I refer to language. Some children never learn to talk; they make only what we call 'animal noises'. These may be language of a kind, but in a human being it is the language of a mental defective. The failure to learn to talk is evidence of an inability to think, for language is not a symbol for thought but the full realization and expression of thought. It is true that parrots talk after a fashion, but when we say of a human being that 'he talks like a parrot', we are reflecting on his brains, because such talking is unintelligent. Instinctive behaviour in the infant is behaviour which, if the infant develops normally, is to be subject to modification, and this is true of animals only to the relatively slight extent to which they can be tamed, domesticated, or trained.

The development of mind is the route to the transcendence of instinct. The biological urges of which Tinbergen gives an account are only the background or raw material of human conduct; they are what is 'given' to us; but it does not follow that the adult is ruled by them as the bee is or that he accepts the gift without modifying it. Tinbergen grants this to some extent when he says that 'mating behaviour in man . . . [is] basically dependent on sex hormones and external stimuli, and it is on these agents that our rational powers exercise a regulating influence'.[1] The words 'regulating influence' do not, in my view, go far enough.

It is true that the regularizing of our life by, for example, having fixed hours for meals may be regarded as exercising a 'regulating influence' on the hunger instinct which many animals satisfy by a restless and continual quest for food. But it is difficult to bring within the scope of Tinbergen's discussions the case of the scholar who may go on working long after his mealtime, quite oblivious of anything but his work; eventually his wife interrupts him: 'Are you not hungry?' And he answers: 'Well, now that you mention it, perhaps I am.' I do not know at what point, if at all, in this example Tinbergen's neuro-physiological mechanisms begin to operate. At the level of adult self-conscious life we are dealing no longer with the regulation of instinct. Instinct has been transformed into appetite and desire, and these involve self-consciousness and for that reason become amenable to what Tinbergen calls 'our rational powers'.

Animals, we grant, have instincts, and their behaviour is dominated thereby (except, as I said, in so far as they can be tamed or domesticated). But men know what instincts they have. And it is this knowledge which delivers them from the tyranny of instinct. Here is one example of how knowledge *changes* its object. Knowledge of an instinct which we have robs the instinct of that compulsive power in virtue of which alone it *is* an instinct. The behaviour of an animal dominated by instinct can be foreseen. A vine-grower or a beekeeper today can learn the elements of his job as easily from the *Georgics* of Virgil as from the latest handbooks on vine culture or beekeeping. Whatever may be said of infantile behaviour, however, the course of human history cannot be foreseen. Knowledge presents man with alternatives and gives him freedom. To know instinct as instinct transforms its character. What at the animal level is an instinct becomes for mind not an instinct but an appetite. This advance of mind must now be described. We begin with where human mind begins, namely with feeling as the body's consciousness of its condition.

[1] *Op. cit.*, p 208.

CHAPTER 3

THE GROWTH OF MIND FROM FEELING TO CHOICE[1]

I. FEELING

Any organism has a rhythmic life of its own. Of this life the plant is not conscious, though its biological rhythms may be regarded as mind in embryo. In Chapter 1 it was maintained that body is a way of describing the presage of mind, and it may be well at this point to make clear that mind is not a sort of apparatus for thinking, a kind of machine. It is a complex of activities which emerge gradually as mind develops. Mind is not something over and above feelings, consciousness, desires, thoughts, or something which has these. It is these. It begins with feeling, which implies consciousness, but soon becomes a consciousness of a self which feels. At this stage we have risen above the animal and the infant. These feel, but they do not say *I* feel. Somehow, and I do not profess to explain how, the infant grows up to the knowledge of itself as an individual. After referring to itself in the third person by saying 'John is hungry', it one day evinces its consciousness of individuality by saying '*I* am hungry'. But this stage of feeling is still a very elementary stage in mental development.

Feeling, as I am defining it, is simply awareness of a bodily condition. 'I am tired.' 'I am hungry.' In other words, it is an awareness of what at that stage is the 'given'. It is awareness of a matter on which mind imposes a form. On Tinbergen's neurophysiological mechanisms, consciousness imposes the form of 'I am hungry'. This is an awareness of an immediate bodily condition, of this, here, and now. I feel hot, in a fever, or so numb with cold that I cannot think, or I feel simply weak after an exhausting climb. Indeed the feeling may be so strong that my individuality disappears, and I am simply hunger, or cold, or weakness; and at that level when we have regressed to infantilism there is no distinction between self and others or self and environ-

---

[1] My treatment of the growth of mind, and especially of feeling, appetite, and passion is based almost wholly on the third part of Hegel's *Encyclopaedia*, especially the *Zusätze*, and the first part of R. G. Collingwood: *The New Leviathan*, Oxford, 1942.

ment. We are so hungry or cold or ill that consciousness of the fact obliterates everything else. Smitten with a high fever, we may feel 'rotten', and asked by a doctor to localize the feeling, we cannot.

Nevertheless, if we try to think ourselves back into the experience of mere feeling, we may distinguish between what we feel and how we feel, or between content and form. The feeling of lying in a warm bath, the glow after a walk on a frosty day, the repletion after a good dinner when we have been hungry, all these are different in content. In form they are all pleasant; but the sort of pleasure differs. The same is true of feelings of discomfort; they are painful in form, but the sort of pain differs. The importance of this consideration is that it is an error to speak of pleasure and pain as feelings. At this level of experience they are the forms of which the feelings of various sorts of comfort and discomfort are the content. And the feelings are associated with our bodily condition; they are feelings of comfort in so far as they are awareness of the organism's activity, and of discomfort in so far as they are awareness of the organism's frustration or need. The organism is not always active. Its energies run down and it needs rest. Or its activities may be frustrated by those of another organism, so that its energies are refused their natural outlet. In such situations the organism is passive and not active, and the feeling is one of discomfort and not comfort. In adult life there are many pleasures and pains of other kinds; but at this primitive level of mental development, the level of feeling, pleasure and pain are forms of feeling essentially linked with, as awareness of, the biological rhythms of the organism.

At this stage, the stage at which mind is just body becoming conscious of itself, pleasure and pain are closely linked together as opposite moments in a single experience. While the pure immediate consciousness of the agent as active is pleasure, pain is the negative side of the same experience. There is an urge to overcome and master the pain, and this urge has pleasure as its coefficient. The pleasure is the overcoming of the pain. Both moments are present in the total experience, even at this low level.

However this may be, the level of feeling is essentially the feeling of this bodily condition here and now. Feeling rotten with a high influenza temperature is oblivious of past and future, of the environment, of others. It is just simply an immediate experi-

ence, suffused with rottenness. That is what we *feel*. But it is not
the truth of the situation. Life is a continuum; the organism is
always in process. We may feel ill, but we are in fact getting better
or worse; we feel tired, but in fact the exhaustion is getting less
because we are resting. To become aware of the process of which
we feel only this moment, and then the next one, is to transform
feeling into appetite, and this is the first step towards the mind's
consciousness of itself as a unity of difference, as a self, and
ultimately as a person.

2. MIND OVERCOMES THE EXTERNALITY OF NATURE

The transformation of feeling into appetite is an activity of mind.
This earliest development of mind exhibits the distinctive
characteristic which differentiates mind from nature. This, as was
hinted in Chapter 1, is mind's power to overcome the externality
of nature. This power must now be illustrated and, to that extent,
explained.

Hegel was right to describe nature as the realm of self-
externality. In nature everything is external to everything else.
Two bodies cannot occupy the same space. This moment of time
is external to the next one. The living organism is external to its
environment; if it absorbs the environment as food, and so
assimilates it, it destroys it in the process and still is external to
the environment that remains. In nature inner and outer oppose
one another and are as external to one another as the billiard balls
that are made to collide with one another. Now consider what we
call a sound, e.g. what happens when we strike a note on a piano.
A wire is hit; the wire vibrates in a certain rhythm and the
physicist will tell us how many vibrations there are per second for
a given note. The vibrations are all numerically distinct, separable,
and calculable. But hearing these vibrations as a *sound* is appre-
hending them as a unified pattern; we overcome their externality
and hear them as a unity.—The ear may be regarded physiologic-
ally as a mechanism for receiving vibrations. The physical fact of
the vibration of the piano wire is repeated in the physiological
reception of these vibrations in the ear. But mind overcomes this
externality and is conscious of this physical and physiological
phenomenon as the *unitary* phenomenon of a *sound*. Here mind
has not only unified the series of vibrations; it has also overcome

the difference between inner and outer. The vibration pattern of the wire when struck has no sonority until it is fused into unity by the percipient. Sounds exist only as heard; and colours exist only as seen. Yet it is a mistake to say that sounds and colours exist only in the mind. They are both physical and mental, both inner and outer. The vibration of the wire is something natural; but it is potentially a sound; this potentiality is realized only by mind. Mind does not impose pattern on nature, despite what Kant has said; it actualizes the pattern potentially present in nature. The world of sounds and colours exists for the mind which overcomes the externality of nature and so realizes what is potentially present in nature. Nature comes to itself in the mind which actualizes the potentiality of nature. History exists for mind alone. It has its background in nature. But it is only for mind that 'one damned thing after another' is transmuted into history. Notice also that it is mind's power of overcoming externality which makes unitary consciousness of my life possible. Schizophrenia is a mental collapse. Hume, whose philosophy still fascinates so many, regarded mind as a bundle of sensations, a succession of impressions and ideas; but, as he admitted in Part IV, Section vii of his *Treatise*, he could never get beyond this multiplicity to the actual experience of everyday life. His initial mistake was to think of mind as something natural, a succession of things outside one another, and thus he could never reach the level of mind at all. Kant knew better than this.

Now just as mind transforms certain discrete phenomena in nature into sounds and colours, so it transforms a series of separate feelings into appetites. Feeling is of the this, here, now, but the organism is in process. The development of mind beyond feeling becomes an awareness of this process, and so an awareness of appetite.

This development of mind is the dawn of reflection. When our mental powers are limited to feeling as such, there may be scarcely any consciousness of the *self* as feeling something specific. Depression or gloom may be so intense that we are sunk in it. It is only when we somehow force ourselves to reflect on our feeling that we become conscious of feeling gloomy and of the urge to rid ourselves of it. It is by reflecting on feeling that we overcome its atomicity and become conscious of process, conscious of hunger and the urge to eat, of weariness and the urge to rest, of reviving energy and the urge to renew the climb. It is by reflection that we rise from a consciousness of feeling to a consciousness of appetite.

We do not at this stage choose to reflect. Mind at its full development is a complex of activities; feeling is the earliest and least of these. But the climax of mind's development is present potentially at the start, and it is the inadequacy of feeling which makes mind dissatisfied with it and so produces the growth of mind, i.e. by producing the new activity of reflection. We grow from feeling to appetite. It is this clash between what is and what might be, between the actual and the potential, which is the key to all mental growth and achievement. The infant is meant to become an adult and it grows because the goal is implicit at the start, and demands to become gradually more and more explicit. All effort is rooted in a dissatisfaction with what is and the attempt to transform what is into what it might be and into what it potentially is. The ideal is present within the real as its heart and essence, and the growth of mind is the growing consciousness of that fact. Mind's power of overcoming externality is its power to reflect. By reflection the stage of feeling is transcended; reflection on the next stage produces further advance still. And the advance may be called dialectical, because reflection on what has been achieved is always the rejection of what has been achieved, since that achievement still falls short of what might be. No finite achievement can satisfy mind, which is potentially infinite.

3. APPETITE

Feeling, as we have seen, is simply consciousness of our bodily or organic condition. Appetite, as the product of reflection on feeling, is still essentially linked with that same condition, and therefore it is still a primitive sort of experience, far below that, for example, of sophisticated desires. Although it is a product of reflection, it is, as such, unchecked. It occurs in adult life as something by which we may be carried away. We regress to it when for some reason our mental powers are inhibited. For example, people released from concentration camps in a starving condition fell ravenously on roots in the fields. They were too ravenous to discriminate; starvation carried them away. Appetites are all concerned with the growth and maintenance of the organism; there are for example

D

appetites for food, drink, rest, and sex. And this would seem to identify them with instincts. But there is a crucial difference. The bee cannot help acting on instinct. Appetites, however, as the product of reflection, are potentially controllable as mind develops. Their operation can be modified; but they cannot be eliminated. The life of mind in this world is always lived in a natural environment. Against the limitations of that environment the moral life is a perpetual struggle; but that environment can never be destroyed. This I have said before, but it is important enough to be repeated.

An appetite gratified produces satisfaction. This is the formal characteristic of gratification whatever the content of the appetite may be. Food will not gratify thirst, nor will drink gratify hunger. The content differs, but the formal character of satisfaction is the same. This satisfaction differs from the formal character of pleasure accompanied by some feelings, just as appetites differ from feelings. Feelings are atomistic and pleasure is momentary. Appetite is a process, and its gratification takes time. Satisfaction is more enduring than pleasure; it endures, for example, through the process of gratifying hunger. Hunger in form, if food is available, is neither pleasure nor pain; it is the movement from one to the other, the positive overcoming of the pain and the producing of satisfaction instead of pleasure. If you ask whether the hungry man wants food or satisfaction, the answer is easy. He wants food. Satisfaction supervenes on his attainment of his end. The formal character of his experience in getting food is satisfaction. It is a mistake to call this a 'feeling'.

4. PASSION

An appetite may not always be gratified. Shipwrecked mariners may be put on starvation rations. The oasis may prove to be a mirage. The loneliness of solitary confinement may be torture. When an appetite is not gratified we experience dissatisfaction or frustration.

Consciousness of this frustration takes the form, at this level, of *passion*. Passion is by derivation something suffered. Here we come up against what I have said is a recurring difficulty in an attempt to describe accurately the stages in the development of moral experience. 'Passion' is often used as a synonym for appetite or desire. Love is described as a 'passion', and we speak of a man of 'strong passions' when we mean much more than that he is often angry.

Passion has two forms; fear and anger.[1] It is inadequate to call these 'emotions', because that word is too subjective and too wide. An emotional person may just be one who bursts into tears on trivial occasions.

Appetite seeks satisfaction. It does not get it. Our reaction is either negative, fear; or positive, anger. Fear is a paralysis; anger is dynamic. Neither contributes directly to the satisfaction that is sought. The one is impotent; the other acts but to no purpose. Stamping the feet, brandishing the arms, shouting curses—none of these advances matters or solves any problem. Action accompanying this display of wrath is blind and can be effective, if at all, only by chance.

Anger, however, is a way of overcoming fear and, to that extent, it represents a mental advance. I recall my fear of a snake, and then attacking it in a fury, beating it with a stick long after it was dead and harmless. A man who had got further towards rationality would not have used the unnecessary violence. The anger in this instance overcomes the fear.

In order to illustrate this doctrine which I derived from my tutor, I quote some considerations in its support:

(i) At this still somewhat low level of mind the passions of fear and anger may have no clear object. They may appear groundless, coming on us we know not why. Sudden outbursts of temper in people who are usually equable are often very perplexing, especially when the occasion for them is trivial. This is why we speak truly when we talk of *falling* into a passion. It implies a regression below the level of self-control. Here the psychologist may come to our aid with the suggestion that some trifling criticism touches some sub-conscious nerve; and the result may be the fear involved in self-contempt; anger then supervenes, only it is anger with oneself and not really with the apparent object. This is why we say to an angry man, with good reason, 'you forget yourself', or ask him to count ten, i.e. we give him time for reflection, and so for surmounting the level of passion.

(ii) Even in a happy and united family, an eldest son may be guilty of outbursts of wrath against his younger brothers and

[1] I am adopting R. G. Collingwood's terminology, *New Leviathan*, pp 67 ff.

sisters. Here again the psychologist helps. The eldest is subconsciously afraid of being supplanted by his juniors in the affection of his parents.

(iii) Walking along a towpath with a friend and coming to a bend in the canal and a bridge over it, I was very nearly caught between a tow rope and the masonry of the bridge, and was within an ace of being cut in two. I lay flat on the ground in the nick of time and the tow rope passed over my head. To my astonishment my friend cursed me in language more violent than I had previously heard. But I now realize that he had feared so much for my life that the anger was the reaction to the fear.

(iv) Never have I been so frightened as when I sat inactive in an air-raid shelter during a raid. Those with duties to do had no time to feel fear. The fear came on because I was inactive and my activities were frustrated. When I gave up going to shelters I recovered most of my equanimity.

It is necessary to distinguish between fear and awe, and between anger and indignation. Awe and indignation may both lead to constructive action; they may provide a stimulus to reason. A 'passionate' interest in something, which may provide the motive power for a life devoted to scholarship or medicine, has nothing to do with the passions with which I have been dealing or with the level of experience which I have called passion. What is often called a 'passionate' interest is a strong desire.

Fear is a blind guide, with futility as its outcome. Anger is just blowing off steam. It therefore follows that we ought never to allow our course of action to be dictated by fear or anger. To act effectively is to act rationally; we must rise beyond the level of passion, and we rise by reflection, just as it was by reflection that we rose above feeling to appetite.

5 . DESIRE

Fear and anger are alternative reactions to a frustration of appetite. They are therefore reactions to what frustrates and so to something not ourselves. Reflection on this experience introduces us to the distinction between self and not-self, and, in general, to the distinction between alternatives. The experience of passion is disagreeable; it does not contribute to the satisfaction at which appetite aims; it may only intensify dissatisfaction. Reflection on this quandary produces the question: What *do* I want? The answer to this question transforms appetite into desire.

This is a considerable *mental* advance, because reflection has risen to self-conscious thought. And this is the key to emancipation from the blindness of feeling, the tyranny of appetite, and the frustration of passion. For example, to discover by reflection, as some would suppose that we do, that we are slaves to appetite, is to be no longer a slave. If I were in fact a slave and no more, I could never discover the fact.

Desire is knowing what I want and knowing that I have not got it; its aim and its satisfaction is happiness. It is characteristic of desire, as an achievement not only of reflection but of thinking and self-consciousness, that it implies aversion. *Hunger*, as we saw, is for food, and as pure appetite it is for any food; the roots satisfied the victims of concentration camps. *Desire* is selective: it rejects what is not precisely the object of its quest. Appetite was concerned only with the maintenance and well-being of the organism. Desire, the creature of an advance in mind, has a far wider range. The organism's needs are there still; but they come under control because desire may be for what will bring happiness to the personality, i.e. for mental and spiritual objectives.

The intrusion of thought into our life is a disturbing element. The animals appear to be enjoying themselves all the time in what they do. But for us to ask ourselves how we do what we are doing is often to fail. It is fatal for the amateur pianist to reflect and ask himself what comes next in the piece he is playing from memory. Thought makes us dissatisfied with the present and it concentrates desire on the future, not on pleasure now but on happiness then. Well is it written that he that increaseth knowledge increaseth sorrow. Thinking alters the world; it is a gross error to look at externals and to suppose that because the cow chews the cud, and infants suck and men go to dinner parties, 'instinct' will explain all these phenomena. Just as in nature there are no sounds or colours but only the potentiality of them which mind alone can actualize, so in infantile life there is only a minimal freedom, hardly more than the potentiality of freedom, which mind in its development will actualize by translating feeling into appetite and appetite into desire.

The way in which reflection, or mental activity, changes the situation has been mentioned already; 'Are you not cold?' 'Now

that you mention it I think I am.' But at a different level it is
possible to be aware of one's situation and yet not to know what it
is. When the prodigal son 'came to himself'—note the phrase, for
it implies reflection—he saw that he was not really enjoying himself; he was wasting his substance in riotous living. Consciousness
of what the situation really is alters its character. The pleasure of
the prodigal turns into self-reproach. Whenever there is a *prise
de conscience*, as I believe the French say, the world is altered.

While it is true that the intrusion of thought, into what otherwise might have been in human life a process as harmonious and
placid as that of animal life, produces 'sorrow' or discontent, there
is, as always in the life of mind, a compensation. To ask 'What do
I want?' makes it possible for us to *choose*, because I have already
pointed out that the transcendence of appetite brings with it a
consciousness of alternatives.

Desire is for what we want. And it is a drive towards getting it.
But the question which created desire, namely: what do I want?
is a question which may receive a wrong answer. We may get
what we want, and find that it does not bring happiness. There-
upon an unsatisfied craving persists. But what sort of craving is
this? It is by an advance of mind that we have reached the level
of desire. At lower levels it looks as if the motive force to action
operates *a tergo*. But this is only appearance. What produces the
development of mind is the end or that which it may ultimately
become as its potentialities are realized. Mind is not so much
driven by instinct or appetite from the rear as drawn upward by
the clash within it between what is and what may be. This becomes plain at the level of desire, where the question: what do I
want? may be wrongly answered. It may be wrongly answered
because the ego here is growing in self-consciousness and in
reflection and the wrong answer may have been given in obedience
to appetite, or, in other words, to an urge which would inhibit the
development of mind and draw the ego downwards towards its
natural origin.

6. THE ROUTE TO FREEDOM

If I answer wrongly the question: what do I want? and find that,
in pursuing what I think I want, I am foiled of happiness, only
one recourse is open to me, namely, to use John Oman's great

phrase,[1] to say NO to desire, i.e. to domination by desire. This denial is the triumph of mind over the given. It is the assertion of the rational self against instinct, feeling, appetite, passion and desire. It is the liberation of the self from these forces and is the beginning of true freedom. Freedom of a kind there is at lower levels when we attain pleasure or satisfaction. But only freedom of a kind. It is not freedom *from*; it is only freedom *to*. And true freedom must be both of these.

At this point I must enter a *caveat*. The thinking which produces a discontent which may be called divine in the sense that it releases us from animalism and sets us on the road to spiritual life—our destiny—does indeed give us freedom from the *domination* of instincts and appetites. But it does not destroy them. Any attempt to get rid of these, by what is called 'repression' brings on itself its own nemesis. In this world we cannot lead a purely spiritual life. All we can do is to control natural forces. We cannot get rid of them. I have said this before more than once, but it bears repetition. In repeating it, however, I would emphasize that the power of mind does make control possible, and therefore does make possible the moral life which is the presage of the spiritual.

I have said that saying *no* to desire is a precondition of freedom. It is freedom to choose, and this is what is often called 'will'. About the freedom of the will there have been interminable and not yet terminated controversies. But the real question is not whether the will is free, but whether I as an individual person am free. Will is not a faculty and so *one* faculty of the self; it is the self in action. To talk of the freedom of the *will* is to imply that the individual is a bundle of capacities, desire, will, reason, and whatever others a psychologist may wish to distinguish. But this splitting of the self into diverse faculties outside one another is to reduce it to nature all over again and so to fail utterly to understand what men, as distinct from animals, are. If by saying *no* to desire, *I* find freedom, it is the whole conscious self which becomes free, free from the domination of appetite, passion, and desire, but not from their existence; free to choose whether to satisfy this desire or another, not free to satisfy none. Desire, or, as Hegel would have said, using a different terminology, 'passion', is the mainspring of all fruitful achievement, for it is the motive force of endeavour. As Hegel said in his own terminology: 'Nothing

[1] *The Natural and the Supernatural*, Cambridge, 1931, pp 298, 313.

great is ever achieved in the world without passion'.[1] Unless we hunger and thirst after righteousness, we are unlikely to live much of a moral life.

7. NEGATION AND EDUCATION

It is at this point, when negation releases us from the domination of desire, that the negative moment implicit in what has hitherto been called 'reflection' becomes explicit. The growth of mind beyond the stage of feeling is the actualization of potentiality, and this development occurs through what Hegel calls the 'power of the negative'. Negativity is the price of advance. Freud saw this when he said that the 'price of civilization is the denial of instinct'.[2]

At first, in the development of the infant and the child, the negative has to be imposed from without as discipline. Psychologists and educational theorists who suggest that the infant and the child should be allowed to develop naturally, without that negation of nature which discipline is, are in fact advocating a policy of inhibiting moral and spiritual development. This psychological doctrine is not so recent as is sometimes supposed; it was current in the late eighteenth and early nineteenth century when it was adopted by humanists, and it seems still to be held today in many quarters. Its holders begin with the belief that man is by nature good, and capable of indefinite advances towards perfection, given a good organization of society.[3] This is nonsense. By nature, or at birth, man is not what he ought to be or, in another terminology, is meant to be. He is not yet a person, a self-conscious moral agent. This is the truth of the Christian doctrine of original sin. In order to become a moral agent, and so to lift himself on to the plane of goodness, man must reject or negate his original nature. Humanists ignore this essential negative in man's development. It is only by negating our origins that we rise to a spiritual life. This is why discipline in youth is an inescapable pre-requisite of a moral order; it is also why juvenile delinquency is such a grim problem today at a time when so many parents have been bemused by psychological and other doctrines about natural goodness

[1] *Ph. d. Gesch., Ww.* [1] ix. 28, [2] ix. 30.
[2] Quoted in R. and M. Knight, *op. cit.*, p 189.
[3] See, e.g. W. G. de Burgh: *Towards a Religious Philosophy*, London, 1937, p 193.

and natural development. Development is impossible without negation, which in this context means discipline and punishment, especially the corporal punishment which is either the only one effective in a child, as in a dog, or else the one which humiliates and therefore impresses the growing mind of the adolescent. It is a fact that it may fail in its purpose, but any alternative seems likely to produce a still worse failure.

8. HABIT AND CONVENTION

What has been said about appetite, passion, and desire may be regarded as a study of the springs of action which are preparatory to choice. But, so regarded, the account is incomplete because a large part of our life is governed by none of these but by (a) habit and (b) by convention.

(a) Habits may be either good or bad. (An attempt is made in the next chapter to state what these adjectives mean.)

Habits are good in so far as the habitual action is itself good; for example, a Christian or a Moslem saying prayers regularly and abiding by other religious observances is good; or a habit may be good when it is one which accords with a rule in some matter where a rule is necessary for an ordered life, but where *what* the rule is does not matter morally, e.g. driving on the left-hand side of the road in some countries and on the right in others.

A bad habit, on the other hand, is bad because the habitual action is always unjustified as, for example, unpunctuality. Bad habit is a product of appetite or desire undisciplined and unchecked by reflection. It is a mark of failure in the moral life, that is to say that it is not 'natural' but a development above the natural level which has gone awry. It is a controlled activity, but one controlled wrongly, distortedly, or in the wrong direction. It is a sad circumstance of our human life that it is easier to form bad habits than good, and easier to change good habits for the worse than bad habits for the better.[1]

It is to Aristotle that we owe the best account of the importance of habit in moral education. A stone, he points out, cannot be

---

[1] Some bad and neurotic habits may have their origin in some traumatic experience in childhood, and behaviour therapy has ways of counteracting them by creating pleasant associations with what had hitherto been an object of neurotic fears.

habituated to move upwards, but men can be habituated to justice
by the regular performance of just acts. 'It makes no small
difference, or rather all the difference, what habits we form from
youth onwards.'[1] If you perform virtuous actions until you begin
to take pleasure in them and do them habitually, you acquire
moral virtue. The wise man, the man who has risen to intellectual
virtue, can tell you which actions are virtuous, and when they
become habitual to you, you see that he is right.

Another moralist who stresses the importance of habit is Bishop
Butler, who, although the dullest author ever, and still, prescribed
to students of ethics, is even now held in high regard in some
quarters. In his *Analogy of Religion*[2] he writes: 'We may consider
habits as belonging to the body or the mind and *the latter will be
explained by the former*. Under the former are comprehended all
bodily activities or motions, whether graceful or unbecoming,
which are owing to use; under the latter, general habits of life and
conduct, such as those of obedience and submission to authority
. . . those of veracity, justice, and charity . . . and habits of the
latter kind seem produced by repeated acts as well as the former.'
This disastrous attempt to illustrate the higher by reference to the
lower has been mentioned already in Chapter 1. But it is worth
noticing that Butler's description of justice as a habit of mind
would have been repudiated by Aristotle. In his view we become
just by performing just actions. Habituation was the process
whereby we became just, and this is quite different from saying
that justice is a habit.

The cultivation of a good habit is one of the foundations of the
moral life, and to that extent it is not without some moral worth.
Indulgence in a bad habit may lead to moral decline, and to that
extent it is not exempt from moral condemnation. The importance
of a training in good habits is that it enables us to settle how to
act in matters of moral indifference,[3] and so enables us to keep
our ability to choose for occasions of moral importance. Habits
liberate us from the necessity of spending time and effort on
reflecting and choosing all the time; they economize mental
exertion and so give us time and energy to do our proper work;
without habit we would have to spend half our time swithering

---

[1] *E.N.* 1103^{b}25. [2] 1, section 6.
[3] Whether to smoke cigarettes or not may be a moral choice. But the habitual
selection of one brand rather than another is one of the ἀδιάφορα

and might indeed starve to death like Buridan's ass. Consequently habit is valuable as a regulator of life. For example, it is as well to make a habit of raising one's hat to a lady in the street, or of rising from one's seat if a lady enters the room; it is as well to make a habit of being punctual for meals or of answering letters promptly or of returning books we have borrowed. And this introduction of order and regularity into life is part of moral education. It is a disciplining and a training of impulse. It reduces the pull of appetite, passion, and desire and so facilitates the entry of choice. It is itself not so much morally worthy as a precondition of moral worth. It affords, as might be said in another context, the *praeambula fidei*. Or it might be called the soil out of which choice grows.

We must notice, however, that habit is always something from which we can depart. A bad habit can be cured. If a good habit is justified solely by its orderliness, we can depart from it without moral censure if departure is for the sake of rising to some higher moral level. The Sabbath is made for man. The man whose habit it was to play golf every Saturday morning and who therefore could not attend his wife's funeral when it took place on that day because he played as usual is not to be commended. Hence a habit must be distinguished from a mania or from domination by appetite. This is not observed by a well-known exponent of Christian ethics, who writes: 'We encourage good habits in our-selves and predict that x will do y on a specific occasion'—we may predict but what is the specific occasion? Our prediction may be falsified if it is based on observance of habits. He goes on: 'within certain not very closely defined limits we regard others as creatures of spontaneous reaction to stimulus'.[1] This is non-sensical phraseology. We learn how to ride a bicycle, and having learnt this we mount it with confidence and ride it, without think-ing, habitually. But there is here no reaction to stimulus, still less spontaneous reaction, whatever that means. This takes us back to the instinctive sucking of the infant and has no relevance to habit. Still less does it have reference to regular action on principle, which in fact is easier to predict than action on habit, because a man *may* decide to depart from habit, whereas he has clearly *decided* to act on principle.

In matters which are morally indifferent, i.e. those where

[1] K. E. Kirk: *Crisis of Christian Rationalism*, London, 1936, p 88.

regularity is required but where what the regulation is does not matter, provided there be one, habit has its proper place and to it there must be ascribed a degree, though only a low degree, of moral worth. This is why it may be necessary to break or change a habit in the interest of achieving a higher degree of moral worth.

(b) Much the same must be said about convention. But there is a difference; it is easier to defy convention than to break a bad habit, and to abide by convention than to create a firm adherence to a good one. It is true that many people abide by the conventions of their milieu unreflectively and that, if challenged, they might regard the conventions as morally obligatory. They then elevate some conventional line of conduct into a moral law, and this is an error, which brings convention into disrepute. Convention is not to be confused with rule. This is why we hear so much from moralists and others, about a 'stuffy and conventional atmosphere'. It is important neither to overrate nor to underrate the worth of convention and its importance.

Lord Chesterfield's commendation of the graces, and his reiterated injunctions to follow a code of gentlemanly conduct, incurred a severe and well-known censure from Dr Johnson. But Dr Johnson, whom I revere, had only a little right on his side, and Lord Chesterfield, whom I do not, had more. Dr Johnson's eccentricities may have been unavoidable, and anything could be excused to genius, but we cannot help thinking that in polite society he might have acquired some at least of the graces of which Chesterfield had so much to say. *Per contra*, Chesterfield might have tried to inculcate some sort of moral principle over and above the graces on which he dilates so tiresomely. To be fair to Chesterfield, he does also preach vigour, and exhort to excellence, and therefore he regards observance of the conventions of polite life as a means to an end; though we may have doubts about the end and the cynical procedure which was to attain it. But this must not close our eyes to the importance of convention.

To abide by the conventions of one's milieu is at least in some respects to order one's life, and here the discipline and training of habit is useful; because the good habit, in matters morally indifferent, will cohere with convention, another master of the sphere of the morally indifferent. Those who defy convention are of two kinds: (i) the selfish individualists who reject not only social but also personal order, who fancy themselves as the *avant-garde*, whereas they are regressing from the moral level of their contemporaries to some form of natural savagery; and (ii) those who are genuinely in the van and who are rejecting convention on the basis of some new insight, and this insight may be social rather than moral. An example of the latter may be certain changes in women's fashions since the mid-nineteenth century.

The inference from this is that reasonable men and women, unless they are possessed of the compulsive power of genius, will abide by convention in the everyday things of life which involve relations with neighbours and those met in the street. Here, to abide by convention regulates life and keeps order. Perhaps an apology ought to be entered here for regarding 'keeping order' as a good, for this has not so far been argued. Order is kept, somehow, no one knows how, by starlings which in enormous numbers in Trafalgar Square or on the Tay Railway Bridge wheel in an instant, when if one failed to obey the call—but what call?—all would collide. In human affairs, order is not kept so easily, but if it were not kept at all, we would have the war of all against all, and the life of man would indeed be, as Hobbes long ago foresaw, nasty, brutish, and, above all, nowadays, short.

From this Hobbesian fate, observance of convention is a primitive kind of deliverance. Hobbes appealed to enforcement of law by an absolute ruler. But he would find things more difficult, if not impossible, if his subjects were not first schooled to obedience, by control of appetite and desire, and so by observance of convention. Law can never be enforced (save perhaps by military rule) unless the vast majority of those to whom it applies are law-abiding. Thus acceptance of convention is one of the foundations of the moral life and of political security. If it is conventional, as it was in my youth, to have an aspidistra in the window, the pressure on the one in the street who had it not became very strong. Resistance to this pressure may have been morally right, just as today the refusal of one person in the street to have a television aerial may have good moral grounds. But those who are so unconventional as not to have a television mast, and who may plume themselves on their moral superiority, must reflect, that this 'keeping up with the Jones's' is one way in which society is ordered and made peaceful. To be conventional is to achieve only a very low degree of morality, but it is better than to be a futile rebel against law; it is at least to recognize the worth of an ordered life. Up to a point it is reasonable, right, and virtuous to abide by the conventions of one's milieu. Here again as with habit, we have one of the *praeambula*. Just as habit is not good in itself but may be judged as good or bad, so convention is always open to moral criticism from a higher standpoint, and from that standpoint convention may be defied, just as habit may be changed.

On these matters, to Butler as the apostle of habit, and to anyone who espouses the worth of convention, there is a reply from John Stuart Mill, who is quoted here the more readily as some of his doctrines will come in for later criticism: 'The human faculties of perception, judgment, discriminative feeling, and even moral preference are exercised only in making a choice. He who does anything *because it is the custom* makes no choice. . . . He who chooses his plan for himself employs all his faculties.'[1] This hits the nail on the head. Choice is on a higher moral and spiritual level than habit or convention or custom; 'spiritual' rather than 'intellectual' because this latter word might imply that only university men could be good, whereas we know the contrary to be more usually the fact.

[1] *On Liberty*, Everyman Edition, 1931, pp 116–17.

CHAPTER 4

CHOICE AND FREEDOM

1. CHOICE

To say *no* to desire is to be liberated from its compulsiveness. This is an advance of mind. Reflection on this experience makes choice possible, and this is an advance of the first importance. If we followed the dictates of desire alone, we would be caught in an endless process which, because it is endless, could never satisfy. Drink of this water and ye shall thirst again. But the reason for dissatisfaction with thirsting again, since thirsting again could be satisfied, for the moment, by drinking once more, is that while desire surmounts the earlier levels, which we described, reflection on desire is now something at the level not only of consciousness, but of self-consciousness, and so of reflective mind. It is the emergence of choice. Choice, or if you like to call it so, will, or practical reason, involves a reorientation of both appetite and desire, and it makes possible not only pleasure, satisfaction, and happiness, but goodness, whatever that may mean at this level. It was after *choosing* each stage in the creation that God 'saw that it was good'. Goodness is the creature, in the first place, of choice and is its continuing correlative. We may ascribe goodness to the aim or object of appetite or desire, but only because that aim or object has been chosen.

There is a sense in which to do what we choose or what we will is to do what we desire, i.e. it is to do what we really desire. It is to do what our whole self desires; there may here be a harmony between reason and appetite. But *this* desire, this self-conscious choice, or our will, is on a far higher level than immediate craving, and is as distinct from it as desire is from appetite. Just as there is a nisus in nature which is revealed in the course of biological evolution, and, indeed, in our appetites, so there is a nisus in mind pressing us forward towards that full development which may properly be called the life of spirit. We attain this, if at all, not by leaving appetite behind but by its control and reorientation to moral and spiritual ends.

Choice implies rejection. It is thus the discovery of good and evil. The good is what we choose; evil is what we reject. But this must raise for us the question: are things good because we desire them and choose them, or do we desire and choose them because they are good? Are we to accept the subjectivism of 'nothing is good or bad but thinking makes it so', or the objectivism of supposing that things are good or bad in themselves? If good is simply what we choose, it seems odd to ask whether a given choice is good or not; and yet we do ask this and proceed to argue the point. On the subjectivist theory, this is very hard to explain. On the other hand, objectivism is no easier to defend, because it will always be possible to ask how the objective quality of goodness is to be identified. If I maintain that a good apple is a hard, tart, cooking apple, and my wife says that this is rubbish and that a good apple must be fairly soft and sweet, it looks as if we are not arguing about anything objective, but only about tastes—which are not reasonably disputable at all. And the subjectivist will use the same argument in relation to moral conduct. *Quot homines*, he will say, *tot sententiae.*

On this plane argument can go on indefinitely between subjectivists and objectivists. The way out of this impasse is to reflect on mind's power to overcome externality. Just as colours and sounds are neither subjective nor objective but both, so also good, potential objectively, is actualized by mind's subjectivity. Good exists for mind alone, for mind that has risen to the level of choice; but this does not mean that it is just subjective. The same is true of evil. Mind can make mistakes. It can choose wrongly. What it actualizes may be evil. Later still mind can choose the bad, knowing the good; at that stage it does not make a mistake, it perpetrates not a blunder but a moral evil or, in religious language, a sin.

Nevertheless the subjective side of choice must be given a certain priority. It is to ignore the creative moment in action to assume that choice is between fixed alternatives already endowed in themselves with objective characteristics like goodness or evil, rightness or wrongness. 'The objectivist leaves out of account the creative process of thought by which we gradually make up our minds what we want or feel our way to a decision, for it is often during this process that the very alternatives, from amongst which we choose, actually come into being . . . To endow with an objective rightness or wrongness the inchoate possibilities whose very definition takes place only during the process of feeling one's way to a decision is' just a superstition.[1]

A day-dreamer may describe as good some experience or some way of life which he makes no attempt to enjoy or attain and which therefore he does not choose. But he is only day-dreaming: he is not thinking or making a judgment. If he said he was, we could only reply that his actual choices belied his 'judgment'.

On the other hand, it may be urged that we call some things good which we have not chosen at all, for example a birthplace; and some people accept their lot in life as good, although they would say that they had had no choice in the matter. In such instances what has been chosen is an attitude towards what could not be helped. We can choose to accept what we have, to learn 'with what we have to be content', or we can make ourselves into discontented, disgruntled, frustrated, and angry young men. It is a mistake to say that attitudes of this kind are just uncontrollable emotional reactions and so not chosen at all. Self control and the discipline of habit have to be learnt, and it is those who have not grown up who lack them. Instead of envying our neighbours, we can reflect on the advantages that we enjoy ourselves. The advance of reflection is the control of emotion and the choice of what we have to accept and what, thus chosen, is seen to be good.

If good is correlative with choice and evil with rejection, we still must recognize different sorts of good. And this is what enables us to ask whether a choice is good. Choice is of good of a kind. But choice of a lower moral good where a higher moral good should have been chosen may be castigated as bad. Pleasure, satisfaction, happiness, these are goods, correlative to feeling, appetite, and desire. But when mind has risen to choice, and so to judgment, and so to new demands above those of the lower levels, it must, if it is to maintain itself and not sink to animalism, choose goods higher than these. It is at this stage that these lower goods become evil. What is rejected, when a man sacrifices his comfort to help his parents, *is* good, but it is a good lower in degree and kind than that which he chooses. In saying that good is what we choose and evil what we reject, we must recognize that our choice may be bad. We may have chosen the lesser or more tempting good, and it is then justly called evil from a higher point

[1] T. M. Knox: 'Action', in *Philosophy*, October 1937, pp 416–17.

E

of view. Evil as the negative of good is not any positive reality. It is a good of too poor a kind.[1] Similarly a bad argument is still an argument and so within the sphere on which a logical judgment may be passed; it is not just nonsense.

It is impossible to make a list of the goods we ought to seek. Anything is good—in some way or other—which we choose. When we have worked hard for a long period, we ought to relax and please ourselves. And in that situation the minimal good of pleasure is at the same time a moral good—if here I may introduce the beginning of the moral life whose foundations I have been trying to lay.

In describing the advance from appetite through desire to choice I have tried to show that this is an advance of mind; the development of rational self-consciousness is not as it were a veneer on physical needs; it alters their character. This is what is overlooked or ignored by those who, possessed of a little psychology, would try to explain away some of our higher moral experiences by such concepts as 'rationalization' and 'sublimation'.[2]

Suppose that a climber encounters a difficult obstacle, and funks it. He may later say that he had to abandon the climb because the physical obstacle was insuperable, and this explanation may simply be a rationalization of an unacknowledged fear. This may or may not be true, because sometimes the physical obstacles are insuperable, while at other times there is plenty of evidence of the strange results consequential on repression. What is illegitimate is an attempt continually to use the weapon of rationalization to explain away any and every conscious decision. Suppose that a man conscious of special knowledge, experience, and ability, aspires to a certain high position where he thinks he could do a good job. His detractors may say that his thinking is no more than a rationalization of his mounting ambition and his lust for power. This is illegitimate. The man may be aware that he is ambitious and that he wants power, but his aspiration is not simply the gratification of ambition; it is ambition modified and qualified by the determination to do a good job. His choice of the position when it is offered to him is a choice; and the reasoning consciousness within the choice is not something superadded to a desire or an appetite; it is a constitutive element in the choice. If the ambition or love

[1] R. G. Collingwood: *Essay on Philosophical Method*, Oxford, 1933, p 82.
[2] See Chapter 9.

of power may be said to be 'rationalized' in the choice, the essential point is that they are altered by the reasoning.

Similar care is necessary with the concept of sublimation. For example, strong sexual desires denied their normal outlet may be sublimated in devotion to religious exercises, but it would be a mistake to regard such devotion as just the fulfilment of desires. A person driven into a course of conduct without knowing why, and being conscious only of a blind compulsion, may have the situation explained if he is made conscious of the desires or appetites which have thus been sublimated. But a *conscious* choice is not to be explained by sublimation alone. The influence of the unconscious is not to be denied or minimized, but it is to make nonsense of the doctrine of the unconscious to deny or to minimize consciousness itself or the transformation and liberation which consciousness provides. Choice is not to be explained away as merely appetite all over again. Psychological investigation may uncover the unconscious motives that lie behind caprice; but to use this fact in an attempt to explain away rational choice is to run counter to experience and so to desert experience for theory.

Choice is rational conduct, the exercise of practical reason, and with such conduct we reach the notion of obligation. Reason, by which I do not mean *Verstand*, but Hegel's *Vernunft*, on its emergence and on being now conscious of lower levels which it has *aufgehoben*, if I may use a compendious and convenient Hegelianism, constrains itself to *be* reason and to rise to the level of choice and choose well. Reason is aware of the stages through which it has been brought into being and at the same time is conscious of the ideal immanent in itself, the ideal of truth and goodness. The moral agent knows that he is not all that he could be; and this inner tension between achievement and potentiality produces the idea of obligation. 'Become what you are', as the ancient Greek put it, is the moral command. The discovery of this command is the product of reflection on choice, on the route by which we have reached it, and perhaps still more on our failure to maintain this level of experience.

For example, in crowds we may regress below the human level altogether and act on animal instinct; if fire breaks out in a theatre some people may be trampled to death. Again, if we are worn out, we may simply become a feeling of weariness, not *desiring* to sleep or to do anything else. Again, deprived of the normal satisfaction of appetite, we may be so enslaved to it that choice is impossible; this dire situation is self-produced by certain ascetics; consider the tales they have told of their dreams and their temptations. In a sudden crisis we may fall a prey to fear or anger. A failure of self-knowledge and a resultant psychological repression may inhibit choice and produce raging desires, and manias like claustro-phobia. But at all these times the moral life requires us to know ourselves, to *choose*, to master nature in the interests of a moral and spiritual life, to be men and not animals, mind and not nature.

In Chapter 1 I said that the moral consciousness was not some-thing which emerged fully grown like Athene from the brain of Zeus. By this time it must be clear that the same is true of mind itself, or of what I have just been calling 'reason'.

The stars move in their courses in accordance with natural law; they cannot fail to do so: 'it is their nature to'. But mind is different. It has to struggle in order to attain and to retain its 'nature'. Mind tries to become itself: its nature is possessed potentially but it has to aim at actual possession. It does not work automatically by natural law. It is simply under an obligation to acquire and exhibit its own true being. In other words mind may fail to be itself, as a planet cannot. We do partially and inter-mittently fail to be minds; we sink to the animal level. The life of mind is thus a struggle for existence. In struggling to be intelligent and good, we are struggling to realize our true potentialities, to give reality to the ideals which are already immanent in us at the start, though undeveloped. Its theoretical and practical activities are simultaneously actualized; the development of one is the development of the other. As Gladstone once remarked: We should 'tread the floor of the earth with an upward and not a down-ward eye'.[1]

2. DETERMINISM AND FREEDOM

Because in my view all the higher ranges of man's moral and spiritual life depend on his freedom and so on choice, I must now explain why I reject determinism. This is in essence a theory which thinks of man as solely a part of nature, concentrates, as some psychologists do, on behaviour, and therefore regards human

---

[1] Quoted in G. M. Young: *Victorian Essays*, London, 1962, p 95.

conduct as determined in much the same way as happenings in the physical world are. This is an old and well-worn topic, and I cannot hope to offer anything new, but the topic cannot be ignored as arguments in favour of determinism have increased within my own lifetime.[1]

What I propose to submit by way of positive argument is very simple. Human freedom in action is on all fours with human freedom in thought. The latter is not possible unless the former is possible, because thought involves freedom to choose between a false theory and a true one. Theory and practice cannot be severed; although, as I have already said, practice may have a logical and sometimes a temporal priority. If we wish to maintain that all our actions are determined by physical or biological events, or by unconscious complexes (themselves with biological roots), then we must maintain the same about our thoughts. This is to say, however, that our theory is not the product of weighing evidence, but of unconscious influences; in other words it cannot claim truth; it is not a theory but something more like an unconscious prejudice.

If after surveying the evidence we say that a certain conclusion is forced on us, we are using a misleading expression, because we imply that the force is in the evidence; but it is not. The force is the force of our own thinking. The verdict, guilty or not guilty, has been chosen. It is true that if we think at all we find ourselves compelled to accept certain logical rules; but the compulsion is still internal to thought itself. It is not an external compulsion like that exercised by propaganda on immature minds or that exercised on us all by unconscious complexes or unconscious prejudices, or illness.

The same is true about choices in conduct. If being the men we are, with our own history and our reaction to our upbringing and education, we say with George Washington 'I cannot tell a lie', the inability is not due to an external influence of any kind. If I cannot tell a lie, it is because I can will myself not to tell it.

[1] When a summary was published of the lecture on which this chapter is based, Professor M. Ginsberg kindly drew my attention to an argument similar to mine in his book *On Justice in Society* which I had not seen. As his book was published in 1965 and my lecture was first drafted in August 1964, it might almost seem as if we were in telepathic communication. I might also refer to a useful article on 'Freedom of Choice' by Mr R. C. Skinner, in *Mind*, October 1963.

Nowadays we may be more circumspect than Washington; we may admit that we *can* tell a lie, for example under the influence of fear when our will is in abeyance and choice is impossible; we may admit that refusal to tell a lie may be equally unwilled if, for example, it results from some 'passionate' enthusiasm, and so from below the level on which choice is possible. But, knowing the possibility that our conduct may not be chosen but may be dictated by impulsiveness or passion, or physical weakness, we are in a position to guard against that danger, and by reflection to free ourselves from these forces which even if mental are unconscious, or pre-conscious, or sub-conscious, or at any rate not self-conscious, and so to rise to the level of choice, and choose either to lie or to tell the truth, though in physical weakness action may be impossible and moral responsibility at a minimum.

The language of determinism is always dangerous when we are describing choosing or reasoning, and it is better avoided, but there are some who would say that when we choose we may have a reason for choosing, and that, if so, the choice is determined by the reason. Phraseology like this does less than justice to the fact that choice is often simply the making up of one's mind. The reasoning goes into the process of choosing. But even if this were denied, the only sense in which reason determines choice is that I, as thinking, determine my choice. The choice is not enforced by any external influence whatever. In choosing I am self-determined. As mind I am free from the external domination of nature, and one of our main tasks in life is to make ourselves minds which are so far as possible exempt from *un*conscious inner controls too.

Reflection, choice, and will have been closely associated in what has been said here about freedom. No attempt is being made to defend the theory that everything in the universe is a chain of ineluctable causes and effects, *except* the will which is then regarded as a faculty supposedly exempt from the laws of nature. What is being maintained here is the freedom of man as mind, and so not as nature but that for which alone nature *is* nature. Man's life begins on the natural plane, but he is potentially spirit too; in virtue of his developing self-consciousness he achieves at least a measure of self-transcendence, so that his natural being becomes recessive. The realm of mind or spirit may be a realm of law too; but it is not, as in nature, a law that is invariably obeyed;

it is one which ought to be obeyed. And it is not a law imposed from and operative from without; it is a law adopted by mind itself. In the great phrase of Immanuel Kant, everything in nature works in accordance with laws, whereas man as mind determines himself by his *consciousness* of law. It is this self-consciousness which makes it possible for man to order his life anew as the tides cannot and as even the bees cannot.[1]

This thesis I now proceed to illustrate by a series of comments on determinism, and I must begin by pointing out the strength of the theory which I am rejecting.

Natural science began to make great progress when it jettisoned the notions of chance and purpose which had played a prominent part in Greek science and especially in the Aristotelianism which came to dominate European thought in the later Middle Ages. The eighteenth century, obsessed with machines and chains of causes and effects, often speaks of man as determined by heredity, environment, and by physical, including even phrenological, characteristics. To this however, there is an easy reply; heredity does not seem to work mechanically or automatically; what influences us is rather our reaction to our environment than the environment itself; and no modern philosopher would think it worth while, as Hegel did in his *Phenomenology*, to point out the inadequacies of phrenology. In some of this eighteenth-century thought, the fallacy of *post hoc, propter hoc* is not uncommon.

It is the progress of science in the last century or so which has made determinism more formidable. Law, rather than causality, is the *leit-motiv* of this progress, and it seems plausible to bring man under natural law as soon as it is discovered that man has evolved from animals and they from matter, so that man is part of nature. Psychological investigation has shown how effective certain unconscious mechanisms are in the life of human mind; and sociological enquiries, based on accepting the hypothesis of natural law in human society, also appear to have made some progress. Electro-physiology and the development of electronic computers, said sometimes to be brains with memories, have also encouraged the belief that laws of the working of the human mind

---

[1] My emphasis on self-knowledge and self-consciousness in this discussion gains some support from Mr S. Hampshire's lectures on *Freedom and the Individual*, London, 1965, but, in my view, he befogs the issue by confusing desire with appetite.

may be discovered as the effect of changes in the brain, its material basis. Leucotomy has completely altered a patient's personality. It is thus neither unnatural nor unreasonable, at first sight, to hold that further enquiry into the whole range of man's activities ought to proceed on an examination of behaviour and on some deterministic assumption, in the hope that in due course proof will be forthcoming that the assumption is valid everywhere. One is bound to admit that this procedure is more reasonable than that of those who would try to refute it by quoting Hume on causality or Heisenberg on indeterminacy; the first of these quotations is a vain attempt to put back the clock; the second is mere ignorant misunderstanding. Nor is it beyond cavil to say that science can predict eclipses but it cannot predict human affairs. Mr R. Robinson, in his book *An Atheist's Values*[1]—a book to which I am much indebted and to which I shall have to return—says that no one could have predicted the Suez crisis in 1956 and that a science of politics is therefore impossible. But believers in scientific sociology and politics are entitled to retort (whether we believe them or not) that as their science develops, as their statistical methods improve, laws of revolutions or crises may be discovered, and prediction, as of election results, may become more and more reliable. It is not by Mr Robinson's route that scientific determinism is to be refuted.

Having now described Cerberus, I will throw him a sop. It is sometimes said that if determinism be true, morality is impossible and that good and evil disappear. This is an error. Even if all a man's acts are determined, what he does may still be good or bad and he may be called good or bad for doing it. It is not moral distinctions that are obliterated if determinism be true, but only the doctrine of individual responsibility. Some theories of divine grace have produced systems of morality without including that doctrine. It has also been alleged against determinism that, if it were true, punishment would have to be abolished as either cruel or unmeaning. This need not worry the determinist who might view with equanimity the disappearance of punishment. But in fact the argument is false. We kill snakes that are a danger to us and on a similar ground we may execute or incarcerate criminals who are a danger to society. There is no need to attribute malevolence to the snakes or freedom to the criminal.

[1] Oxford, 1964.

To Cerberus I can concede no more. I now move in to the attack.

It is sometimes held that determinism cannot be refuted because freedom is something that must be believed on faith alone, or alternatively that 'Sir, we know the will is free and there's an end on't'. My reply to this has been indicated already. A theory claims to be true; its sponsors ask us to choose it and to reject as false a theory that contradicts it. Determinism is a theory which denies the possibility of choice, and it therefore refutes itself. However, *per abundantiam cautelae*, I offer some further considerations.

Determinism identifies mind with nature. Man, it is alleged, acts in accordance with the laws of his nature, and these laws underlie the impulses or instincts of which he may be conscious. With the exception of consciousness, so the argument goes, the life of man is on all fours, in principle, with the life of bees or ants. Men may discover what instincts they have, or the laws underlying them, but this is just a discovery that conduct is determined, and the discovery makes no difference to the fact. If a stone were endowed with consciousness, Schopenhauer says,[1] it would still fall in accordance with the law of gravity, and knowledge of the fall would make no difference to the falling. A view of this kind used to be held by economists who talked of the 'iron laws' of economics which received an encomium from Hegel. But economists have since discovered that there is no 'iron' in them. A given economic system will have certain implications and these will be inevitable within that system, but not otherwise. But economic systems change. Why? One reason is that there is a difference between men and stones. A man will fall like a stone if he suffers defenestration, like people in Prague, and his consciousness of falling will make no difference to his fall. But the falling is something that happens to him, not something that he does. A stone endowed with consciousness would no longer be a stone, and this is what Schopenhauer failed to see. Man can distinguish between what happens to him and what he does, and it is because of this that man can change his world, and with it his economic systems. The situation we are in sometimes happens to us without our having had any influence on it, for example the situation we are in at our birth. But usually what happens to us is the result of something we have done; and in virtue of our

[1] Edn. *cit.* (i. 126. He is partly quoting Spinoza: *Ep.* 62).

knowledge of what the situation is, we can change it. The point was neatly put by Walter Bagehot in a cruel epigram: 'A man's mother is his misfortune; his wife is his fault ' When we lose hope, we may just let things happen to us; and some people live on tramlines because it has never occurred to them to act differently. But let them realize what their situation is, let them realize that they are men after all, and hope will revive with the realization that their situation is alterable by their choice. The sleep-walker does not know where he is going; he is indeed determined: but by waking up he becomes conscious of where he is, and this knowledge sets him free and enables him to choose either to prolong his walk or else go back to bed. The determinist takes us to be sleep-walking all the time. If this distinction between the things that happen to us and the things we do is an illusion, as it is for determinism, how does it arise? and why does it persist? The illusion that the stick in water is bent can be scientifically explained, and it does not persist. We do not *think* that the stick is bent after we hear the explanation.

We react differently to people we like and to those we dislike. Why? The determinist presumably answers: Because different people in virtue of their characters or physical appearance produce different reactions in us. This cannot be accepted. The goods wagons react to the stimulus of the shunting engine, and mechanical reactions similar to this may occur on the biological level too. But an individual feels likes and dislikes and is conscious of them, and it is these feelings which endow persons, and physical objects too, with attractiveness or the reverse. The determinist will decline to accept this and will hold that our feelings are themselves reactions to qualities in the persons or objects, whether we are conscious of these qualities or not. This is dogmatism. How can it be known? The goods wagons do not react to all the qualities of the engine; they will react whether the engine is steam or diesel driven. If our feelings are reactions to qualities in other persons or objects, we must know what these qualities are, and our consciousness of these qualities may then produce the feeling. Consciousness makes the difference which the determinist denies, and he denies it because he is seeking an explanation of human conduct by reference to its most primitive levels, i.e. to those which precede the discovery of alternatives *via* the frustration of appetite and the experience of passion.

It may be urged that our consciousness is determined by our physical condition or by our glandular metabolism. A man may be quite unable to help being lazy, although he knows he ought to be active. But he knows about his condition and for some glandular troubles he can take the doctor's tablets. His responsibility may be diminished in ways that he cannot help. But his knowledge of his physical condition will nevertheless enable him to take the tablets and thus to restore some at least of his responsibility. We are not determined by our social class or by our physiological make-up but can be free, at least to some extent, by our reaction to these.

The deterministic theory is sometimes put in the form that men are 'just conscious machines'. To talk of a conscious machine, however, is an absurdity, a direct contradiction. The various cogs of a machine are so designed as to do their work if the proper force is applied. Now it is true that a driving force can be applied to man; propaganda may be used to stimulate the driving force of his appetites; threats may be used or rewards offered in order to stimulate fear or greed. But the application of these driving forces works only if the agent is not reflecting, if he is not fully self-conscious, if he is allowing himself to act mechanically. His self-awareness as a man, like his power to choose, his conscious mind, is in abeyance. In so far as men react to stimuli, they are indeed like machines. But we can become conscious of these external stimuli, and that knowledge together with our power of reflection enables us to react to them as we choose. We can decide to go in the direction in which we are being propelled or else to go else-where. It is because, *qua* thinker and *qua* mind, man is capable of choice that dictators endeavour to destroy the minds and the intelligences of their victims by stimulating their appetites and so putting them at the mercy of forces which only self-conscious reflection can control.

The determinist may try to strengthen his case by adducing the power of men's habits to which I have alluded already. It is true that a man's spontaneity of action can be reduced to a sort of mechanism if habit governs his whole life. But life is full of surprises and a man may be 'shaken out of his habits' by mis-fortune or grief. 'Shaken out of his habits', however, is an expres-sion that concedes too much to believers in mechanism in human affairs. Grief or misfortune may so numb a man that he sinks into habit more deeply than ever. All will depend on his attitude to his misfortune. He may reflect on his situation and as a result spur himself to renewed effort and change his habits accordingly. The reflection, once more, makes the choice possible. A man may be shaken out of his habits; but he may also set himself to change them deliberately, actuated only by his own choice, and not forced by any external stimulus.

The determinist may reply: If a man does change his habits, he changes them only because he is a person of a certain kind, i.e. the change is determined by his character. A similar sort of argument has been advanced by Professor Ayer when he says, in effect, 'of course I can do what I want, and therefore I am free; but what I want is determined by my character and therefore I am determined'.[1] But what evidence is there for an underlying character, there all the time, determining all the vicissitudes of a man's life?[2] A man's character is his history up to the point he has reached at any given time, and what makes his character is just either his failure to rise above the appetitive level to the level of choice, or his success in so rising and the choices he makes thereafter. Even if I choose x today because I am the kind of man I am today, that is no proof that I do not choose. And my choice today will affect what I am tomorrow. It is my choices that determine the kind of man that I am. There is no permanent underlying substratum of the self. The determinist argument just takes us back to impulse again and ignores the growth and development of mind. A man's character is not a product of heredity, environment, upbringing and so forth, but is formed by his *reaction* to these, i.e. by his mental development.

Professor Blanshard has told us[3] that he is a determinist. Every action, he says, is caused, but causes differ in level. Mental causation is not like the clash of billiard balls. He instances logical inference and the work of an artist. Aesthetic and logical work is

[1] See K. T. Gallagher: 'Choosing to choose', *Mind*, October 1944, pp 480–1.

[2] Professor H. J. Eysenck thinks that there is some, derived from the ancient doctrine of temperaments. But when we survey the characteristics of each and try to apply them to persons we know, or even to ourselves, our doubts increase. An intelligent man's reaction to any temperament he may have is liable to give him a mixture of temperamental characteristics. Professor Eysenck, concerned with behaviour, abstracts (usually) from the power of mind. (See, e.g., *Fact and Fiction in Psychology*, Penguin, London, 1965.)

[3] In his contribution to *Determinism and Freedom in the Age of Modern Science*, edited by S. Hook, New York, 1958.

successful in so far as it becomes the instrument of a necessity lying in the subject-matter. As for moral experience, when a man does his duty he has caught a vision of the good. The good necessitates certain things as integral parts of itself. The saint is most free when he is most a slave.

The admission of causal levels shows that it is only in a Pickwickian sense that Professor Blanshard is a determinist. But it is surprising that he does not see that we are not compelled by the evidence or by a logical ideal, but only by our conception of these. And if a man fails to do his duty, is this because he is necessitated by a vision of the bad? Determinism ought to imply predictability of human conduct, as of eclipses, for example, and Professor Blanshard does not claim this.

The strength of determinism lies in the fact that our freedom is not absolute. We are not free *from* the ravages of disease. We are not free *to* become invisible. This has long been obvious; but what physiology, psychology, and perhaps sociology have done in this century is to show that our freedom is more circumscribed than has often been admitted in the history of thought. Mankind, as I have urged before, has feet of clay. It can never wholly transcend its natural origin or attain in this world a purely spiritual life. The determination of some of our thinking by unconscious complexes, etc., and of some of our actions by appetite, has been too amply demonstrated for it to be ignored. A natural life would indeed be one as much dominated by natural law and as much determined as nature is itself.

But we need not live a purely natural life, and failure to realize this is the weakness of determinism. By the process of increasing self-consciousness, by the development of mind and reflection which I have described, we can win our way to choice and to freedom in part at least of our life, and it is our moral task to enlarge the area of choice and of freedom to the greatest possible extent.

To this the scientist may retort that I have forgotten that human conduct too is 'behaviouristic'.[1] We observe how organisms react to their environment. A plant hit by the sun's rays may turn its

[1] These notes on behaviourism are taken from E. B. Holt: *The Freudian Wish*, London, 1915, but Professor Ryle in his *Concept of Mind* seems to be tempted to a similar view in his anxiety to destroy the 'ghost in the machine'. And the view is explicit in the work of Professor Eysenck (see, e.g., *op. cit.*).

leaves until they lie at right angles to the sun's rays. The hen has
a retinal image of a hawk and clucks to her brood; shoot the hawk
or remove the brood, and the clucking stops. A man is walking
past my window; observation will reveal what he is really doing,
e.g. going to a pillar box or waiting for a girl friend. In all these
instances it is behaviour which is observed. In all these instances
the behaviour is the result of the working of integrated mechanisms in the nervous system, and these can be observed by experiment, as in animals, and they can thence be inferred to be present
in man. The fact that man is conscious of purposes is irrelevant
to the fact that these are really determined by the workings of the
nervous system producing an appropriate response to the environment.[1] The electro-physiologist who removes part of the brain of
a grasshopper, then observes how, coming into contact with an
electric charge a few times, the grasshopper gradually withdraws
its legs from this contact, and then quotes this as an instance of
memory, is adopting a dubious procedure if he is trying to cast
light on human memory and the workings of the human mind.
The procedure is dubious because it implies trying to interpret
the higher by reference to the lower, and there is no obvious
analogy between an impetuous recoil from a disagreeable stimulus
and subsequent avoidance of that stimulus and the procedure
whereby a child may be taught to memorize the multiplication
table. Nevertheless a younger child puts out its hand to the candle
flame and withdraws it quickly on feeling pain: when it knows that
the flame is hot it has an impulse to avoid it. The parallel with the
grasshopper is perceptible. As applied to animals and to unconscious or infantile human conduct, this theory may serve. As
applied to adult life, it is self-destructive. If the theory is a
product of mechanisms in the nervous system, we have no
reason for believing in its truth. The electro-physiologist cannot
apply his theory to his own procedure. The 'learning-theory' of
which Professor Eysenck has so much to say[2] may have some
relevance to the acquiring of habits in infancy, but I am at a loss
to see its applicability to the conscious and intelligent endeavour
to learn anything.

[1] The argument of G. Madell (*Mind*, 1967, pp 34 ff.) does not shake me.
He seems to think, though he does not argue, that consciousness makes no
difference. Moreover, our interpretation of the *behaviour* of the man passing
my window is entirely dependent on my experience of *action* and purpose.
[2] *Op. cit.*, p 140.

Nevertheless the electro-physiologist's procedure is highly ingenious and is a testimony to his own ingenuity in framing the experiment. He is in control; the experiment is not constructed by random guesses or external stimuli. His whole procedure is carried out on a level above any on which determinism can have any relevance. The scientist who avows a deterministic theory of conduct is tacitly exempting himself from the theory, and he is there as the best witness against its truth. The social scientist, searching for laws of social and political action and drawing attention to the success of certain public opinion polls in predicting election results is drawing attention to something which may make the search for the laws of history vain. If you ask a man how he is going to vote, he may have made up his mind and may have reasons for his intentions; and the prediction that that is how he will vote will be tolerably reliable unless there is some startling change of circumstances. The prediction of human conduct is thus possible not because it is determined, but because it is reasoned. And the fact that a choice may be foreknown is no evidence that it is not freely made. If men were determined by appetite alone, they would be governed by a chaos of unordered and changing whims, and prediction would be impossible. If the social scientist retorts that underlying and controlling this chaos there are laws which in due course he will discover, we cannot say him nay, even if in the light of the process whereby appetite is transcended and choice achieved, a process already sufficiently described, we are somewhat sceptical of the success of his endeavours. Finally, the electronic brains or computers of which we hear so much have their brains and their language and their memories given to them by men who can think and act. If the machines can produce results achieved by a process which in certain respects resembles human thinking, their ability to do this is provided by those who construct the machine. It can do only what its builders and users can make it do. The machines are not in control in actual life, whatever they may be in science fiction. If the determinist proposes to argue that just as electronic computers made by men work mechanically, so men have been made by God to work mechanically too, he is avowing a form of theism which I would not care to defend.

Historians have seldom looked favourably upon studies of history which have proposed to discern in it a cyclical movement, or a recurrence of the past, or laws governing its operation and enabling us to predict its future. These studies are fatalistic in the sense that they ask us to learn from history what *will* happen. It may be true that history teaches that no one ever learns anything from history, but we might perhaps be able to learn from it what in some situation is likely to happen if we do not choose some alternative policy. If we knew the future, the paradox is that the knowledge would enable us to change the future. A man told by a fortune-teller that he will die in a railway accident can falsify the prediction by going to a district where there is no railway and by moving out of it as soon as the construction of a railway is proposed. A man beside himself with anger may be induced to come to his right mind if he can be persuaded to count ten before acting. Knowledge and self-consciousness are the source of freedom. In so far as our choices are caused, they are caused by ourselves, and by our conscious thought; the unconscious complex may compel, but it cannot compel a *choice*. It is no answer to say that if a choice is caused by thought, that thought is caused by another thought, and so *ad infinitum*. This language only darkens counsel. Thoughts do not cause one another in any intelligible sense of the word 'cause', e.g. in the sense in which the electric charge causes water by fusing hydrogen and oxygen.

3. LEVELS OF CHOICE AND ACTION

Having now done my best to establish the reality of choice, I can give some indication of the path that lies ahead of us.

Choice and good are correlatives; and different sorts of choice are correlative to different sorts of good; and these different sorts of good correspond to different levels of moral experience. Suppose we ask *why* we choose what we do. The question is an intelligible one because choice occurs at the rational level. It is purposeless to ask why or for what reason we seek to gratify an appetite. I mention five different reasons which, on different occasions, we may give for our choice. I choose x; first, because it is pleasant; secondly, because it is the fashion or the done thing; thirdly, because it is a means to some end; fourthly, because it is right; fifthly, because it is my duty.

These reasons are not mutually exclusive. One example will serve. When I discharged the plantation manager, my first reason was that this was a means to transforming a loss into a profit; my second reason was that this was the right thing to do, it accorded with the rules of the economic sphere; but my ultimate reason was that this was my duty, i.e. my duty to abide by the rules of the sphere in which I was earning my living. Duty has claims in every level of experience; otherwise it would be devoid of content.

The five different reasons which I have mentioned lie at the root of different moral theories which conflict with one another when they profess to account for, or to cover, or to justify, or to explain morality as such. They may be reconciled if each is regarded as true of one level of moral experience, but false in supposing that that level is moral experience as a whole. For example, consider promise-keeping. If the conception of different levels of moral experience is denied, then the same principle must be adduced in order to justify both keeping promises and breaking them. On a utilitarian theory, for example, utility on any given occasion may lead to keeping a promise and, on another, to breaking it. An observer may be excused for thinking that, in that case, the real guide to action is not any principle at all, but desire or even caprice. In the moral life, the life into which reasoned choice enters and which it governs, there must be different principles for different levels. It is futile to ask us to act ideally if we have to act within a framework which has its own rules and standards. In a world of spirit, things would be different; but we have to act in a world of space and time and under all the limitations imposed on us by our natural environment and origin. Thus the best we can do is to moralize so far as possible the different spheres in which we have to live. In the example I cited earlier from my own experience, I had to observe the standards of commercial life. I had to consider what compensation could be provided, within commercial limitations, and so on. But I had to abide by the rules of the commercial situation; not by the rules of a game, nor yet by the spirit of a sphere above rules altogether.

Just as with choice we have arrived at obligation and so at moral experience proper, so also we have arrived at action proper. There is something recognizable as action of a kind in each of the spheres of feeling, appetite, passion, and desire. Corresponding to these different levels of experience there is a rising series of modes of action, each successive mode being a higher and better realization of what action ultimately is, namely self-conscious and reflective

F

choice. Moreover different kinds of choice, and the different principles guiding those different kinds, are also accompanied by different kinds of action.

Choice is possible only after reflection on the experience of desire and its negation has introduced us to alternatives. Hence action, as self-conscious choice, is subsequent to this reflection. But action comes before thought; by reflection on the most primitive types of action we are enabled to rise to a higher type, but action must be there first before we have anything to reflect upon. Action makes our world what it is. Hegel's famous remark is apposite: 'Philosophy comes on the scene only after actuality is there cut and dried . . . When philosophy paints its grey in grey, then has a shape of life grown old . . . The owl of Minerva spreads its wings only with the falling of the dusk.'[1] If self-conscious choice and its specifications are to be understood, the nature of action must first be examined, and it may be unfortunate that this theme has not more often engaged the attention of moral philosophers who would certainly have made better music of it than I have done.

[1] *Ph. d. Rechts*, Preface, Eng. Tr., Oxford, 1942, pp 12–13.

CHAPTER 5

ACTION

The problem of the nature of action may be best approached by considering the oppositions between action and (*a*) inactivity, (*b*) thought, and (*c*) movement.

1. ACTION AND INACTIVITY

When action is opposed to inactivity, what may be implied is the opposition between the use of energy and the use of none. In this sense the terms opposed may be used not only of men but also of machines, and hence in that sense the opposition is not of specifically moral significance. The same is true if action is supposed to be conduct, and inactivity to be death. If on the other hand, action and inaction are used as applicable within the sphere of human conduct alone, then it is plain that the opposition is not between action and its opposite but between two different kinds of doing. 'The busy man is active, the idle one does nothing' we may legitimately say in ordinary conversation; but we do not mean that the idle man has stepped outside the sphere of action altogether and thus has exempted his conduct from moral judgment. The idleness may be morally praiseworthy if the idle man is thereby recuperating his energies, and it may be blameworthy if instead of lying on a sofa half asleep he ought to be at his desk. Although he is idle and inactive, he is still *doing* something; he is lying down, it may be, or taking a stroll. A policy of inactivity has been said to be 'masterly', and the 'strength' of the Egyptians was 'to sit still'; in these instances inactivity was an effective form of action, different in kind from the busy running to and fro to which it was opposed, but still a form of *action*. In the only sense then in which the opposition of action and inaction is of moral significance, the opposition is that of one kind of action to another. The inference is that action does not necessarily involve movements which could be photographed; nor need deeds be spectacular. The man who sees an accident and makes no move to help the victims is inactive; but he would by many be judged to have *acted* wrongly in not trying to help. And his action consisted not in doing nothing, but in *standing still* and so doing nothing to help. Inaction is the name which we give to a kind of action, a kind exemplified alike in the cringing of the coward and the forbearance of the meek; and since the coward is reproached and the meek has been called blessed, inaction may be either evil or good, born of weakness or strength, so that its opposition to action cannot be that of evil to good. If we can distinguish kinds of action, as the opposition we have been studying suggests that we can, then we must observe that the opposition between good and evil recurs within each kind. A dichotomy of actions into good actions and evil actions obscures the differences of level on each of which the opposition of good and evil breaks out.

2. THEORY AND PRACTICE

The opposition between action and thought, between practice and theory, has a long history; it would seem to be presupposed by the traditional distinction between logic and ethics as philosophical sciences, and it is enshrined in philosophical teaching in the provision of separate Chairs of Logic and Moral Philosophy with their divergent fields of enquiry. 'Common sense' clings to the validity of this opposition when it says of a scheme that it is 'all very well in theory, but hopeless in practice', or when it distinguishes between 'thinkers' and 'men of action'. Nevertheless, despite the weight of tradition and the prejudices of common sense, it must be affirmed that, while a distinction there may be between theory and practice, opposition there is none, and that the attempt to assign separate spheres to action and thought as if one of them were a reality without the other has been one of the most fruitful sources of philosophical error.

What is really meant by the distinction of practice from theory? Aristotle distinguished between the theoretical and the practical life, between the philosopher and the politician, and gave primacy to the former. But this is as clearly a distinction of two kinds of practice as the distinction between action and inaction was one between two kinds of action. For philosophizing is none the less a type of activity; it is what the philosopher *does*. He asks himself questions and works out solutions. The politician does the same. But, it may be argued, the politician, having solved his problem (e.g. decided how to keep prices down), proceeds to give effect to his solution, i.e. to propose measures in the House or to give orders to his staff to take certain steps; while the philosopher need not, *qua* philosopher, proceed to write a book or give a course of lectures on his problem and its solution; and it is herein that a difference between theory and practice is thought to lie. The philosopher and the politician both think; and their theoretical activity may be practical in the sense that it is an activity; but the politician's thought issues in practical measures, while the philosopher's need not and often does not. But is it really true that there is no practical consequence of the philosopher's thought? Suppose that his problem is logical, and suppose that the result of his investigation is a proof that a certain type of reasoning is invalid or produces conclusions only probable and not certain. The consequence must then be that he ceases to use that type of reasoning or uses it only where probability and not certainty is his aim, or that his theory is but the crackling of thorns under the pot. His theoretical enquiry, if he is a man of sense, has had as direct an influence on his practice as the politician's has. The practical activity of thinking issues in theoretical results which themselves are the mainspring of future practice. Theory and practice are moments in the single activity of living, distinguishable moments, but inseparable.

To escape this conclusion, it may be suggested that there is surely a difference between the practical activity of the philosopher or the scientist in framing a theory and the theory itself. The theory (thought) is one thing, the theorizing (action) is another. But theory is the product of the activity of thinking, and the distinction here is that between an activity and its product, not the commonsense distinction between theory and practice; and while it may be possible to sever the working of a machine from the product of that working and to consider the two separately, in the case of thinking and thought there is no possibility of effecting this severance; for what is a thought, a theory, if not thinking, and how is it to be understood and so known to be a theory except by thinking? The marks on the paper on which the scientist's theory is printed become the theory for us only when we interpret them and think them; i.e. when we transmute what seems to be a product into the very activity which gave it birth.

This will be dismissed as sophistry by those who still cling to an 'obvious' distinction between theory and practice, and they will perhaps now point to a difference between a theory, e.g. about conduct, and the practical facts which the theory is supposed to cover. There is surely, it is argued, a plain difference, and a possible divergence, between conduct and a theory about conduct, between practice and thinking about practice, or theories about practice. We shall be reminded of the drunken minister who preached against intoxicants and begged his congregation to 'do as I say, not as I do'. A man's theories are one thing, his character another. Is not common sense justified in such instances in clinging to its theory-practice distinction? There may seem at first sight to be no direct connection between a scientist's theory of the remoter nebulae and his character, although further reflection might make us wonder whether reliance should be placed on the factual observations of a man whose relations with his fellows had made them dub him unreliable; or his own selfishness of character might lead us to doubt whether he ever had sufficient objectivity of mind to be a thorough investigator. But, however that may be, let us examine the supposed divergence between the moralist's theory and his practice, between his thoughts and his actions. In the first place, we are concerned with his theory and his thought, not with a divergence between *his* practice and the theory of someone else which he has never made his own and which he repeats only as 'the drunk man quotes the words of Empedocles.' (In the latter case there is, to be sure, a divergence between the theory-practice of Empedocles and the theory-practice of the drunkard; and if this divergence be called the divergence of practice from theory, we are again confronted with a form of words which, whatever it *says*, means a divergence between two different types of theory or two different types of practice.) Now my theory of conduct is a theory of a field of a special kind. If I theorize about my observations of the remoter nebulae, I theorize about phenomena remote from me and external to me. They are intelligible, if at all, only from without; I cannot 'get inside' them as I must get inside the mind of the agent whose conduct I try to follow. A theory about conduct is an attempt to understand not only deeds but the purposes which lie behind them. In other words, what makes conduct conduct and distinguishes it from natural phenomena is purpose or thought. What constitutes practice as distinct from the swaying of trees in the wind is thinking, i.e. is theory.

And my theory of conduct is simply my apprehension of my conduct's theoretical background. Further, while physical movements are always external to me, I am myself an agent; I am myself practical. And my theory about conduct, if it be genuinely my theory, must in turn affect, govern, and illumine my conduct. If it does not, then it is condemned as a theory, for if my conduct diverges from my theory, I have not made my theory fit the facts, i.e. I have not been thinking at all, but only imagining, or dreaming. My theory would be as clearly condemned as a scientist's theory would be which, no matter how self-consistent, or however ingenious, yet failed to account for observed facts. And the construction of such a theory is not evidence for a divergence of theory from practice, for, even if formally a theory, it would, of necessity, have fact and practice of some kind for its content; and the divergence would be between the facts on which the theory was based and the facts of my own life; in other words it would be the divergence between Empedocles and the drunkard over again. The man who preaches, 'do as I say and not as I do' will not find many listeners, for he will invite the reply that what he says must somehow be at fault. If it be 'common sense' to hold that theory and practice diverge, it is also common sense to hold that the theory which does so diverge must be false and hardly worth calling a theory at all. A theory, to be a theory, must be a theory of the facts; the theory of conduct must be the crystallization of the thoughts and purposes which make that conduct what it is.

A remark may be added on the phrase, 'all very well in theory, but hopeless in practice'. This is said of schemes which profess to be practical, e.g. of a scheme for an incomes policy, and the question at once arises: in what sense is such a scheme truly said to be 'all very well in theory'? If it professes to be practical, then the only theoretical standard properly applicable to it is that it is a thought-out scheme for attaining practical ends. To say of a scheme meant to be useful that it is theoretically sound but useless in practice is meaningless; for there can be no theoretical soundness about a practical scheme except its utility. What the phrase seems to mean is that the scheme in question would be a practical scheme in Utopia but not here, i.e. whatever the phrase says, its meaning is that theory *cum* practice may differ from place to place or from time to time. Here again we have no warrant for a cleavage between theory and practice, action and thought; there is only an indication that there is more than one type of thoughtful action, more than one type of conduct.

Once action and thought have been severed, the problem arises: how do men come to act? The severance and the problem are the philosophical heritage of ancient Greece. For Plato, good action is something consequential upon thought. Knowledge of the Good is the prerequisite of the good life. But what he fails to explain is *how* the knowledge of the Good leads its possessor to any activity other than that of contemplation. The men of golden intelligence wish to live their whole life in the pursuit of philosophy and it is only under compulsion that they forsake philosophy for the practical tasks of politics. Ruling, like practical activities in general, is a *pis aller*, an irksome necessity ancillary to human life, but only a brute necessity, not something intelligible and worthy in itself. This world, only a shadow of the genuine reality, contributes nothing of value to the reality itself; acquaintance with it may remind us of eternal truths, but our task here is essentially a preparation for death and then for the immortal life wherein action will give place wholly to contemplation. In this picture, action becomes unintelligible, even futile. The activity of thought remains, but although Plato speaks of the philosopher as ruled here by the ἔρως τοῦ ὄντος, the *desire* for reality, this is only a metaphor because, for him, desire lies outside intelligence, so that to be moved by desire is indistinguishable from being moved mechanically. Reason's task is to subdue and control desire so far as possible in this life in order to attain an immortality in which desire will have vanished with the body. The soul which is immortal, is not the tripartite soul of desire, spirit, and reason, but reason alone. The body with its desires is temporal and perishes like the whole of the temporal world; what is truly intelligible is not the perishing, but the eternal; and action, rooted as it is in the flux of temporal events, becomes essentially unintelligible. If the Good exists transcending this world and is not immanent in it as well, and if this world is shadow and not substance, then to make changes in this world, i.e. to act, is not worth while; for it amounts to substituting one shadow for another and contributing nothing to the substance. If the Good is there, whatever we may do, we have no *reason* to do anything except contemplate its goodness, and in such circumstances action may even be sinful. That there is another side to Plato's thought is doubtless true; his moral fervour, his eagerness to stem the moral decadence of Greece, his passionate concern that men should love justice—these are far more prominent in his dialogues than the depreciation of action which, as has been indicated, is the logical consequence of his psychology and his severance of thinking from doing, theory from practice. But this underlying scepticism of the value of human effort comes out clearly enough in the *Republic* itself when the philosopher is bidden to shelter under a wall when the dust storm blows and when Socrates remarks that nothing in human affairs is worth much concern.

We may perhaps descry the Platonic depreciation of action in favour of thought in certain aspects of medieval monasticism, and still more clearly in some of the ideals and practices of India, where the good life is regarded as strenuous contemplation and where asceticism has gone to extreme limits in its suppression of the body and its desires. In the west, however, life has become more rather than less active, and pursuits which the free-born Greek despised have become honourable and normal parts of our life. But Greek influence has continued to make action a problem. Aristotle taught that while theoretical reason moved nothing and so led to no action, there was also practical reason, a fusion of reason and desire, which did lead to action; but the original dichotomy of theoretical and practical reason remained unexamined, and we find in Kant, as late as the end of the eighteenth century, the remark that how pure reason can become practical is an incomprehensible mystery, though that it does become practical is a fact. Western thought has preferred to speak rather of 'the will' than of 'practical reason,' and it is often said that what is chiefly lacking in Greek ethics is a clear conception of the will. But (*a*) either the will is, as Kant held, simply the practical reason, and thus its relation to pure reason is an unsolved problem and the unity of the self or the personality is split into pure reason and practical reason without any connecting link between the two, so that they become as it were, two taps, though who turns on now one and now the other, and why, is left unexplained. Or (*b*) the will is regarded as non-rational, a *voluntas sibi permissa*. This view of the will is elaborated specifically as a criticism of Greek thought. The Greeks had usually conceived of God as a demiurge, a craftsman imposing rational and intelligible forms on given unintelligible matter; and they had thought of human action similarly—the agent apprehended the self-existent intelligible form of justice and then attempted to impose it on the given raw material of human society. The characteristic of action, whether human or divine, is thus craftsmanship, not creation. The Jews, on the other hand, had believed that God created the world out of nothing, and this Judaic doctrine became part of Christian teaching. It was then held that reason apprehended objective realities, whether Plato's forms or the entities studied by mathematics, while the creative power was will. Now if it is believed that human action matters (as it does matter to the Christian who believes in the immanence of the Spirit in men and who rejects the pure transcendence of Plato's God), it is easy in an attempt to explain action, to supplement Plato's mathematical view of the nature of reason with a doctrine of acts of pure will. But this is only to add one abstraction to another in the vain hope of reaching the concreteness of human experience. To be sure, it is possible to find in human life instances of what appear to be (*a*) thinking alone without willing, and (*b*) willing alone without thinking; and it may seem to a hasty observer that thinking is one thing and willing another, even in instances where they accompany one another or become interfused. But we must ask of what order is this pure thinking or pure willing.

Consider, for example, the assertion, which we encountered in Chapter 1, that the work of scientists and mathematicians is inspired by a purely intellectual interest; they have no thought of any possible utility in their investigations: they desire not to *do*, but only to know; and they may describe their researches as 'purely theoretical.' That this interest in knowing for the sake of knowing is a reality we can hardly deny, for we possess not only the testimony of those in whom it is strong but also the commendation which many moralists pass on the 'disinterested quest for truth'. None the less, the value of these purely theoretical studies must be questioned. The disinterested curiosity which is felt by the pure mathematician in the properties of a tetrahedron or by the biologist in the varieties of the butterfly has been denied to me; but, as I hinted earlier, I feel it in our railway system, in the speed of trains which I will never catch, in the time-table of trains to places I will never visit. When we consider these instances and add to them the logician's anxious probing of problems whose solution will never enable him to think better but which are of 'purely intellectual' interest, we may well conclude that we are dealing not

with thinking at its highest or best but with what is either a hobby
or else an intellectual exercise occupying on the scale of thought the
same level as gymnastics occupies on that of practice. Why do we
seek truth? Because it will make us free. We thirst for knowledge
and search for it disinterestedly in that we search for it single-
mindedly or without fear or avoidance of the results of our enquiry, simply because we may thereby be enabled to be better
men, to be free in the world, and to build a better world as a result
of acquiring that freedom. Pure thought, if there can be such a
thing in human life, is abstract thought, or thinking which turns its
back on the concreteness of human life with its ever recurring
practical problems and which, therefore, belongs to the level of
recreation only.

Pure will, we need not be surprised to find, is on the same low
level of practice. A willing which is not shot through and through
by rational motives becomes indistinguishable from impulse. If
the will be not practical reason but an activity parallel to, though
distinct from, reason, then the distinction must rapidly become an
opposition. For it will be futile to ask what reasons lie behind an
act of will; such an act will lie outside the field of rationality
altogether and then will be opposed to reason whether it be regarded as infra- or as supra-rational. If it be regarded as the former,
then will and irrational impulse become identical, and acts of pure
will are not the highest but the lowest and most trivial of our
actions. If, on the other hand the will is supposed to be supra-
rational, the result is much the same, because to put something
above reason is to depreciate reason and to exempt from rational
criticism whatever is elevated above it. We thus have in either case,
the conception of a *voluntas sibi permissa*, a will which wills as it
pleases (not as it *thinks* fit), and which, having exempted itself and
its actions from rational control, denies the rationality of moral
choices and must make good synonymous with its own pleasure.
Here we have the sentimentalism which ascribes to the heart
'reasons' which the head knows not of, and here also is the fascist
exaltation of the call of blood over reason.

Schopenhauer's criticism of Kant is open to a similar description. The attempt to adhere to the mathematical view of reason and
to supplement it with a doctrine of a pure will is an attempt which
fails to explain human conduct as a whole. It presents us with the
pure thought of hobbies and intellectual exercises and the pure

will of impulse or non-rational desire, i.e. with the thoughts and actions specially characteristic of a juvenile. The upshot, then, of this discussion of the distinction between action and thought, practice and theory, is that while there is a distinction between different systems of action-thought and practice-theory, the attempt to sever action from thought, practice from theory, will from reason, only results in abstractions which may be true of abstract (i.e. of lower) levels of human experience but out of which the concreteness of adult experience cannot be built. Once the original abstraction, e.g. of will from reason is made, *fehlt das geistige Band*.

3. ACTION AND MOVEMENT

We may now ask what differentiates an action from a movement. Suppose that I strike a gong. My action is a movement, but something more. There may have been a mechanism arranged to strike the gong at a certain moment, but my striking of it is different, even if I do it at the same time. On the other hand, if a man strikes me and I fall, my falling is a movement which happens to me; it is not *my* action. What is the difference between these two instances? If we ask: why did I fall? the answer is that someone struck me, i.e. one object has impinged upon another *ab extra*, and my movement, falling, is describable in the same physical terms as those which describe the falling of the stone which we fling over the cliff. But if we ask: why did I strike the gong?, there are various possible answers, e.g. because I wanted to make a noise, or because I wished to find if the gong were cracked, or because I was to summon guests to dinner. Each of these answers presupposes that the striking of the gong was my action, the fulfilment of my purpose, and that the movements involved in striking the gong were intelligible only as the expression and fulfilment of my inner purpose. In short, these answers presuppose that my striking of a gong was not a movement explicable in physical terms, like the operation of a mechanism, but an action, the subject matter not of physical science but of history.

Another type of answer, however, is conceivable. It may be said that I struck the gong because I was moved by a psychological stimulus operating in accordance with a mechanical law comparable to the laws governing motion in the physical world. Such an answer presupposes that there is no difference in principle between action and movement, that in fact an action is simply a physical event, so that the proper study of action is not history but physical science. Instead of speaking of human conduct, it would be more accurate to speak of 'behaviour', and to hold that there is any difference in principle between what happens to us and what we do is an error or a superstition. With this behaviourism I dealt in the preceding chapter. What is called 'action' by behaviourism, is in fact a series of movements, some physical, some psychological, determined by the operation of mechanical laws. If this attitude be sound, then not history only, but moral responsibility also, is an impossibility. It would be as reasonable to call the tide bad because it had not risen so far today as it did yesterday as to call a *man* bad because he had been impelled to move in such a way as to kill his neighbour. In the mechanical picture painted for us by those who deny that the methods of studying human affairs must differ from those of studying the physical world, there is no place for deliberation, for thoughtful conduct; there is only impulsiveness. And if we now ask why Hannibal did not march on Rome after Cannae, we shall no longer try to fathom his reasons, e.g. to ask whether he overestimated the Roman power of further resistance, or whether his troops needed rest and were quickly made effeminate by the luxury of Campania, or whether his own indecision was prolonged past the hour when a blow could be struck with effect. All these attempts to probe the mind and purpose of Hannibal we shall dismiss as misconceived, and instead we shall say simply that he was impelled to remain where he was by his psychological make-up or, as in the play *The Path to Rome*, by desire for a woman. In other words, we shall abandon as not worth while the attempt to *understand* history, and for such attempts at understanding we shall substitute explanation, but this in effect, means an unexplained hypothesis, like the phlogiston theory; we shall disguise our ignorance of the moving principle of history by giving it a psychological name.

In the light of these considerations, we may be tempted to say that what differentiates action from movement is 'the thought behind it' or 'the thought whose outward expression it is'. It may be admitted that without the inner side (thought, motive, impulse, choice, decision, or whatever other form that inner side may take) there is no action there at all, but only a movement or a physical event. An action is always someone's action; the sparks which fly

upward do not act, and though we may speak of the 'action' of the
tide in eroding a coastline, we are then using the word meta-
phorically and interpreting nature anthropomorphically. And if an
action must be some person's action, i.e. if it is something for
which he is prepared to accept responsibility, it must possess the
inner side without which it could not be 'his', because the ego
itself, to which the action belongs, is itself nothing external,
nothing which can be photographed; it is the *body*, which the
anatomist can dissect, now become *conscious* of itself, and this
consciousness may be described as inner, in contrast with what is
passive under the scalpel. If this be doubted, we may consider
whether we would call actions the things which the patient says or
does under an anaesthetic or which the dreamer may mutter in his
sleep. Here there is a subject who possesses consciousness and who
moves, but the subject has no awaking consciousness of the
movement and may therefore be justified in repudiating it as not
his. And his repudiation will decrease in rigour when the degree of
his consciousness increases as he begins to awaken or to come out
of the anaesthetic. In extreme depression after child-birth a
woman may destroy her child and herself. Is this her action? Is she
responsible? There is a similar reluctance to speak of the 'actions'
of an infant; its movements are just as little 'actions' as its mentality
is self-conscious. As its mentality becomes clearly conscious and
then self-conscious, so its movements gradually become not events
merely but its actions. In short, in human life, the difference
between action and movement is a difference not only in kind but
also in degree. As thinking develops from the rudimentary
consciousness of the infant to the self-conscious reasoning of the
adult, so action develops from what is hardly more than mere
occupancy of space, i.e. bodily action, or reflex action, to the deliberate and self-conscious execution of purpose.

While, as we have seen, inactivity is a form of action, so that
action need not involve movement, we have treated action as a
synthetic unity of inner and outer; inactivity, for example, may
be inwardly a determination to be quiescent and outwardly
simply 'sitting still'. On this view moral predicates would apply to
the action as the simultaneous actualization of inner and outer
moments. On the other hand, however, it is sometimes maintained that moral predicates apply not to concrete actions but only
to their inner side, i.e. to intentions or desires. Attention is drawn

to the discrepancy which may exist between (*a*) what is intended and (*b*) what is effected. I may intend to help a man injured in a street accident and be prevented from doing so by being run over myself; or I may produce a good result without intending anything of the kind. In such cases, my morality or immorality seems to depend on what I intend, not on what I outwardly do. Or again, to take a different type of instance, Leontius, in Plato's story, was tempted during his walk to look aside at dead bodies which he knew to be at the roadside. Suppose he resisted the temptation and walked steadily on without looking, and yet still wanted to look. The man who 'sinned in his heart' did nothing; yet he was said to be culpable. Can we say that he was culpable though he did nothing? And is morality then a matter of intentions or desires merely and not of movement at all? i.e. is there really no such thing as action, but only a difference between intentions (some of them causally connected with movements) and move-ments (some caused by intentions, others occurring in accordance with physical laws)?

We perhaps ought to pause before rejecting as mistaken a belief in good and bad, right and wrong, *actions*. In mathematics we can distinguish between triangles and squares and consider their properties in isolation from one another; to take one in separation from the other does no violence to either, because they are not simultaneously actualized. The anatomist, similarly, can dissect a dead body and consider its organs *seriatim*. But we must be more cautious when we come to the concrete, to life. Here we may distinguish, but we must be careful not to separate. And the danger is that once we distinguish in an action an inner and an outer side, we go on to ascribe the latter to the causal efficacy of the former and so to ascribe a self-subsistence to the former; but, owing to circumstances outside the agent's control, it fails of its effect. If thought, as we have been maintaining, is an integral moment in an action, then action is a concrete whole, not divisible into parts, even though distinguishable into moments. We may ascribe priority in a logical sense to choice, but not in a temporal sense. If we bend our arm at the elbow, the wrist rises. Here we have two movements simultaneously actualized, though one is logically prior to the other. So an action is a concrete whole of inner and outer moments, where the inner is logically prior, but not temporally so.

Let us look from this point of view at the examples quoted above to substantiate the separation of choice from movement which here is being denied. (*a*) It is alleged that we deserve credit for a good intention which through no fault of our own we are prevented from executing. But this allegation is insufficiently precise. We sometimes say of a man that he was well-intentioned, and mean that what he did was in some way unsatisfactory, though his intention was sound; i.e. the intention for which he is given credit is one which he *has* carried out, though inefficiently. What he did is explicable only in the light of the intention; it may be a success or a failure, but in either case we can assess the meaning and significance of what we see done only when we take into account the intentions with which the deed is connected either positively or negatively. If I hit my thumb with a hammer, the reason may be that I did it deliberately because 'it would be so nice when I left off', or it may be that I meant to hit a nail and bungled it. The act is intelligible only in the light of the intention. The same reasoning applies to a bad intention. The intention which is worth calling bad and which justifies us in imputing badness to the agent is one which in some way the agent has begun to execute. Intent to commit a felony becomes an offence when it is evidenced by 'loitering'. And, though a temptation is less definite than an intention, there is something to be said for the view that a man who does right, though tempted to do otherwise is worse than one who does right without being tempted at all; even if the temptation does not lead him to do what he was tempted to do, it still has its effect on what he does actually do. For example, he does it with less zest, or it takes up attention which he ought to be devoting to other things, so that what he has to do is to wrestle with temptation instead of doing what he should. In any case, though at first sight the temptation may seem to be wholly inward, it is clear on reflection that it is not; the action as a whole is in some respect or other different from what it would have been had no temptation to do otherwise been there. (*b*) If I do good 'unintentionally', the good done is not my action; to deny this is to confuse action with movement, to forget that an action, in order to be an action, must be *mine*. The good done unintentionally is as much a 'happening' to me as the bad I 'do' if I am knocked over and in my fall injure someone else. Here again, however, my action is something concrete; if I intend to give a beggar a penny and inadvertently give a half-crown, my action is certainly giving and the action has an inner and an outer, or more precisely a subjective and an objective aspect, but giving half a crown is not my action. Responsibility for giving the half crown is only partially mine; the position here is the same as when I assess my degree of responsibility for the consequences of an action of mine. If I deliberately give the beggar ten shillings which he uses to get drunk and if in his drunkenness he flings a bottle at the driver of a bus and causes a fatal accident, I may repudiate all responsibility for the accident, and yet I may reflect that indiscriminate almsgiving is a folly and that I have therefore by my action contributed something to the accident. This instance shows the need for rather more precision in our conception of action, for it suggests that there may be some difficulty in regarding action as an atomic event which we can consider in isolation (a) from preceding intentions, and (b) from consequential events.

4. INTENTION

Intention plays such a large part in ethical discussions that it deserves a longer treatment.

(i) If my intention is a genuine one, i.e. if it is more than a vague wish and has been explicitly formulated in my own mind and so taken the first step towards objectivity, then the second step follows forthwith. The decision to act is the beginning of the action, not the last step before the action starts. And it is this passing over of the subjective into full objectivity which distinguishes the firm intention or resolve which persists throughout the action from the vague wish. There is no gap in continuity between the crystallization of intention and the doing, the objective side of the action, and the crystallization is incomplete until the intention passes over into action. When this is denied by those who cite a decision made today to do something in the future, what is forgotten is the fact that our intention if genuine does affect our conduct between its formation and what is *prima facie* called its subsequent execution. I keep the intention in mind, arrange my work in accordance with it, avoid making engagements which will clash with its fulfilment. That is, the intention, if genuine, begins at once to be fulfilled, though the fulfilment may not be complete until days or even years afterwards. Sometimes I intend to do something and forget, but is there not truth in the view that we

G

forget what we want to forget? That is, the intention we forget is the one which is not genuine—it is only a vague wish which remains unreal as an intention because it is not objectified at all.

It is to give greater firmness and reality to the intention that we tie knots in handkerchiefs, make diary entries, and so forth. Unless the intention in this way governs our outward conduct and becomes real in the process, it fades away and becomes as vague and tenuous as an imagination or a dream. These phenomena will be admitted, but, by some, otherwise explained. The intention, it will be urged, is firm, but the flesh is weak; but it is a weakness of spirit not to objectify itself. The spirit which does not affirm itself by the mastery of the flesh in and through which it finds objectification is doomed itself to evanescence; and the divisions of the personality into spirit and flesh (i.e. into two substances, mind and body) has a bad philosophical history. So much we must concede to Professor Ryle. The terminology of spirit and flesh is a useful metaphor, but it is no more. The self, as Plato taught, has the task of winning its way to unity out of a multiplicity of experiences—desire, impulses, awareness, thoughts, etc.—and not until it has done so is it genuinely a self; when I can say 'I' and recognize that it is same self which fails, is hungry and tired, thinks, strives, resolves, the same self which is pulled in two ways at once when 'spirit' and 'flesh' conflict, when I recognize this unity of the self, and not until then, am I genuinely a self and a person.

(ii) Our intentions may be frustrated, however, by our stupidity in not taking account of possible actions by others or by our own bungling or inefficiency. This is no argument for ascribing moral worth to intention alone and not to action.

We are concerned here with intentions to perform actions on which a moral judgment may be passed, and therefore not with intentions which fall within the sphere of play. I may firmly intend to climb a hill but find that success is beyond my physical strength. A golfer may firmly intend to send his ball straight down the fairway and yet foozle his drive. In such instances the intention is real enough. The truth is otherwise when the intended action has moral overtones.

We must lay our account with externality; we are not disembodied spirits leading a solipsistic life in a vacuum. Our mental or spiritual life demands objectification for its realization and continued development. And if our intentions fail in the world because of inefficiency, it is because they are not after all real intentions, framed to meet the objective situation in which we find ourselves, but only dreams or ineffectual wishes. If we blunder, we have failed to objectify our intention, in a sense; and yet what we have really done is to actualize an imperfect intention, one not adequately framed to meet the demands of the situation; but, we must observe, its inadequacy is known only through the whole complex of subject and object, through our *objectified* subjectivity. To fail in this way is to fail to give reality to what we should be, i.e. we are letting ourselves sink to the level of a thing acting and reacting on other things in accordance with physical laws, instead of rising to the spiritual level of the mastery of the physical. Bungling means that intention has not been disciplined out of dreamland into the seriousness of life. If this were not so, 'inefficient' and 'clumsy' would not have a bad sense, nor would it be an adverse judgment on a man to say that he had 'bitten off more than he could chew'. 'Clumsiness' is not an attribute of character with which a man starts in infancy; he becomes clumsy through his actions, and these are the actualization of a defect of character shown by its failure to transform wishes into intentions by taking adequate account of the external media which are the vehicle of spiritual or mental achievement. It is an easy way out of a difficulty to hold that inefficiency and stupidity are not defects of character but only of skill or mentality. But this means once again dividing a personality and holding that one of its parts is without influence on the remainder, i.e. it means a denial of personality altogether, the substitution of a sort of committee for the person whom we know and love or hate.

(iii) Even if this be admitted, however, it will still be objected that sometimes our intentions are frustrated by *force majeure*, e.g. by sudden death, or a stroke of paralysis, or by political action which may make it impossible for a beneficiary to profit from what we had intended, e.g. if an intended endowment for a public school is made of no effect by the absorption of public schools into the state system. Surely, in such instances, the intention has moral worth, even though it is never objectified and realized in fact. This may be admitted, up to a point; an examiner may give half marks for an uncompleted answer to a question. Nevertheless, there is something to be said on the other side. If the death or the stroke or the political measure occurs before there has been time for the intention to start on actualization, how can we be sure that it was a genuine intention and not a mere subjective aspiration or wish which was never to be carried out at all? Under the influence of an eloquent preacher or an attractive woman, a man may make a resolve and intend to carry it out, and yet, even at the time, he may know himself too well to believe that he will ever really do what at the moment he intends. If an accident happens to frustrate the intention, some may then blame not themselves but external circumstances. And yet it remains true that they may not themselves deserve credit for an intention which, because it failed of its proper objectification, may after all be one of those with which the road to Hell is said to be paved.

5. OUGHT AND CAN

But, it will be urged, 'ought' implies 'can'; the fulfilment of our intentions is sometimes outside our power, our best efforts may be frustrated by accidents for which we have no responsibility; hence it is on our intentions that moral judgments must ultimately be passed. If we do all we can, then our moral guiltlessness is unimpaired. This implies (what is here denied) that intentions can be assessed in respect of their moral worth independently of their objectification, and further that inefficiency is not necessarily a moral defect. This doctrine depends on the acceptance of the axiom that 'ought' implies 'can'. It is true that there is no point in addressing a moral command to an entity which has no choice; 'ought' certainly implies 'can' in the sense that it implies our ability either to heed or to neglect the claims of morality. But, to me at any rate, it is far from self-evident that we can actually accomplish all that we ought to accomplish.

Some moralists seem to take it for granted that moral experience implies our ability to fulfil the moral law. The grounds of this belief of theirs seem to have escaped their scrutiny; the axiom is taken as 'self-evident' or as requiring no justification. And yet it has against it the teaching of orthodox Christian theology. Man, Christians have held, is dogged by original sin; he is an unprofitable servant; and it is the saints who most frequently and sincerely have bewailed their sins and shortcomings. This theology after a period of eclipse in the Protestant world is once again being taught (e.g. by Barth and his followers); but the moralists who hold that 'ought' implies 'can' seem to be rejecting this doctrine and it seems possible that they have been rejecting it without realizing that they were doing so in the interests of a humanism which should require them to recast their moral system to a far greater extent than they have actually done. An ethics which attaches importance to individual decisions but knows nothing of original sin is an ethics of egoism and pride, not an ethics of humility. However that may be, the question arises whether the doctrine of original sin is not in its meaning nearer to commonplace facts of moral experience than the doctrine that 'ought' implies 'can'. If we consider the choices which we make in life, the plain fact confronts us that only too often they are choices between evils and that this is the inescapable lot of men because they are men, finite and imperfect beings. It may have been a cynic who said: 'Whether a man marries or not, he will regret it', but the truth in the statement is that in choosing x and rejecting y, we choose what in some way will fall short of perfection (so that we are at once led to choose again, to act once more—the imperfection of our choice is the spur to renewed action and so to the continuance of life), while what we reject has advantages and attractions of its own which we are compelled to forgo. How could it be otherwise in a world which spirit ever tries, though with only partial success, to master? We may choose an academic career with its leisure for thought and enquiry, but we must then reject the ease and comfort which the financial rewards of industry might procure. We may 'want everything our own way' until life undeceives us. The achievement of an ambition may promise contentment, but is contentment ever realized? 'It is better to travel hopefully than to arrive.' Achievement of any kind entails sacrifice; the infinite possibilities of youth must be restricted and reduced if anything actual is ever to be attained. The choice between good and evil seems to some to be as clear as the choice between black and white, and in a sense it is; but we shall never understand it unless we realize that it is a choice between things which differ in kind only because they differ so far in degree. Even in an evil choice there is satisfaction and so good of a kind; and the choice of good entails self-sacrifice and self-discipline. However we may describe it, the fact is that our best choice has in it some evil, some imperfection—spiritual pride, perhaps, over-reluctance to abandon the attractive, though evil, way; no choice is so good that it might not have been better—

if we do not realize this, is that not in itself a proof of a self-satisfaction alien to the spiritual life? The moral law is sometimes held to be a counsel of perfection, and many have attempted by such a subterfuge to whittle down the commands of Jesus; but so to regard it is tantamount to disclaiming the absoluteness of moral commands and substituting for them the whims of the individual. Even so, the very phrase 'counsels of perfection' is an indication that there floats before the mind of its user a hint of the truth that ought does *not* imply can. We need, therefore, not be dismayed by the reflection that the view here taken of intention and action precludes us from attempting to ascribe *full* moral value to an intention unfulfilled, i.e. unobjectified. The fact that there is a sense in which 'ought' does imply 'can' will come before us in the sequel.

What has been argued here about action is that even if it is possible to distinguish between a subjective and an objective side, between an intention and its fulfilment or frustration, the distinction does not justify our dividing into two parts the concrete whole of action and then passing separate judgments on the two parts. An intention may not issue in a movement that could be photographed or even in a change of overt behaviour, as when a man may intend to be less envious of his neighbours and succeed in carrying out his intention, though his loss of envy may go unobserved. Nevertheless, it is to make a false abstraction to pass judgment on the subjective side alone and to suppose that it is that side alone which is to be credited with praise or blame.

There are, however, types of action of the first importance which may seem to be wholly subjective and in which no distinction of the kind discussed above can be drawn. I refer to the actions whereby mind achieves its self-transcendence. Tempted by appetite, it may be mind's duty instead to choose, and to choose to choose. This battle may take place entirely within the agent's consciousness; if mind wins the day where is the objective element in the action? For action it is. It is the act of mind in establishing itself against nature, in actualizing its own potentialities, giving fresh actualization to the ideal of goodness. Thus the act of choosing to choose and not to be dominated by appetite is at the same time an achievement. Choosing is the doing; the thing done is the advancement of mind. The act is the synthesis of subjective and objective moments.

6. WHAT ACTION IS

In the light of this discussion of contrasts drawn between action and (1) inactivity, (2) thought, and (3) movement, it may be possible to come to some positive conclusions about what action is. The story of my life is perhaps the story of (a) my actions and (b) the things that happen to me. But if I ask what *I* am, then the answer would seem to be the series of my actions; for the things that happen to me help to form and mould *me* only in so far as I react to them. The objective situation formed by the happening is the setting in which I act; what forms a man's character is his reaction to his environment, not the environment itself or, as St Augustine puts it, it is not the sufferings which matter but the sufferer.[1] The action may take the form of 'initiating a change', or of a negative reaction to the existing state of affairs; or there may be no change (i.e. the action may be the disobedience which refuses to desist from present idleness), and in that case the reaction is positive. But whether positive or negative, my action is my response to objectivity. As my response, there are in it all the constitutive moments of my personality—thought, emotion, desire. Moreover, as mine, the action is not a bodily movement plus a mental state (as if my personality could be divided into body and mind as its separable elements); it is on the contrary the action of mind, a synthetic unity. This synthetic unity—a human person—grows from infancy to manhood in an objective environment. Its actions are both its reponse to that environment (i.e. to happenings) and also its own work in the modelling of itself and in the creation of an environment to suit itself. No account of action can be complete which ignores either action as response or action as creativity. And it may be that since action is the life of a human being it always involves these two elements; no human action is wholly devoid of creativity because the human being is mind and not nature; and yet as the human being is nature too (set, as Aristotle said, between the beasts and God) no human action is wholly creative; and mind is not pure spirit; it cannot away with its environment in nature altogether, cannot live wholly and completely on the creative, i.e. spiritual level. If it is in action that the human person grows, in mind and character, then it is in action that it comes to realize its potentialities. What happens is

[1] *De Civ. Dei*, 1.8.

that subjective potentiality actualizes itself in and through the process of objectification. This process is action.

Action at its height in moral choice is something creative; if the creative moment is lacking, there is just a return to the semi-mechanism of habit or to the mechanisms of the nervous system which have been mentioned already. Action is always the assertion of the self in face of what seems to be the purely objective and real—the translation into actuality of a purpose, the actualization of an ideal, or even in a given case the actualization of the majesty of the law. Life at the moral level is creative activity, not deducible from law or from any list of objective goods, but something lived, with an inner dynamic.

The hedonist is not wrong in putting 'I want' at the heart of the matter, though at the moral level, to which the hedonist does not rise, we must substitute for 'I want', 'I choose'. The difference here is due to the advance of mind. 'I want' does not necessarily imply any consciousness of alternatives: to these we are introduced, as we have seen, in the process of mental development which leads to choice, because the choice of x is the rejection of y, whether explicitly or not.

The spur to action is an inner one. It is a fiction to suppose that we find confronting us a number of alternatives whose merits we assess intellectually, and then proceed to choose the one discovered to be best. We only know their merits in the act of choosing. We make up our minds what we want; this is the process by which the choice is produced; but the choice *is* the mind made up. The selection of this or that external object is an outward expression of a choice which is establishing an inner character. The clash between what I am and what I would be is an inner clash or tension and it is this which urges us to act at the conscious level.

In order to actualize our moral and spiritual potentialities, we must act, and act creatively. Without this, our potentialities remain implicit and we revert to animalism. Action is mind translating itself into actuality. We create ourselves as moral beings in and through self-conscious choice, so that action, not right or good or character, is the centre of ethics. It is also the centre of metaphysics. To make thinking the centre is to leave out individuality. My thought and yours may coincide. But my action is always exclusively mine.

You cannot foresee what your friend will do in a given situation, though you may be sure that he will act reasonably and morally. There will be rationality in his choice which you may be able to discern subsequently, but his action is not logically deducible from his character, because there will be a creative moment in it. History is not foreseeable, for a similar reason; and yet it is not a tale told by an idiot or a series of accidents. History would be an impossible study if it were merely a series of facts without rhyme or reason, and yet, but for the creativity of human action and so of the human mind, it could be foretold. You cannot foretell the future because the future is not yet made, and what the future will be depends on how men are going to make it. We fashion our future out of the materials left to us by the past. (I say fashion, in case someone supposes that by 'creation' I mean creation out of nothing. We speak, and rightly, of creative artists, but that does not imply that they have no materials of any kind.)

Choice is not a selection for some reason or under some form of compulsion of one out of a number of given courses of action, because this view of choice ignores initiative and creativity, and forgets that a choice is not in essence the choice of any given thing, but an act of self-creation, a further determining of what I shall be or of what society shall be. Action is the very reverse of man's adaptation to his environment. We have read *ad nauseam* works about the influence of geographical and other natural conditions on human life. The point is that man as creative activity, i.e. as a thinking and moral being, adapts and moulds his environment to his will. He imposes his will on his surroundings, harnesses the tides and the waterfalls, flies in the air like a bird, levels mountains with the plain or raises them out of it. The highest moral codes are those of peoples who have interfered with nature most. It is not in peoples of helpless resignation or amid the self-indulgence of quietism and idleness that man's mind progresses to enter the kingdom of the spirit. Moral triumph through action is self-discipline, not the adaptation of thought to natural drives, but the schooling of those drives to subserve the requirements of mind; and this moral discipline has run *pari passu* with the disciplining of nature. The Greeks assigned work to slaves and to the vulgar, because they had no theory of action; if contemplation and the intellectual life is given primacy, then the assertion of the self can only be error. The Greek distaste for individualism, exemplified in the fact that their statues are eyeless and simply ideal figures,

is tied up with their distaste for action and so for work as that
process by which alone man's potentialities can be realized.

As we survey the field of human action we find that men,
possessing both memory and imagination, act in accordance with
tradition, customs, laws, and also for the sake of realizing ideals
and making a bad world better. Hence certain moral concepts
arise at once from this survey—good, right, law, evil, wrong.
Further, if we survey action on the subjective side, we find men
impelled by cravings, desires, calculations of their interest, and
by a sense of duty. Now these nouns, good, right, etc., interest,
duty, etc., all arise in the context of the verb to *act*. To forget this
is to fall into the dangerous error of supposing that morality is a
code, something permanent, like a fossil, rather than what it really
is, a creative *life*.

7 · THE IDEAL AND THE REAL

Action is essentially bringing into existence what does not yet
exist; can it then have as its dynamic the ideal: how could something non-existent provide a motive for actualizing it? What is the
nature of a moral ideal and what is its relation to the real? Consider two examples: (i) 'In Heaven there is no sea.' I have repeated
these words hopefully as I have lain seasick in my bunk, but they
are a poor picture of a sailor's ideal life. Here the ideal is just the
converse of present experience, and it is more like a dream than
something which urges us to action. What interests us in ethics is
the ideal which in some way does influence action. (ii) As an
instance of such an ideal consider 'perpetual peace' or the elimina-
tion of war. The Greeks had no such ideal; they regarded war as
a normal and inevitable feature of human life, as inescapable as
the sea in the natural world. By the end of the eighteenth century
when this ideal was explicitly formulated by Kant, the advance
of natural science had extended man's control of the physical
world, and this led to a hope that international relations might be
brought under a similar control. The point is that perpetual peace
begins to be an ideal rather than a dream when it already shines
in or is partially realized in human affairs. When political life in a
large country becomes strong (especially after a period of civil
war), and men settle their disputes by legal process instead of by
force, the idea suggests itself that a similar method of settling

disputes between nations might be introduced and war thus eliminated. We act to realize better what has been partially realized already. We are not dragged forward by a transcendent ideal, i.e. by something non-existent; it is the actually, though partially, realized ideal which leads us to act, because of our discovery of imperfection whether in ourselves or in our world. We express our thought in words, but then revise the words in order to express better what is partially expressed already, and in this process we discover further what our thought really is. Our conception of moral goodness is deepened and enlarged as a result of endeavours to become better men than we are. This may well be the discovery that moral goodness transcends human achievement, but we discover this only because moral goodness is immanent in us in some degree at least. If, as Kant thought, in doing our duty we are constraining ourselves to obey a universal law, it is a law already, in one terminology, written in our hearts, or in Kant's terminology, a law of our own reason, binding on us as rational beings. If the ideal were not immanent in the real, we would have no reason to change the real; we could just go on contemplating the Good like Plato's philosopher kings after they have been released from their kingship. And it is choice which discovers to us this clash between ideal and real in the world or in ourselves. Choice is also rejection, and it is by reflection on our choices that we come more and more to realize where goodness lies. Man knows his finitude and imperfection only because the infinite and its perfection somehow dwells within him as spirit warring against nature.

I said that action was the process whereby our subjective potentialities were objectified and so realized. The process of objectification is twofold. We sometimes hear of thoughts too profound for words or of the poverty of language as a medium to express thought; but we may legitimately doubt the reality of inexpressible thoughts when we consider the labour and difficulty involved in capturing one's thought and giving it adequate expression; for we find that in this process we are giving precision and clarity of outline to what previously was like a cloud, impalpable and evanescent. The attempt to express is the attempt to make real, and if the expression is a muddle we are fairly sure that the original thought is a muddle too. What we have thoroughly thought out in advance is not difficult to write, as any author knows. In becoming clarified, i.e. in becoming thought instead of a vague mass of confused reflections and feelings, what we write has become what we really think; our thinking has risen from potentiality to reality in the process of its objectification, i.e. in being put into words. Until it is put into words, it is not *my* thought at all, and when faith in the value and importance of the individual is weak, there may be no effort to put thought into words, or into intelligible words. For thought we may be offered the language of mysticism, for the attempt to realize my thought we may have the attempt at self-cancellation in the interests of absorption into the All, and the concrete mentality of the individual person may give place to the mental vacuity of the ascetic who has succeeded in becoming one with the infinite.[1] Personality in such a case has died; it has lacked all objectification; in its quest for universality and its denial of the individual, it has forsaken human life for an experience of a different sort, sub- or supra-human according to the faith of the onlooker.

The first step in the process of objectification is the crystallization of the stream of consciousness into words or some other expressive medium. But a second step is no less necessary. My thought, even if made clear to myself through its objectification in language, is still in a sense subjective and incompletely realized until it is communicated in speech or writing to others. Not until this happens is it genuinely mine as distinct from someone else's; not until then am I assured of its objectivity as thought, for it might otherwise be only the consistent subjectivity of a dream. It is for this reason that, e.g. philosophers feel the need, when they do not write books, of discussion with one another; it is for this reason too that men feel the need for human companionship, that the lonely roadman in a distant glen brightens up when the vanman calls with the weekly provisions—he is thereby not imprisoned in a subjective cell which grows ever narrower if there is no communication with others; on a desert island a man will write on the sand in the desperate endeavour after the objectivity in which alone his subjective life can be made real and so preserved. Aristotle devoted one fifth of his ethics to discussing friendship, despite his belief that the wise man should be self-sufficing, and he is at pains to show that the weakness of humanity is such that

[1] Cf. Hegel's treatment of the 'beautiful soul' in *Phenomenology*, Glockner, vol. ii, pp 504 ff., and *Ph. d. Rechts*, section 140 *Anm.*

the thinker needs to find his thought objectified for him in the mind of another; the friend, he holds, is a second self, and the reader may wonder why he should think that a second self is necessary. The reason seems to be the need which the subject feels for objectivity if the subject is to be genuinely real. Or again, to take a different example, we may consider the history of the Christian Church. Again and again there is a reforming movement, protesting against forms, ceremonies, institutions, organizations, which seem to choke the life of the spirit. And yet the reforming movement survives only by organizing itself afresh and so making itself a target for other reformers later. Revivalist movements sweep through a village only to produce in the end a further deadening of spiritual life because they stimulate the spirit but, lacking objectivity, give it no genuine reality. They are thus weakening instead of strengthening it. The letter killeth, the reformer says, and yet the spirit needs forms through which it can work.

If we are to think of the spirit not as a self-subsistent constant entity imprisoned in the flesh but as growing and developing, as becoming progressively more real in objectifying itself, then the physical is not simply the vehicle for the realization of the spirit or a medium in which the spirit works; the connection between physical and spiritual is closer, so that in human life they must be regarded as an indissoluble unity if either is to be fully understood. For the purposes of scientific investigation, we may think of nature as self-subsistent; we may abstract it from the mind or spirit which knows it and works upon it. But if instead we think of life as we human beings live it, then physical and spiritual become fused together in action which is the spirit realizing itself and *eo ipso* transmuting the physical into the objective side of the concrete whole of action. In this way we escape altogether from the conception of action as movement plus intention, of two things coupled together from time to time like two railway carriages. Instead we have an objectified intention (i.e. something no longer purely subjective) or a purposive movement (which is not in the physical sense a 'movement' at all because it is transformed by the purposive moment within it). The task of mind is to come to grips with objectivity and overcome its externality and this is possible because, as we have seen, mind is implicit within it from the beginning. The object is transformed from a mere externality into the objective side of that spiritual experience which is the objectifying and *eo ipso* the realization of the spirit. Without this reference to the objective, spiritual experience forsakes thought (which professes to be true and objective) for dreams, and ultimately, since even these do not wholly lack objectivity, for lunacy and mental vacuity.

Action thus conceived develops through at least the following forms: (*a*) Bodily action, i.e. body's occupancy of space, the vanishing point of action; (*b*) Reflex action; (both of these have been described already); (*c*) Appetition; (*d*) Gratification of desire; (*e*) Choice, which in turn is specified as (i) caprice, (ii) economic action whose measure is utility, (iii) political action whose measure is compromise effected in law,[1] and (iv) moral action proper, or duty.

It is to these higher specifications of action as specifications of choice that we now turn, while noting first that action at each level has justification at that level. In play we are acting to amuse ourselves, and although it may be a duty to amuse ourselves at times, it is amusement and not duty that is the measure of play itself; similarly it is an error to suppose that morality and not compromise can be the measure of politics. By acting, the self is gradually realized and objectified, and in and through acting the self discovers and actualizes the ideals of truth and goodness[2] which are immanent in man and the spur to his development. Thus the higher the type of action which we come to achieve, the more rational the action is, i.e. the more satisfactory to self-conscious reflection. Action then as self-creativity is at its best rational choice, the expression and actualization of what it is to be a human being.

---

[1] The boundaries between these specifications are not clear cut. There is something of play or caprice in the zest of an enthusiastic salesman, whose activity is economic, and there is in a merger between large companies, which may produce a near monopoly, something political even although the merger may have had a purely economic motivation. On this point and on the nature of economic laws see my article on 'The Study of Economic Activity' in *Philosophy*, April, 1936. See also below, p 147

[2] On these ideals and their influence on action see my article on 'Action' in *Philosophy*, 1937.

CHAPTER 6

ACTION FOR PLEASURE

I. HEDONISM

Choice in its most elementary form is caprice; I choose from the menu the dishes that I want. My choice is rational in so far as it is a choice, but it is incompletely rational; it is made because it pleases me and not for a reason, although a psycho-analyst may find *determinants* of my choice in my unconscious. A reason, however, is suggested by those hedonists who find in *pleasure* the governing principle of action.

Hedonistic theories are various and widespread. The fundamental objection to most of them is that either they endeavour to explain the higher by the lower, the more developed by the less, or else they are deterministic and so involve not an explanation or a theory of choice but a denial of its reality.

Hedonism is derived from a Greek word and it originates in Greek philosophy, but its Greek manifestations need not detain us long. They teach that pleasure is *the good*; men first come to *know* what pleasure is and then they will seek it and thus lead a good life. Epicurus is often identified with advocacy of a sensual life, but this is an error. Pleasure is intellectualistically conceived, and the good life for him becomes one of philosophy and a philosophic absence of care, fuss, and worry (ἀταραξία). This is open to the same objection as any theory which puts knowledge first and action second. This makes action unintelligible.

Hedonism becomes a formidable doctrine in the modern world. Its emergence almost contemporaneously with the Protestant claim for private judgment in religion and with Descartes' placing of the individual self at the centre of knowledge is no accident. The formidable type of hedonism may be stated as follows: men act because they crave. To get what they crave is to enjoy pleasure. Hence men act to satisfy their cravings or to please themselves. And 'whatsoever is the object of any man's appetite, that is it which he for his part calleth *good*'.[1]

Here action is dictated by appetite. It is not being argued that

[1] Hobbes: *Leviathan*, I, vi.

we first embark on an intellectual enquiry into what will please us and then proceed to seek it. Pleasure is the objective side of a subjective-objective relation, but it is the subjective side which comes first. This is the reverse of Greek hedonism.

This is a formidable doctrine because it is based on the true insight that action is *self*-assertion against the real. It is a mistake to try to distinguish between selfish and unselfish desires. My desire to give pleasure to my friend is still my desire, my craving; and on the hedonistic theory my craving is not for his pleasure but for my pleasure in giving pleasure to him. This theory is not refuted by referring, for example, to martyrs. Even if I shun martyrdom and have no craving for it, the hedonist is entitled to claim that the true believer exults in martyrdom and craves it, and this sort of thing is true enough of those called masochists.

The hedonist emphasizes two facts about action which intellectualist theories ignore:

(i) Pleasure is one ingredient in any choice. If we are coerced we suffer pain, the pain of passivity, of not acting, of not being ourselves. My choices are mine; no one can impose action on anyone: Hobson's choice is still a choice, and to that extent it involves pleasure, no matter how much bitterness as well.

(ii) All actions are self-interested in the sense that they involve this pleasure and contribute to my character and my satisfaction. Self-sacrifice is still self-interest in the sense that they who lose their lives shall save them.

The error of the hedonist is to attempt to deduce the whole truth about action from these facts. For one thing, we must not confuse the results of an action with the reason why it is done. For another thing, we ought to ask why we feel pleasure in doing this rather than that. The hedonist takes the martyr as a martyr possessed of a curious taste for the pleasures of martyrdom without asking why he has such a taste at all. He takes a man's character as something ready made and does not scrutinize its development.

To suppose that all action (and not merely capricious action) is guided or produced solely by immediate cravings simply does not account for the facts. If immediate craving is what produces action, then a victim of sea-sickness will never again go on a boat; and it will be impossible for anyone to forgo a pleasure of his own in order to meet the wishes of someone else. In both cases, reflection would have to supervene and control or deny the immediate craving.

Moreover, the hedonist is supposing that immediate craving always indicates what we want. No doubt it does so sometimes, but 'do what you like' is often a hard saying. We are confronted on occasion with a situation in which we are conscious of contradictory cravings or impulses, and in order to have some sort of reason for choosing between them, and so for taking action, we may toss a coin. It is useless for the hedonist to retort that this is unnecessary and that the strongest craving will win. 'Strongest craving' is only a form of words; it explains nothing: the strongest craving can only be the one that does in fact win. Impulses always conflict. Even believers in instincts tell us that we have instincts both combative and gregarious. This is why it is an educational crime to leave children free to do what they like. This just enmeshes them in a tangle of impulses, whereas they should be taught to act on rule, e.g. to get up at a specific time and to be punctual at meals. We escape from the impasse of impulse only by reflection.

Impulse or appetite is an initial urge towards acting, and the hedonist is right to stress the fact. But he is wrong in ignoring the process whereby reflection on impulse transforms it until we reach the level of will or choice. It is only because the martyr has by reflection reached certain beliefs that he can 'enjoy the pains of martyrdom'.

If we were in fact at the mercy of immediate craving, as the hedonist supposes, we would never know the fact. In an experience of intense pleasure, we are not conscious of being pleased. We may look back on an experience and describe it as pleasant; but in the experience itself what we are conscious of is its content and not its form. After hearing Richter play Schumann's Fantasy in C we may say that the experience of hearing it was pleasant, but at the time we are simply lost in the work itself. The act of hearing it was the pleasure of hearing it: but consciousness of the pleasure came after the work was finished, and it came because we reflected, not because we felt the urge of another craving.

The distinction between the form and the content of experience is important. The fact that they are simultaneously actualized is no reason for not distinguishing them or for failing to recognize the logical priority of one of them. Consider some examples. I

H

draw a curve, and concavity and convexity are actualized together; but the act of drawing has logical priority. William James tried to show that the blush was logically prior to the embarrassment, though I am not aware that he and Lange have had much of a following. This is relevant to the question of what the hedonist would have to say about remorse. Why is remorse painful? Only because we believe that we have been false to a moral conviction. The pain is logically consequential on the reflection and dependent on it; it is not the thwarting of a craving. Hence to say that I am telling the truth because I want to avoid the remorse that I may feel if I lie, is too elliptical. The pain of remorse is only the form of the experience, and is not isolable from it. The content is a reflective consciousness of a moral failure. This sort of experience is totally different from a craving to be rid of the pain of toothache, though even there the pain is the form whose content is a specific ache. It does not help matters to say that what I crave is to shun the pain of being false to conscience, because, if this were true *simpliciter*, conscience would just be an unreasoning appetite. Unless I really want to do what I judge to be moral, there is no pain in disobedience.

One consequence of ignoring this difference between the form and the content of an experience, and concentrating instead on the feeling which is the form only, is the confusion of suffering with evil. This puts on to one and the same level the pain of disease, the pain of self-denial, the pain of suffering punishment for an offence. Why is torturing others commonly regarded as wrong? If hedonism is right then the answer must be: because the pain of the victim outweighs the sadistic pleasure of the torturer. But how is this known? If the victim cannot feel pain—and there are instances of this—is the torturer fully justified, even though it is pain that he intends to inflict? The suffering of the justly punished criminal cannot be wholly evil. Attempts to diminish suffering may be laudable; but they are not necessarily so. It is not open to a hedonist to say that the suffering is justified by the reform or education or future good of the sufferer, because a strict hedonist knows nothing of means to ends; he is thinking in terms of immediate craving and immediate satisfaction or the reverse. Moreover if the cause of suffering be moral evil, attempts to diminish it will fail if they are directed solely towards relieving physical pain. Physical pain is an evil of a kind but it is as low in the scale of evils as immediate pleasure is on the scale of goods. Such scales, however, the hedonist cannot recognize.

Some hedonists think they are telling us the obvious when they say that 'men act for pleasure'. But what does this mean? Pleasure is a form of feeling, existing when felt. It cannot possibly be an end. Men cannot be moved to action by a craving which pleasure stimulates. The pleasure I feel now does not stimulate action; all I want may be to go on enjoying it. If pleasure is not present, it cannot exert any force on me at all. So the hedonist may mean that I act in order to bring into being a contemplated pleasure which does not yet exist. In so far as this is true, it makes thought or reflection, and not immediate craving, the spring of action. This is truer than a theory that denies reflection altogether but it is not open to the strict hedonistic doctrine which I described as 'formidable'. That doctrine is true of some human action and therefore it is more plausible than a revised doctrine, sometimes adopted by hedonists, that pleasure is selected as a guide to human action, that men do deliberately seek pleasure and avoid pain, or that what they choose as a policy is the course of action which they expect to give them the most pleasure.

It is true that we sometimes choose the line of least resistance; there are also those whom we call pleasure-seekers. But the very fact that we do this implies that we do not always choose the line of least resistance and that some people are not pleasure-seekers. We must distinguish between the pleasure of a warm bath and the pleasure of having succeeded in a difficult task; we must distinguish again between the plight of a prisoner of war who, though tortured, refuses to give information to the enemy and who thereby does enjoy the pleasure of fulfilling a painful duty, and the situation of a man driven by hunger or sexual appetite. The latter is urged or impelled forward; if he tries to reflect he may find himself overwhelmed by appetite; he is conscious of his craving, and his whole consciousness may just be this craving. Even this is not a craving for pleasure but rather for food or for a woman. The prisoner chooses; the sensual man does not—he is a creature of appetite. The prisoner's choice is the rejection of everything that the sensual man would call pleasure; and the pleasure he does get he gets only because pleasure was what he rejected. The hedonist ignores differences in kinds of pleasures because he never asks why a thing pleases us or considers the difference between the satisfaction of an appetite and the pleasure which comes unsought and is supervenient on some achievement as its form.

Some might grant this and yet still try to hold that pleasure is a guide to action in the sense that we always deliberately seek what will give us the maximum of pleasurable feeling of any kind and so the fullest satisfaction. If this were what we did, however, it would be relevant to ask why. The answer might be that we think pleasure the chief good and take it for granted that the sensible thing to do is to seek it. This is a hedonistic attempt at morality but it fails, partly because it is a reversion to Greek intellectualism, and partly because it seems to be at odds with the facts. It is true that when a person is asked to do something which, in his view, brings him no obvious reward, he not uncommonly asks: 'What do I get out of it?', where he need not be expecting 'cash' as an answer but would be content if the answer were 'pleasure'. Nevertheless, there are others ready to do work offered to them without asking this question; the work seems to them to be worth doing on its own account; and the satisfaction which comes from the doing of it is the kind which comes only because it has not been sought at all. Self-fulfilment comes only from an unseeking self-sacrifice.

To take individual satisfaction as the chief good means regarding as highest good not the struggle of the spirit against matter, not the triumph of mind over nature, but the emotional accompaniment of that triumph; importance is ascribed not to the work of art produced by a genius but to his satisfaction as he contemplates it; not to the moral character of those whom we respect, but to some individual satisfaction of their own. Can this be believed? Once we elevate the incidental satisfaction to the chief place, we will rapidly forget its incidental character and so slip back from morality to the satisfaction of cravings once more. This really is a regression and in so far as hedonism tries to be a moral theory it is self-contradictory in not realizing the fact.

Craving and its satisfaction is a chaotic and constantly changing sort of life. If craving and a quest for its satisfaction be taken as a guide to life, the experience of mankind is that it is only a guide to misery and therefore to self-frustration. It is a commonplace to hold that the only way to be happy is not to seek happiness. It is only when we reflect on impulse that we begin to introduce order into life and so to substitute intelligence for emotion as a guide. In so far as hedonism proposes to stick to facts, as it did when it emerged as a formidable doctrine, it is incomplete because it is too selective in the facts that it studies. In so far as it is a theory about life it is an attempt at understanding, but by professing to give control of life to impulse and not to understanding or intelligence it is of necessity incoherent.

There has been an attempt to combine hedonism with choice on the following lines: we choose the action which will be productive of most pleasure, and we choose it not because of any reflection, but because we naturally select the course of action which is most attractive; and the attractiveness of a course of action resides in the action's capacity to provide a pleasure which is not yet existent.

This implies that of three possible actions the first may have ten units of pleasure-giving capacity, the second five, and the third two. We do the action with ten because it is the most powerful of these three magnets. If this be so, choice is impossible, because even if we are said to 'choose' the one with ten units, the difference between choice and rejection would be a matter of degree only. We would whole-heartedly choose the one with ten units, and half-heartedly the one with five. This sort of situation would always arise because no course of action is wholly devoid of advantage and therefore of attractiveness. Choice and rejection, however, are opposites, different in kind and not in degree alone. This attempt to keep choice and hedonism therefore fails.

There is one final modification of hedonism which needs to be mentioned, namely that which is frankly determinist and with which, therefore, I have dealt in principle already. This is essentially a theory of conduct in its simple form as momentary feeling with the formal character of pleasure or pain, and the process of appetite with the formal character of satisfaction or frustration. In other words it takes conduct at a level below that of choice and looks on human action as determined by impulses and urges or cravings of various kinds. It is not surprising to find many psychologists, who are so preoccupied with sub-conscious and unconscious drives, taking for granted in their books a hedonistic theory of ethics which at bottom is determinist.

I have now tried to show the origin of hedonism in Greek philosophy and have argued that it became formidable in the modern world as the theory that men act because they crave; they crave what will satisfy their craving; hence men act to satisfy their cravings or to please themselves. I have argued that there are insuperable difficulties in this doctrine and have discussed various modifications of it which have been adopted by its sponsors in an endeavour to meet these difficulties.

2. EXPERIENCES OF WHICH HEDONISM IS A TRUE ACCOUNT

Nevertheless, I wish to point out that the formidable hedonist doctrine does provide a true enough account of some human experiences, and it is to this fact that it owes what plausibility it has and also its continued popularity.

There are four such human experiences:

(i) *Childhood*. Until it learns better, the child's life is one of craving. Often enough it does not know what it craves, whether food or drink or sympathy; still less does it know that it craves the pleasure or satisfaction which the right one of these will bring. But an observer, seeking an objective analogue of the subjective craving, is not unreasonable in finding it in pleasure.

(ii) *Action induced by propaganda and advertising*. The propagandist and the advertiser are very seldom appealing to the intelligence. Their task is to create a demand or a craving, and to give the impression that the satisfaction of the demand or craving will be pleasant. Here again the victim is conscious of wanting some specific thing, and not pleasure, but it is not unplausible to use pleasure as an omnibus name for the object, even though it is only the formal character of the experience which possession of the object is expected to bring.

(iii) *Action induced by psychological or pharmacological stimuli*. Similar remarks apply to this, and it is not necessary to condescend on detail.

(iv) *Play*. This is not quite the same as the other three. It is a more self-conscious activity, at any rate in adult life. We play because we want to, and we play because it gives us pleasure. Hedonism may be regarded as the ethics of play, erroneous only because of its assumption that play is the whole of chosen conduct. It may be a completely true account of the play of young children, but not of the play of grown-ups. Although we play because we want to, play involves the moment of utility as well as pleasure, because it provides relaxation or exercise and so is a useful means to a healthy life. It also involves the moment of rationality, because it proceeds on rules. The rules are more rigorous in adult games; a child's rules may be altered or over-ridden to suit changing circumstances. The author of a penny dreadful has a licence that is not allowed to the author of the detective story which is to amuse the leisure of the intellectual. The essential thing in play, however, is the pleasure it gives; utility and rationality must be recessive elements in the experience. No game gives pleasure until the rules are so thoroughly mastered that their observance is almost automatic. To have to wonder what the rules are transforms play into an irksome social obligation or even a piece of hard work. Utility too must be kept out if the game really is to be an effective relaxation. It must be played for its own sake. The man who really plays golf for exercise, and does not merely say that that is his reason, is not really playing at all; he is simply taking a means towards the end of health. It is reasonable to play for the sake of playing; and play, in its place, requires no justification other than the pleasure it gives. This too then is a sphere where some form of hedonism is at home.

Although I have granted that hedonism can give an account of these four experiences, I add that these are all immature or primitive types of action. To suppose that they are the essence of action, as hedonistic theories do, is to fall into the genetic fallacy once more.

To rise above the level of feeling and appetite, and above these primitive forms of experience, is to rise above the entire sphere envisaged by hedonism, namely the sphere of caprice, and to reach the higher moral level of reflective choice where we have reasons for our choices and where we encounter things that we ought to do, not because they satisfy us, but in spite of that fact. Obligation helps us to order and guide our feelings and appetites, and to choose our pleasures. But pleasure and the thought of pleasure cannot determine our obligations, for the very notion of obligation arises only for reflection, i.e. after the stimulus-response level of appetite and even the higher level of desire have been transcended. This may be the place to insert a lady's remark which has been transmitted to me: 'Gifford Lectures can be reduced to the dictum that when you particularly do not want to do something, that is your duty.'

CHAPTER 7

ACTION ON RULE

1. RULE AND BENEFIT

In the last chapter I said that it was an educational blunder to leave a child at the mercy of its caprices and that it should be taught to act in accordance with rules, e.g. to get up in the morning at a specific time and to be punctual for meals. Rule is thus one negation of the sphere of caprice.

Rule, or rightness, in its turn may be negatived by the quest for benefit or utility. *Fiat justitia, ruat caelum* is rejected in the interests of human welfare.

An attempt may be made to avoid this polar opposition between right and benefit by asserting, with G. E. Moore[1] that 'right' means 'useful'. This is nonsense.

The opposition is evidence that each of these conceptions is inadequate as characterizing moral life, and that they must both depend on some higher synthesis. The bitterness of their opposition, however, is due to the fact that each has the other implicit within it as one of its moments. Rules are constitutive of social life and to that extent are necessarily beneficial. Utility or benefit cannot be secured without rules of some sort; to suppose the contrary is to revert to selfish individualism and caprice. Moreover, both the opponents find room for obligation, but have little or no interest in motive.

It is tempting to regard rule as the first negation of caprice and to regard benefit, as the negation of rule, as a good higher than rightness. But this is not the truth. By denying that law-abidingness as such is a good, utilitarianism is taking lower ground. It seems safer to regard right and utility as on the same level with one another and criticizing one another. Law, or right in its pure form, i.e. in a society where law is sacrosanct, as among the Medes and Persians and the Jews, came on the scene earlier than utilitarianism, and therefore it is convenient to deal with rightness first and benefit or utility second. Nevertheless, much of the truth

---

[1] *Principia Ethica*, Cambridge, 1929, p 146.

about rightness appears only through its contrast with utility and therefore not until the end of the next chapter.

If right does not mean useful, what does it mean? It means what is in accordance with rule. Obedience to rule, or right action, is recognizably good. Men are born into families and social groups, and acceptance of caprice, instead of rule, would disrupt their functioning.

Consider a different example—the distribution of a charitable fund to its beneficiaries. Some trustees are disposed to say that every case should be dealt with 'on its merits'. But how are these 'merits' to be assessed unless they fall under some rule? To try to deal with the individual case 'on its merits' and to give £50 to one applicant will soon prove to be unfair to other applicants for whom either less or nothing will be available. To administer the fund for the 'general' benefit of the beneficiaries becomes impossible unless the administration proceeds by rule and on principle. The specific rule or principle adopted may be criticized on the ground that it is too complicated and therefore inefficient, but administration by rule instead of trying to treat every individual case 'on its merits' is a *better* procedure. The having of a rule is good in itself; the results of having this rule or indeed any rule are irrelevant to this goodness. If having some rule or other is a good in itself, then law-abidingness as such must be good in itself too.

Of course, it will be objected that the value of the disposition to observe laws depends on the goodness of the laws observed, and that therefore law-abidingness cannot be good in itself, but is good only if it is abiding by laws that are just. This, however, is a misunderstanding. Law-abidingness is not *the* good, but only *a* good, the one appropriate to the level of experience under discussion. Pleasure is *a* good, even if, as the pleasure of a sadist, it is described from a higher point of view as bad.

The principle that rules should be obeyed needs no utilitarian justification. It is the recognition that order, consciously adopted, is one feature of the good life. This is not likening human life to the ant-hill, because, so far as we know, the ants do not choose the order under which they live. Men can and do; and, in so far as they recognize order as a good, they make their changes in an orderly fashion; the disorder of violence sometimes seems a more efficient route to a new order, but it is a contradiction of order as the underlying good, and this is why revolutions so often crystallize into reactions or into conditions very different from those that their sponsors had in view. This conception of rightness places it on the moral scale, along with utility, below duty. It is the fact that rightness or law shines in the political sphere more brightly than in the economic that makes it impossible to regard politics as wholly utilitarian. It hovers between the spheres of utility and right, and the higher category of duty glints in it too.

2. MEANING OF RIGHT

A conception of rightness as something below duty is not easy to defend because the word 'right' is used as a word of commendation in so many different contexts. For the utilitarian the right act is a useful one and a useful act is the right one; for others the right act is the one which it is my duty to do, and rightness becomes synonymous with duty. In both these instances, however, rightness is still connected with the notion of rule; a rule that promises be kept may be accepted both by a utilitarian and a deontologist, only the former accepts the rule because it is useful and the latter because keeping this rule is one of our duties. Sometimes, however, we are told that the right act is the act that fits the situation. Here the notion of rule seems to have disappeared because those who adopt this conception of right are not saying that the right act fits this situation because the situation is of a certain type and therefore assumable under a rule. The view is that the right act to do in this unique situation is the one that fits. This cannot be accepted. For one thing, 'I shall do what I think fit' is not the same as to say 'I shall do what I think right'. For another thing, 'fit' here is a metaphor. The key fits the lock and the dress fits the woman, but how can the keeping of a promise fit a situation? The metaphor is used in the interests of a form of intuitionism, and it seems to mean: 'I see that in this situation what is required of me to meet its exigencies is to keep a promise'; the act is just seen to be required, in the same sort of way in which the dress must be seen to fit. Although this conception of rightness is unsatisfactory, it has one important feature in common with the conceptions of rightness as utility and as duty; it is alleging that there is something objective about rightness. The right act is the one that in fact fits the objective situation: the right act is the one which is in fact useful; the right thing to do is to obey a law of duty which is objectively binding. Thus although these three views of rightness are unsatisfactory because they do not clearly differentiate it from utility on the one hand or duty on the other, they do point to two characteristics which are essential and intrinsic to the conception of right as such.

These characteristics are rule and objectivity. Whether you know it or not there is a right way to swing a golf club or to tie a knot that will not slip. Whether it is through ignorance or in-advertence that you disobey the rules of accountancy by omitting overhead charges, your statement of accounts will not be right. If it is right to keep your promises and wrong to disappoint others, it is because there is a rule to this effect.

The same characteristics appear in a different use of the word right, as when a person claims to have a right of private judgment or free speech or property ownership. Except in instances where it is legitimate to say to an individualist, 'if you stand up for your rights, you'll be knocked down for your impudence'; a claim to have a right is a claim that there shall be a rule or a law guaranteeing it to him and others, if such a law does not already exist. Thus the so-called objective or natural rights of man cease to be a slogan when they are guaranteed in the Constitution of the United States.

Rightness, in short, is abiding by objective rule, even if only by the rule that people should be law-abiding. A man may be law-abiding and still try to reform some existing law. Respect for law as such does not necessarily entail respect for this, that, or the other specific law; but this respect for law as such is the good, or the moral conviction, which utilitarianism cannot envisage.

3. OBLIGATION

To require obedience to rule or law in defiance of caprice is to introduce the notion of obligation.

It is a commonplace to hold that statements containing the word 'ought' cannot logically be derived from statements of fact (although this is occasionally denied in articles in philosophical periodicals), and it may therefore be asked whence this notion of obligation, now coming clearly[1] before us for the first time, is in fact derived. It cannot be derived from nature; if external observa-tion counts for anything, the bees and the ants, the cows and the

[1] It was adumbrated in Chapter 4.

sheep, the cats and the dogs seem to live their lives naturally, following their noses, seeking their food, enjoying life from moment, and never striving to be other than they are. Human beings, however, are not like that. They look before and after and pine for what is not. They have within them a spiritual potentiality which they seek to realize; their condition is expressed in the words of the collect: 'Thou hast made us for thyself and our hearts are restless until they find rest in thee.' It is this consciousness of inner tension between nature and spirit which gives birth to the conception of obligation. A child may be told by its parents that this is what it must do; it obeys; but it comes to realize that this is something which needs no external command; it lays the command on itself and in so doing it discovers obligation. The discovery is made at a very rudimentary level and it may be no more than the reflection that I ought to do this because my parents told me to, and I rely on their judgment and their love. But it is the discovery of the moral life and the choice of a good higher than that which any caprice can provide. What is at issue here is *moral* obligation. It is sometimes possible to use the word 'ought' without any moral reference: e.g. 'for this job I ought to use a screwdriver, but I have not got one and must make do with a pocket knife'.

4. RIGHT AND DUTY

Hedonism in the modern world is the assertion of pure subjectivity, of the individual's cravings. Rightness, as pure objectivity, is the polar opposite of hedonism. This is a clear sign that as one of a pair of opposites it cannot be finally satisfactory, however great an improvement it may be on what has gone before. 'The right thing' and 'my duty' are not synonymous. English speakers do normally differentiate between right and useful; the utilitarian argument has not been so convincing as to have dominated common speech. But right and duty are not by any means so clearly distinguished. Law-abidingness has been a prominent characteristic of the English; it is a good characteristic; and it may not be surprising that it should be identified with duty, and duty with it. Nevertheless it is a mistake to regard law-abidingness as the height or culmination of morality.

To see the deficiency of rightness, it is only necessary to call it legalism. From a recognition of the worth of law-abidingness and a respect for law it is easy to slip into the position of holding that morality consists in obeying whatever laws there are. (*a*) Difficulties then arise when it is found that in a given situation two laws conflict, and the question arises of how a choice is to be made between them. (*b*) It is also found that the human situation alters, and that this appears to make some laws obsolete. Are they still obligatory? Can disobedience to them be morally justified and, if so, does this mean abrogating the law? If so, is this then a relapse to caprice?

5. CONFLICT OF RULES

(*a*) Conflict of rules is more commonly a conflict between two levels of experience or a conflict arising from what may be called 'special' obligations. The rules of family life may conflict with those of social life or economic life or with the law of the land. And it may be necessary to solve the conflict by deciding to abide by the standards of the higher level (though there may not be universal agreement about which *is* the higher level). For example, it may be a rule that social engagements be kept and another that a man has an obligation to look after his wife: if she falls suddenly ill and he telephones to cancel their dinner party engagement, he would be regarded as Quixotic or worse if he had done otherwise. To his wife he had taken solemn vows, to his friends none; the difference in the relationship justified his regarding one claim, and therefore one rule, as higher than another. In the personal relations of social life, however, we can expect our friends to 'understand' if, for reasons they can appreciate, we break a promise to them.

It is different, however, with the economic side of life; it is less justifiable to break a business engagement than a social one; the sphere of utility is higher than the sphere of play. If the claims of a wife and the claims of a man's employment clash, and the husband believes that the wife's claims are, in the situation, paramount, there is nothing for it but to seek leave of absence on compassionate grounds or even to take it, but the necessity for such a request may arise at a much later stage than some uxorious men will allow. The wife may not legitimately forget the business claims, even if only because it is on the satisfaction of these that her own livelihood depends.

Promise-keeping is in general a law governing the economic side of life, and is considered in the next chapter; but I remark here that a promise may be broken in the interest of fulfilling the law of some sphere which ranks morally higher. Observe, however, that if I fail to keep an appointment because a train is late or because I am taken ill, I am not breaking a promise; I am being prevented by something outside my power from keeping it, and this is a hazard to which human life is always liable. The breaking of a promise can be justified only when it is necessary to abide by some higher principle. Consider an instance where there is a moral but not a legal justification for breaking a promise. I refer to a promise to marry. If in the course of an engagement either party comes to the conclusion that a mistake has been made, he or she has the painful duty of breaking the engagement, not because the future happiness of the parties may otherwise be jeopardized, but because a marriage entered into without a whole-hearted mutual dedication is unlikely to last, or, if it lasts, to be more than a moral mockery and a sham. Nevertheless an action at law lies, in some countries, for a breach of this promise, an indication that the sphere of rightness is not yet at the culmination of morality.

There is one further point about breaking promises. If we are told by utilitarians that the attainment of some greater benefit justifies the breaking of a promise, we should observe that they are making a rule that benefit shall outweigh a broken promise, and a defence of this rule in terms of benefit is circular.

These suggestions about how to solve a conflict of rules, how-ever, all involve using some sort of standard other than that of rightness itself. Just as, at the level of pure subjectivity, there is no way within that level of dealing with a conflict of cravings (as when we want to get up but also want to lie in bed), so at the level of pure objectivity there is nothing in the concept of rightness to tell us which rule to obey if two rules conflict in a given case. In some cases there may be an attempt to solve the difficulty by reducing it to a question of fact, namely to asking which of the two rules, if either, is genuinely applicable to a given situation; but this will not always serve. For example a spendthrift may get himself into a situation where, his resources being so slender, he must either leave his debts unpaid or steal food to support his life. Legalism will not help him here if he lives in a country where suicide is a felony.

In passing, I mention two unsatisfactory justifications of breaking a promise, the first from Godwin and the second from Spinoza:

(i) Godwin: 'It is impossible to imagine a principle of more injurious tendency than that which shall teach me to disarm my future wisdom by my past folly ... I promise to do something just and right. This certainly I ought to perform. Why? Not because I promise but because justice requires it ... If I promise something good and, when the time comes for fulfilment, a "nobler purpose offers itself and calls with an imperious voice for my co-operation", I must co-operate. A promise can make no alteration in the case ... "Gratitude is a vice, not a virtue." '[1] It takes but little discernment to see that the justice here mentioned has nothing to do with law; so far from reaching even the worth of law-abidingness, it is simply a sermon in aid of anarchy, and, in the last resort, of caprice.

(ii) Spinoza: 'The fulfilment of a promise depends on the promiser's will. Therefore if a man judges (whether rightly or wrongly) that more loss than gain will result from fulfilment, he may break faith and is entitled to do so by the law of nature.'[2] Here is an attempt to justify the breaking of a law (*pacta sunt servanda*) by reference to a higher law, the law of nature. The argument thus remains within the sphere of rightness, but maintains that in a conflict of rules the higher is to be kept, and the higher is the law of nature. Now the law of nature may be regarded as a criterion for judging the justice or otherwise of positive laws, but difficulties arise as soon as an attempt is made to give a content to natural law. In fact it is hard to see what difference there is between natural law and what might be called the moral law. Spinoza is attributing a utilitarian justification to *positive* law and saying in effect that a man has a moral justification to override positive law in any instance where to abide by positive law would produce less benefit. Here the concept of rightness seems to disappear between utility on the one hand and duty on the other. If on the other hand Spinoza means that the law of nature may on any occasion override the positive law if an individual thinks, *rightly or wrongly*, that it should, then positive law is being abolished altogether, and we are being exhorted to follow what we

[1] Quoted in A. Gray: *The Socialist Tradition*, London, 1946, pp 120–22.
[2] *Tractatus Politicus* II, 12.

think, rightly or wrongly, the natural law requires. This is still not recognizing the worth of law-abidingness or its objectivity, and it ascribes worth instead not to what a man does but to what he thinks, whether he thinks rightly or wrongly. This emergence of subjectivity may either be a relapse into hedonism, or the presage of conscience and the importance of motive. As will be seen later, a theory which does not explicitly find room for the worth of rightness is poised precariously between the upward path on the right and the precipice on the left.

6. OBSOLESCENCE OF RULES

(b) The second fundamental difficulty in clinging to rightness as an ultimate, or in legalism, arises from the history of law. The laws of the Medes and Persians were unalterable; but the Medes and Persians, and their laws too, are as gone as the snows of yesteryear. To insist that no jot or tittle of the law shall pass away is to make moral progress impossible, and it simply fails to take account of the facts of history. Rightness remains as the principle that rules or laws are to be obeyed, but legalism is always forced to give a content to this general principle and to claim sacrosanctity for specific laws. It may be urged that these are the attempts made from time to time to actualize the permanent and unchanging natural law, or the law of human nature as such. It is as difficult, however, to discover an unchanging human nature, a sort of permanent core underlying all the phantasmagoria of rising and falling civilizations and all the vicissitudes of human history, as to discover in an individual an inner core of character persisting unaffected by his successes or failures, his joys and sorrows, his varying reactions to his changing social or political environment.

A law may be made obsolete by changes in the political situation. Hegel's essay on *The German Constitution* provides plenty examples of how, although the complex Constitution of the Empire as it existed in the sixteenth century still persisted in name at the beginning of the nineteenth, it was only a solemn farce. The spirit which animated the constitution had fled, and the persistence of many old traditions was meaningless. Here was an instance of law-abidingness gone mad; of rightness sunk into an indefensible legalism, and so Hegel's youthful and eloquent indignation led him to advocate making a clean sweep of the lot and the establishment of a new order by a German Theseus. Hegel's proposal was made in the interests of the people, but it was certainly not incompatible with a recognition of the worth of law-abidingness; Hegel was the last man to ignore that particular value. It was a new legal order which his Theseus was to establish.

7. MORAL REFORMERS

Laws are also changed, however, in the interests of morality.

A system of law breaks down and is abandoned because of the conflict of rules which it is found to contain. Contradictions have become too blatant for the system to survive. The disappearance of systems based on the recognition of slavery may be one example.

The discovery of such contradictions has been due, if not always, to the activity and the agitations of moral reformers. And this leads to an important question about the judgment to be passed on their lives. The law requires obedience, and does not care why we obey. Obedience is right. But suppose that a moral reformer believes that a certain law is wrong and he disobeys it. By breaking the law he has done a wrong act, but he might be called a good man on the strength of his motive, and this has been maintained. But this is erroneous. The statements: 'he is a good man but he does wrong acts' and 'he is a bad man but he does right acts, because he keeps the law and yet is a hypocrite' are not judgments but statements of a problem. When the Disciples plucked the ears of corn on the Sabbath Day, they broke the law. But when Jesus said that the Sabbath was made for man, the Disciples and their Christian posterity believed him; they did not say that Jesus was good but still authorized wrong. He had introduced his world to a conception of morality which was higher than legalism. And this was attributed to him for *goodness*. He did not abrogate the law but fulfilled it, but this fulfilment meant the transcendence of rightness as an exclusive moral category. The Pharisees, however, took a different view from that of the Disciples. Jesus disobeyed the law, and therefore he was a bad man and one to be crucified. Here are two opposing moral judgments on the same action, but they are answers to the problem: is a man good if he does wrong acts? They do not regard the problem as a solution, as some modern moralists have done. It is when the conscientious law breaker convinces others that he is possessed of new

I

moral insight, and is not a mere antinomian, that the law is changed. And this is a further indication that rightness is still a subordinate sphere.

8. WHERE RIGHTNESS IS VALID

The inadequacy of rightness has now been sufficiently indicated, but just as hedonism gained its plausibility and worth from being true of one sphere of life, and was a realization, in some degree, of goodness and therefore was obligatory in that sphere, so rightness and law-abidingness have their home and their truth in their own sphere, the sphere of law. It is rightness which the policeman requires; the judge has not infrequently to emphasize that his court is one of law and not of morals; and even if in interpreting the law he is in fact sometimes making it, his task is to apply and interpret the law and not to enquire into its merits and demerits. The advocate doubtless thinks of the interests of his client, but he is bound by the law and must simply try to show that the law as it exists tells in his client's favour. The law is accepted as binding. Rightness is thus the value required and actualized in this sphere. A legal theorist like Bentham, or a legislator, may alter a given law or produce a legal code, and may do this with utility in mind; but this does not alter the fact that the law, whatever it is, requires compliance, and this in itself is an essential feature of the moral life, whether personal or social.

If in what I have said I have over-emphasized the deficiency of rightness and law at the expense of its importance, I must redress the balance by saying that I think that reverence for law, and a sense of shame and guilt in breaking it, are of the highest import- ance. The growth of violence in this country and the frequency of strikes instead of negotiated settlements of industrial disputes are sinister signs of moral decline. Right and law stand with utility below duty, but it is necessary to go half way before the destination is reached. One of our troubles today is that so many people stop at utility without seeing the worth of law and rightness at all. To rise to this level is to feel guilt at law breaking. There are those today who are so anxious to get rid of guilt where in their view there should be none, e.g. in adultery, that they have tended to propound views which would eliminate guilt altogether. And they are meeting with some success. Lord Devlin argued that if there is no sense of guilt in the populace, there is no means of keeping law and order.[1] He said that there were many criminals who, realizing that today only a minority of those guilty of robberies of various kinds were ever brought to justice, the chance of going scot free was high. No sense of guilt in robbing was present. And therefore it was possible to take a calculated risk of escaping detection.

If, however, there is to be a sense of guilt, the law must command respect. In the nineteenth century many Anglican clergy broke the law in relation to vestments and the ceremonial use of incense for example, because they thought it was their duty to do so. They had no sense of guilt in breaking the law, because they thought the law was wrong and ought to be changed. They would not have liked to be classed with the bank or train robbers of today. They would have been the first to say that they respected law as such, so long as it did not conflict with their conscience. The trouble is that so many law-breakers today have no conscience in the matter at all. This may be partly due to the proliferation of laws in a modern society and to the fact that the justification of many of them is indeed merely utilitarian. Such a justification is inadequate to produce the reverence for law which alone will suffice for the keeping of law and order in a modern society. It is a useful rule that no one should ride a bicycle without lights; but an individual brought to court for transgressing this rule is nowadays more often regarded as unfortunate than as guilty and will frequently have no sense of guilt herself. Social disapproval used to act as a powerful succour to the law, because the transgressors were ostracized. But this operates nowadays less and less. Divorcees used not to be received at Court, but in recent years there have even been divorcees on the bench. Easy divorce is a child of utilitarian ethics. If utility is the guide, then it may be useful to keep a promise or to break it, to be faithful to a wife or otherwise. And this is the penalty to be paid if there is a failure to supplement the notion of utility with the notion of law and right. The criminal regresses from utility to his own pleasure; and this may be the case with some divorcees too.

[1] *The Times*, 11.xi.64.

CHAPTER 8

ACTION FOR UTILITY AND BENEFIT

1. THE RIGHT AND THE USEFUL

Historically, utilitarianism is a protest against legalism. Bentham was a legal reformer, desirous of producing a legal code justified by its 'optimific' character and devoid of 'useless' legislation. Once this aim is adopted, it is easy to make the mistake of identifying rightness with utility, and this mistake is commonly made by utilitarians. It may be a very useful thing that people should be law-abiding, but being law-abiding and doing what is useful are not synonyms. It is the general practice in some universities to transact business in committees. When a professor attends, he is abiding by the general practice, but he might well be more usefully employed in his study or laboratory; and the business of the committee could frequently be transacted more efficiently by the administration. To neglect the distinction between being law-abiding and doing what is useful is to make it inexplicable why 'red tape' is a term of abuse. The clerk is acting rightly with his red tape, because he is abiding by the rules of his office, but he is not doing something useful. This may be an argument for discarding rightness and concentrating on utility, but let us see.

The transition from pleasure to utility, like that to right or rule, is a transition to a higher form of good and a higher form of action. Utility is a higher good than pleasure because, whereas pleasure may sometimes be useless or worse, the useful always includes, in some degree, the pleasant. It is also a higher realization of the notion of goodness because, whereas pleasure is a form of feeling and may involve the minimum of mental activity for its enjoyment, utility involves forethought, and to that extent it appears at a higher level in mind's advance than pleasure need do. Pleasure is a realm of caprice. Caprice is momentary, atomistic. Reflection, however, shows that in future we may wish to make other choices which satisfying the caprice of this, here, and now will make impossible. Hence we modify our present action in the light of an envisaged situation which has not yet arisen. This is the transition from pleasure and caprice to the choice of utility, an intellectual transition and advance.

2. ESSENCE OF UTILITARIANISM

The essence of all forms of utilitarianism, and there are many,[1] is the distinction between means and end, and the doctrine that we choose the former for the sake of the latter. The end, whatever its character, is regarded as good, and the worth of our choice of the means depends on the contribution which the means makes to the realization of that good.

Utilitarianism as a moral theory stands higher than hedonism because, as we saw at the beginning of the last chapter, it can and usually does make room for obligation and rules, two vital moments in the moral life and its development.

It is open to a utilitarian to say: 'It is in your interest to do this because doing it is the means to attaining the end that you regard as good.' This is a statement of fact; it does not in itself provide a reason for doing the act in question. Before providing a reason, it must be supplemented by saying, for example: 'All sensible men seek their interest; being sensible is better than being foolish.' Even this, however, may not suffice. 'Why is being sensible better than being foolish?' At this point there must be either a relapse to hedonism in some form ('You cannot help seeking your pleasure anyway, and seeking it is your interest'), or else an advance to morality by introducing the notion of obligation (the origin of which was sketched in the last chapter) by saying: 'You ought to do this because this accords with a rule, observance of which contributes to the good life.'

Utilitarianism is compatible, as has been said, with an insistence on rules. John Stuart Mill, whose name can hardly be omitted from any discussion of utilitarianism, insisted on them. The reason is that it may be argued that to act on a given rule is to choose the appropriate means to the envisaged end. The sanction of a rule, however, lies always for a utilitarian in its results. For him no rule is good in itself; law-abidingness as such is not a virtue. It is a

---

[1] It seems to me that they have all been refuted in D. Lyons: *Forms and Limits of Utilitarianism*, Oxford, 1965. This did not come my way until after my lectures were delivered. *Litera scripta maneat*. But those who have read Mr Lyons may skip most of this chapter.

virtue only if the rules that are kept are rules subserving a good end. If promise-keeping is right, then the only reason is that promise-keeping is a means to some good, whether personal, or social, or political.

3. BENEFIT

For a utilitarian, what justifies an act is its contribution to good, however good may be defined. The great moral principle is thus *benefit*, and no action can be morally justified unless it can be shown that someone or some society or some political order benefits from it. If we have an obligation, it is the obligation to produce as much benefit or good as possible. But we are then faced with the difficulty of discovering what this good or benefit is. For Mill, the end is the greatest happiness of the greatest number. Alas! We are not told why this is the great end to seek, and still less how the precise nature of this end is to be ascertained. On the ground that he that increaseth knowledge increaseth sorrow, the best way to pursue Mill's end would not be, as Mill desired, the provision of universal education, but the reverse. The view that the masses will be made happy by getting what social reformers think is good for them is perhaps not yet dead.

The essence of utilitarianism as a moral theory is that 'right' means productive of good, and this view is not without a certain superficial plausibility. If the reason for keeping a promise, for example, lies in the benefit accruing to the promisee or to society as a whole, it is clear that we have no obligation to keep a promise if to do so is futile. If I say to a friend: 'I will be at the Caledonian Hotel at 7.0', I am not obliged to keep my word if he telephones in advance to say that he cannot meet me after all. The *reductio ad absurdum* of promise-keeping is related in one of Macaulay's letters. A Protestant fanatic had promised to delay as long as possible a Bill prohibiting processions of Orangemen. He insisted on dividing the House seventeen times, although he was in a minority of one or two and saw that his procedure was futile. 'I feel I am doing wrong, but I must keep my word.'[1] Moreover, it is argued, if it is ever relevant, in considering whether to keep a promise or to break it, to weigh the results of either course of action before deciding which to choose, then it seems plain that the ground of an obligation to keep a promise must have some connec-

[1] *Life and Works of Lord Macaulay*, London, 1897, vol. ix, pp 272 ff.

tion with results. Any action, the utilitarian will hold, must produce some good if it is to be justified, and he will also hold that a
rule or a law can be justified only by its beneficial results. It seems
obvious to him that virtues like kindliness or modesty are justified
by their contribution to harmonious social relations, and that laws
against stealing or murder are equally justified by their contribution to the peace of the body politic. He will also urge that if two
rules conflict, so that in a given situation we cannot abide by both,
we ought not to waste time trying to assess the relative stringency
of the rules but simply ask which course of action will produce
most good. In all such instances, the utilitarian may say, there is
no need to go beyond the immediate effects of your action, i.e.
beyond those which you can immediately foresee. If you keep a
promise to a friend, you have benefited him and there your
responsibility ends. Any further consequences or results of your
action will depend on him. Of those remoter results your fulfilment
of your promise may be a *conditio sine qua non*, but your action is
to be judged only by the result of which it was the *causa efficiens*.
Thus stated, a utilitarian theory gains in plausibility and it is
exempt from many of the criticisms urged against Mill, but it is
still hopelessly defective as a theory of moral action.

To begin with, let us examine the notion of benefit. Health is
commonly regarded as a good, especially by people of a utilitarian
frame of mind. A town's sewage system is a means to health,[1] and
therefore the work of the sewage engineer is right, for utilitarians,
in exactly the same sense in which keeping a promise to a friend or
being grateful is right. This implies that efficiency in dealing with
the means to a good end has for the utilitarian the same moral value
as a choice to keep a beneficial promise. This puts technical skill
and moral character on the same footing. If a pianist uses the
wrong fingering, he is morally to blame, just as if he had failed to
pay his debts. The classical argument against this position is to be
found in the first book of Plato's *Republic* where it is argued that
skill is one thing and morality another, if only because skill is the
ability to do opposite things well, and it may be used for good or
bad ends, whereas the fruits of moral character are always good.
It may be true that a moral action ought to be efficient, but can it
be made moral by its efficiency?

[1] This is derived from J. Laird: *Enquiry into Moral Notions*, London, 1935,
pp 288 ff.

If morality is a technique, as the equalization, in principle, of sanitary engineering and morality implies, then what is called a conflict of obligations is reduced to a matter of fact. The decision about which of two conflicting obligations to fulfil is similar in principle to a decision about which of two different sanitary systems to adopt; in both cases our task is to choose the most efficient method of attaining some benefit. We may ask, however, whether the parallel can be exact. A woman may ask herself whether she should continue to look after her parents or accede to her fiancé's request to marry now. To accept either horn of this dilemma is to fail somewhere, and it matters to her which course of action she adopts. She is conscious of different claims on her. The engineer, on the other hand, has perplexities of another kind. Neither alternative sanitary system has any claim on him; both may be rejected as unsatisfactory or too expensive and he may devise a third. The means he selects need only be efficient. If two systems are equally efficient it will not matter which is chosen; the engineer is not in a dilemma. He may make a mistake in his choice; but the woman's choice may be a *sin*.

The utilitarian who holds that what justifies a rule or a specific action is the resultant benefit must still be asked why one benefit rather than another is chosen. This is the difficulty which ought to haunt social planners. The choice of one benefit rather than another is not simply the choice of one end rather than another; it may also be the choice of one means rather than another. For example, let it be admitted that it would be beneficial to diminish the deaths from road accidents. There are then various means of contributing to this result, for example: (i) abolish all road vehicles which can travel at more than ten miles per hour, (ii) make special roads for fast vehicles only, (iii) enforce by rigorous penalties a Highway Code. Now which of these ought, on utilitarian principles, to be selected, and why? The answer might be: 'select the one or those most in the general interest', but we then have to ask what that interest is. Fairness may be more important than efficiency. For example, is the tyranny of abolishing motor cars worse than a continuation of, or an increase in, road deaths? If the tyrannical overriding of public opinion is to be avoided, this implies a preference for liberty over an effective means of diminishing road deaths, and it may imply a belief in the worth of justice for all, pedestrians, cyclists, vanmen, and motorists alike. This implication that liberty and justice rank high as social benefits needs justification in turn. Some would say that the reason is that they are moral ideals, higher in the scale of goods than any form of material welfare. But the utilitarian cannot say this; he must say that liberty and justice are means to benefit and owe their worth to the end that they subserve. Their goodness must consist in their efficiency—but efficiency for what? It is of no use to speak of the general benefit all over again. Liberty and justice may be useful, but that may not be the reason why we value them.

4. THE GOOD

It does not improve matters if the end is not described as the general welfare, but as the good, for the problem then is how this good is to be described. Bentham was at least candid when he said that a proof of the rectitude of the principle of utility is at once needless and impossible: the principle in question is that approval or disapproval of an action depends on the action's apparent tendency to augment or diminish happiness.[1] It is still characteristic of those disposed to utilitarianism to take the end for granted and so to fail to give any reason for the choice of that end. R. Robinson, for example, has no doubt that the obvious end is the diminution of misery.[2] Others who are not utilitarians have just as few doubts about ends, but they would hold that they do not take the nature of the good for granted; they simply see it. We can enumerate things that are good, just as we can enumerate things that are yellow; but if we are asked what goodness is or what yellow is, we cannot go beyond this enumeration; the questioner must just *see* for himself.

But one difficulty is that different people *see* different things to be good, and this cannot be explained away on the analogy of colour-blindness, because people argue about good and bad. When the Scottish Advisory Council for Education 'saw' that it was bad to suppose that the fundamentals of education are the three Rs, I would gladly have argued the point. The intuitionist is likely to reply that when different people see different things to be good, they are not differing about what good is but only disagreeing about what the things are in which this quality is instan-

---

[1] *Principles of Morals and Legislation*, ed. W. Harrison, Oxford, 1948, pp 126–8.   [2] *Op. cit., passim.*

tiated. This, however, is impossible. Universal and particular cannot be understood in separation from one another. Knowledge of both proceeds *pari passu*. The real reason why people differ about goods is that good is correlative to *choice*, but this is what objectivists like G. E. Moore or utilitarians who take the end for granted will not believe.

5. INTUITION

If we enquire what this moral intuition is which enables us to see and so to be assured of moral obligations, we are usually given an analogy from mathematics. There is no proof that two straight lines cannot enclose a space, but we 'see' the truth and the necessity of this axiom as soon as we understand the meaning of the words. In the same way, it is argued, we 'see' that promise-keeping is right or that giving pleasure to others is good. It seems doubtful if the analogy will hold. The mathematical axiom is concerned with straight lines, i.e. with abstractions accurately defined in advance, and its truth follows from the definition, taken together with the notion of enclosure. The necessity of the axiom and its truth for all intelligences depend on its abstract definable content. But when we come to the alleged moral intuitions we are in a different sphere, that of the concrete; and at once we discover that there is no universality of agreement. G. E. Moore 'sees' that aesthetic enjoyment is among the few things that are good in themselves.[1] Plato was of a different opinion and banned Homer from his state, despite the beauty of the Iliad and the Odyssey, because of their immoral influence, i.e. because they tended to lead men not towards the Good but in the reverse direction. Again, Sir David Ross asserts that it is one of the clearest facts about our moral consciousness that we ought to give pleasure to others but not to ourselves.[2] That we should give pleasure (or happiness) to both has been argued by J. Laird,[3] and others might with equal plausibility urge that we have no duty to give pleasure to anyone (attempts to do this so often fail), and that our duty is to act justly and mercifully and kindly to others.

Intuition corresponds to and is on the same level as caprice, and is thus irrelevant to the understanding of rational action. Intui-

[1] *Op. cit.*, p 188.   [2] *Foundations of Ethics*, Oxford, 1939, pp 272-3.
[3] *Op. cit.*, pp 272-3.

tionism in ethics is often attractive because it makes difficult things easy: 'I see it to be so, and you will see it too if you look carefully.' Unfortunately this is not true. What we see is apt to be dependent on what we are looking for. The intuitionist sometimes tells us that we will see it too, *if we reflect*. This is a very different matter. It is true enough that the cogency of an argument has to be seen before it can be accepted. Sight and reflection are both required; mediation and immediacy are as little to be severed as universal and particular. Intuition is an element intrinsic to thinking. It is only after climbing the hill that we see the view, but a closer analogy with thinking would be to say that at every step in the climb more and more of the view is seen. If we 'see' the solution of some matter that is under dispute, the seeing has been mediated by reflection and discursive reasoning.[1] We may on occasion be unaware of this mediation, because thought is often quick, but we can recover it on reflection. We need intuition in order to grasp the situation in which we stand and so to discern our duty, but intuition here is not a separate faculty; it is our own thinking become luminous.

6. DEFINITION OF GOOD

Of course good cannot be defined as a triangle can. It is too concrete a matter for that. But this is no reason for taking refuge in intuition. Good is a concept which develops through various stages, such as pleasure, utility, right, and duty; it is part of an adult experience, learnt through the teachings of others, through language, through our reading, and ultimately through our choices (to which it is always correlative), themselves illumined by our total experience of life. To define goodness is to describe its various degrees and kinds and the various types of choice which we make, and to enumerate the various things and experiences in which through choice it is instantiated. For example, the goodness of a tool is its efficiency; the goodness of any means is its efficiency as a means to an end. This must be a low degree of goodness, even if it be that commonly envisaged by utilitarians. A torturer can be extremely efficient in extorting information or a confession or a

---

[1] Cf. Hegel: *Ph. d. Rel*, Lasson, vol. i, pp 92 ff.: 'Immediate knowledge is the knowledge in which we have no consciousness of mediation. But mediated it is.'

recantation. To that extent he is good, but few will describe him as good without qualification. Pleasure and happiness, health, prosperity, and peace are also goods and they may be pursued as ends, and not only as means. But nevertheless their goodness is only a conditional goodness. Everything depends on who enjoys them and when and in what circumstances. Thus they may become little goods, inadequate actualizations of the notion of goodness, as for example, when peace is obtained at the expense of honour, and men have often looked askance at the prosperity of the wicked. If these are subordinate or conditional goods, inadequate realizations of true goodness, then true goodness or some unconditional good there must be as a norm for them.

7. MOTIVES

The utilitarian usually admits an unconditional or supreme good, namely that to which all right actions and justifiable rules are in the last resort means. But no such good can be discovered within any single action, since any such action can be justified only by the end to which it is a means. Suppose that a soldier attempts to save his comrade's life at the expense of his own. Both are killed. The sacrifice was therefore wasted. Suppose again that a parent by self-sacrifice gives a child a good education and the child makes no use of his opportunities and becomes an enemy of society. Was the sacrifice bad? In these two instances does the justification or otherwise of the sacrifice depend on results at all? We may reply in the negative but suggest that it might depend on the motive. But this reference to motives is one which the utilitarian would have to reject. Justice Darling once wrote: 'Is too much attention paid to motive when we judge a man's deserts? Some influential teachers of mankind have estimated motives at nothing, for example the Gnostic sect of Cainites. These people worshipped the first murderer on the hypothesis that he must have been virtuous because he was oppressed, but they also adored Judas Iscariot because had it not been for his perfidy there would have been no salvation for Christians.'[1] This might well have suited Austin who says firmly that: 'utility is the *test* and not the motive of action. We are not to say that the lover is to kiss his mistress with his eye

[1] *Scintillae Juris*, London, 1903, p 36.

on the general good'.[1] This implies that an individual's motive may be a quest for his own pleasure or interest, but the test of what he does lies in the action's contribution to the general happiness. This seems to amount to Mandeville's 'Private Vices Public Benefits'. And in any case how does Austin know that the kiss contributes to the general happiness—or does not?

8. RULES AND EXCEPTIONS

Despite all this, the utilitarian may try to show that unsuccessful sacrifices can be morally justified on the ground that they are valuable as an example to others. If so, they are a good example and we must ask why this should be so. The only answer would seem to be that acts of sacrifice redound *as a rule* to the general benefit. But then the question arises whether the rule applies in this particular case; this question presses on anyone who maintains that what justifies a rule is its contribution to some result or end, such as liberty or the diminution of misery. Mill for example tells us that mankind has discovered the kind of action which does contribute most to the general happiness and has thus discovered the rules laid down in the Moral Almanac. Richard Robinson does not go so far as this, but he does at least seem to hold that he can discover which rules or laws are justified, namely those which do diminish misery, or 'tend' to do so, whatever that may mean. The qualification implied in 'tend', which occurs in Mill also, may be an admission that the rules recognized are not infallible, and this may be as well, because even Mr Robinson, who says that 'it seems perfectly clear that states ought to keep their treaties',[2] might find it hard to show that the keeping of a treaty invariably increased human happiness or diminished misery: consider for example Frederick the Great's tripartite treaty for the partition of Poland.

But if exceptions are admitted, and Austin grants that there are 'anomalous or eccentric'[3] cases (though 'comparatively few'), the rules become useless as a general guide and have no justification at all. All action is action in a unique situation; this is one of the differences between man as mind and the world of nature. Therefore I am faced at every moment with a calculation of means and ends, or of the consequences of my action, and the calculation can

[1] *Province of Jurisprudence Determined*, Edn. 2, London, 1861, p 101.
[2] *Op. cit.*, p 171.   [3] *Op. cit.*, pp 47–51.

never have any certain answer; for although I may know what I intend, I cannot be sure that my intention will be realized. How often does someone intend a present to give pleasure to a friend, and how often the present does not please at all! And the difficulty of ascribing moral worth to intentions alone has been discussed already.

9. UTILITARIAN CRITERIA MAY BE INAPPLICABLE

If we cannot calculate what action will in fact produce the greatest happiness or the least misery, the consequence is that we cannot know at the time of acting what action we ought to perform. This is admitted in some quarters when it is said that the right act is the most felicific act though one can never know what that is. This is an admission that the question: which act will produce the greatest happiness or the least misery? is unanswerable, and therefore no sensible man will waste time on trying to answer it. What then would it be sensible for him to do? He can give up looking for utility as a clue to rightness and act for his own pleasure; he can revert to hedonism; and he can back up his decision by espousing out-of-date economics: if every man seeks his own welfare, pleasure, interest, etc., then the general welfare, pleasure, interest will result. In effect this too involves a regression to hedonism, for the social consequences of the universal pursuit of self-interest do not seem to have coincided with the prophecies of *laissez-faire* economists. Alternatively, the sensible man can ask why the question was unanswerable, and he may decide that instead of trying to work with the category of means and end, or to regard consequences as the justification or otherwise of an act, it would be better to ask himself what was the right thing to do, or to rise to higher ground and ask himself what in this situation was his duty. In other words he may conclude that in assessing the worth or otherwise of self-sacrifice a calculation of the actual results of the sacrifice is irrelevant.

If this be so, then unconditional goods are to be sought in actions and not in the results thereof. Virtue in general is unconditionally good, whatever its results may be. It may issue in good results if only because its exercise strengthens the character of the man who possesses it. But virtue is not made good by its results. The virtuous act is not a *means* to establishing good social relations, it *is* the actualization of such relations. But good social relations exist only when we differentiate between the claims of different people in a way which it is difficult for untilitarian ethics to explain.

We are told to do the most good. But I have argued that some goods are qualitatively higher than others, higher actualizations of the notion of goodness, and higher and lower goods are thus incommensurable. It is impossible to determine how much of a lower good is to compensate for the loss of some part of a higher one. To abide by a previous example, how many road deaths are to be accepted? Which will diminish misery less, the abolition of the motor car, or the preservation of the motorist's liberty? A man may give happiness to three friends if he promises to join them for a game of bridge; but his wife may take ill. Is he to give pleasure to three people by keeping his engagement or to one by staying at home? How a decision in such a case is to be reached on the principle of doing the most felicific act it is difficult to see.

10. SPECIAL OBLIGATIONS

What makes the criterion of the general good or the general happiness inapplicable is that although, for example, we ought to work efficiently at any job that we undertake, and although it may be an obligation to help people in a difficulty, whoever they are, we may have a special duty to work at this job (for which we are paid) and not at another which may be voluntary but may appeal to our social conscience. This is what some university students forget when they give excessive time and energy to collecting for charity to the detriment of the studies which the state is paying them to pursue. Mill tells us that each is to count for one and not more than one, and so ignores the fact that a wife may have to count for many more than one; but curiously enough Godwin took a different view from Mill's: 'Justice', he says, 'means that I must contribute everything in my power to the benefit of the whole.' And he goes on to object to the precept 'Love thy neighbour as thyself' on the ground that it overlooks the fact that my neighbour and I may have different values for society.[1] This bold attempt to justify the pursuit of my ends at the expense of my neighbour's shows how easily a utilitarian theory can relapse into hedonism. Of course it may be said that, as a general rule, fulfilment of

[1] Quoted in A. Gray: *op. cit.*, p 119.

special claims works out to the general benefit, but this raises once more the problem of whether this rule permits of exceptions, and also the problem of what benefit is, since benefit is an omnibus term for goods of different kinds which are not commensurable, and, therefore, to speak of benefit conceals the impossibility of calculating quantitatively things that are qualitatively different. Mill was never able to explain what the criterion was for differentiating pleasures by reference to quality. Nor did he observe that any such criterion must have ranked higher in the scale of goods than pleasure. Qualitative differences and special claims are the Achilles heel of utilitarianism.

11. RESULTS, ACCIDENTAL AND NECESSARY

Although I may seem to have made heavy weather of utilitarianism, there are still some things to be said about the results which in utilitarianism are supposed to provide the justification or otherwise of an action. When we ask in this context what an action is, the answer is not obvious. Consider the payment of a debt. I receive a bill. I write a cheque. I put it in an envelope and stamp it. I then post it. Where is the act of paying the debt? Is it the act of writing the cheque, or the posting of it, or what? Presumably it is all of these, along with the receipt of the cheque by my creditor and his payment into the bank, and so on. Hence within what we judge as a single action, paying a debt, we distinguish several actions related to one another as means to end, and the later phases of this complex might be regarded as the necessary results of the earlier, necessary because they are all included in what I plan, execute, and regard as a single act. The whole act may have what might be called accidental results, for example, the use the recipient makes of the cheque when he gets it.

There is another distinction between accidental and necessary results. Gratitude, for example, actualizes a good relationship between benefactor and recipient. Here the gratitude and the relationship are actualized simultaneously, yet the one is logically prior to the other just as, in Kant's example, the cannon ball lying on the cushion is logically prior to the indentation of the cushion. It is possible here to distinguish between means and end, but only as simultaneous moments within a single complex. The result or end is necessary to the means because the two are actualized of necessity together. Indeed any action at all can be analysed in this way.

Now when the utilitarian argues that the worth of an action depends on its being the means to beneficial results, what sort of results has he in mind? Is he thinking of the later phases of what is one act, or is he thinking of results which the act may have later?

(i) If he means accidental results, i.e. if he treats the action, within which means and end can be distinguished, as a single isolable whole and as a means to an end, then apparently it is the end which justifies the means. Any efficient means will do, and even an inefficient means will be acceptable in so far as it is a means. There are often alternative means of attaining the same result, for example, the different means of catching salmon to feed the hungry. If the utilitarian concentrates on feeding the hungry, he gives no guidance on the choice of means and must regard any efficient means as justified. If contributing to good is the sole and sufficient justification of an action, nothing is either right or wrong in itself; all depends on the result achieved. For example, it might be held that war, though in itself an evil, was the efficient means to a new order and would thus be justified by the end to which it was a means. So Hitler might have argued. It is commonly thought, on the other hand, that what justifies a war, admittedly an evil, is the just cause in which it is waged. In 1939 and 1940 what the outcome of the war would be, was for some people in doubt; what was not in doubt in this country was that it was right and a bounden duty to take up arms against Hitler, whatever the outcome. If it be said that a just war is a means to defending a good cause, then here means and end coincide; the waging of the war is *eo ipso* the defence of the good cause. The utilitarian justification could only apply to successful wars, but are we sure that the just cause has never lost? Was the Hungarian Revolution in 1956 wrong because it was soon crushed and therefore unsuccessful? To concentrate on accidental results is to hold that the end, and the end only, justifies the means, and then end and means fall apart, accidental to one another as they are.

(ii) If the utilitarian turns from accidental to *necessary* results, then his doctrine disappears into an attempt to analyse any and every act into two parts, end and means, and an assertion that the rightness of an act depends on the fact that its start is a means to its

K

conclusion. But, to revert to the example of gratitude, why is worth to be ascribed to one moment of a situation where two are actualized simultaneously? The nerve of utilitarianism lies in taking the whole act (the recipient's gratitude plus the right relation between the parties) and holding that its justification lies outside it in the general happiness or welfare or in the 'favours to come' of which La Rochefoucauld wrote. If a single act can be split into its components, and as I have said any act can be so analysed, then utilitarianism has lost its nerve. Utility is intrinsic to *any* action, if we analyse it sufficiently, but so to analyse it and to consider one part to the exclusion of the rest, is not to exhibit its moral worth but to analyse its moral worth away, because it is on the whole act, and not on one part of it, that a moral judgment is passed.

John Laird hit the nail on the head when he said in one of his unjustly neglected books, 'moral excellence cannot simply be one means among others for producing benefit by voluntary action'.[1] It shines in its own right like a jewel, and this is what utilitarianism cannot explain. If a tree is known by its fruits, that is only because the fruits are part of the tree so that the connection between tree and fruits is one of the necessary results to which I have referred. A good character has fruits, but it is not the fruits that make it good. The product of villainy may on occasion be good, but that does not transform the villain into a saint.

12. THE TRUTH OF UTILITARIANISM IN ECONOMIC AND POLITICAL LIFE

Although as a theory of rightness utilitarianism must be rejected, its protest against legalism was to some extent justified. It was justified in the name of welfare, even if it misconceived morality as a matter of welfare. To suppose that morality means no more than keeping every jot and tittle of the law is the characteristic error of Pharisaism, and the utilitarians were right enough in holding that there could not be a duty to do something futile. But instead of considering motives, as Jesus did in opposition to the Pharisees, the utilitarians enter and cannot leave the morass of beneficial results. This, as we have seen, tends to assimilate morality to efficiency and skill, and draws no distinction between the utility of

[1] *Op. cit.*, p 301.

an economic transaction and the intrinsic worth of a moral action,
or indeed of a moral character. What justified the woman's act
when she threw her two mites into the treasury was not the trivial
benefit which her almsgiving would produce, but her own self-
sacrifice. This is what utilitarians may find it difficult to accept
or explain.

The real strength of utilitarianism, however, is that, just as
hedonism and rightness are true accounts of certain levels and
aspects of human experience, it is an adequate account of economic
life, and to some extent of political life, as these two types of
experience are seen from within. Not everyone is a business man,
but everyone has his own finances to look after, and everyone buys
his needs somewhere, and here, as in industry and commerce, it is
utility and not pleasure which is the essential thing. A shoemaker
does not make shoes for the fun of the thing but in order to make a
profit and to supply the needs of his customers. A child may buy
for the sake of buying, and its feminine elders may do the same at
the sales: but a reasonable man buys in order to supply some
specific need of his own. The transaction is a means to an end, and
the transaction depends for its justification on its utility. This is
true of the whole economic sphere. Pleasure, to be sure, may be
present incidentally; no-one's eyes sparkle quite so brightly as the
commercial traveller's when he is handling a good and successful
article (cf. above, p. 110, fn. 1). But the pleasure and romance of
the commercial world are dependent on utility, on the successful
achievement of profits or power (in a free enterprise system) or of
some other end, such as public service or national glory (in
socialistic or communistic systems). The pleasure of a game is not
necessarily dependent on winning; but the pleasure of commerce
is. If commercial activity is not a utility, if it is unsuccessful, the
participants in the activity feel cheated and the zest has gone out of
it. Rules also are to be found in economic life; bargains must be
kept; failure to abide by arbitration awards is an economic crime;
sharp practice is as vigorously condemned on 'change as it is in the
pulpit. But the business man justifies the rules on the utilitarian
ground that honesty is the best policy. Within the economic sphere
this is reasonable.

Political activity has, *prima facie*, a similar utilitarian justification. The state's end appears to be peace and security of life, and
war or civil strife is not the apotheosis of the state but its downfall.

Political institutions are devices framed with a view to securing these ends, and their justification is thus utilitarian. Plato thought that compulsion would have to be exercised on wise men to make them take part in politics, but, strange as it may seem, politicians in these days appear to enjoy their work, especially when they are in power, and there is no lack of aspirants for office. But in a free country the essential task of the politician is not to produce legislation which is inherently right, but to make compromises for the sake of keeping the peace. And the justification of their activity is thus utilitarian.

13. NON-UTILITARIAN ELEMENTS IN ECONOMIC AND POLITICAL LIFE

Although, therefore, utilitarianism will pass as an account of at least the most obvious features of economic and political life seen from within, there are other features in these experiences which it cannot cover, and this exhibits its weakness. It would be a fully adequate account of economic activity if those engaged in it were the economic men of whom economists have sometimes spoken, and of political activity if the whole truth about man were that he is a political animal. Economic man is an abstraction and political man is another. I drew attention in Chapter 1 to a clash in a business man's mind between economic and personal claims. Business men are still men, and therefore are beings capable of reasoning and reflecting on their situation and activities. The quest for wealth or power, or for any other end to which economic activity may be regarded as a means, amounts to a quest which, however successful, is never satisfying or satisfied. Economists speak of 'rational' activity, i.e. the conscious choice of the most economical means of securing profit, power, or welfare. But this is the activity, if I may use an Hegelian distinction, not of reason but of the understanding, and, as Hegel pointed out, it is characteristic of the latter to embark on the false infinite, in this instance a quest for power after power *ad infinitum*. There is no business reason why the business man who is immersed in his expanding business should ever set limits to its expansion.

If there is no business reason, there may be others which come to light when the business man reflects on his activity and sees 'shining' in it, as Hegel would say, the categories of a sphere other than the utilitarian. Rules which from the purely economic view seem to be only useful may become recognized as rational or as having a rational basis. As an example I propose to consider promise-keeping once more. Whatever promise-keeping may be for the man immersed in business, for us, looking at the commercial world from without, it appears as a law of trade and commerce, not useful as productive of certain results, but intrinsic to trade and commerce as its *sine qua non*, justifiable as reasonable, rather than useful, to the extent that the whole economic sphere is reasonable. To sue for breach of contract everyone with whom business is done would be an impossibility; without the keeping of contracts to deliver goods and to pay for them when delivered, trading could not take place. Promises are, at the very least, an intrinsic part of the economic or business side of life. A promise to deliver a Rotary Club address or to keep an appointment is on the same footing as a promise to pay for what we order or to attend a business conference; and the reason for keeping promises is of the same order as the reason for playing a game according to the rules. The rules of the game are as it were the mechanism of the game itself, and promise-keeping is the mechanical ordering of the business side of life. It may be for this reason that those to whom this side of life is an ever-present reality are those who are most punctilious in keeping their engagements. I have a suspicion that business men have the laugh of academic people here. The academic philosopher who maintained that it was not his duty to return a borrowed book but only to 'set himself' to return it would get short shrift not only from a banker who advanced a loan but from the recipient who required it to expand his business.

To make a promise involves intelligence and foresight; it refers to the future and so to the sphere of the possible as such. The nature of the present limits the possibilities of the future to some extent, and a promise is meant to limit them still further. The restriction of possibilities is a procedure of reason (rather than of the understanding). It is only to the child or the uneducated man that *any*thing is possible. The law that promises be kept is thus a rational, not just a utilitarian, law, for on it depends the very being not only of economic life, but the mechanical side of the social life of men, who, being bodies as well as minds, cannot escape that mechanical side. Hence the ground for keeping a promise is not the welfare, etc., produced by the keeping of the promise, but the recognition that keeping promises is part and parcel of economic life and of the mechanical side of social life.

If honesty be adopted just as a policy, it may always be possible to discover situations in which a different policy will produce similar or even better results. As has been pointed out already, the use of the category of means and end in human affairs results in conclusions which can be true, if at all, only ὡς ἐπὶ τὸ πολύ as we learnt long ago from Aristotle. Promise-keeping is not an expediency or a reversible policy. To keep the rules of bridge is not a means to playing bridge; it *is* playing bridge. To keep promises is not a means to economic utility; it *is* living economic life. But there is an important difference from the rules of bridge. Bridge is a game which no-one need play. Economic life and the mechanics of social life are inescapable features in human life. Moreover the rules of bridge are arbitrary. Clubs might have been made to count higher than spades. Some laws which regulate life are also arbitrary; in this country it might have been made compulsory to drive on the right instead of on the left. But the rule that promises be kept is not reversible in this way. Social and economic life would be impossible if the rule were that no promises be kept, for in that event scarcely any restriction would be placed on future possibilities, and economic life depends on some such restrictions being precise. If a customer promises to pay £50 at the end of the month, and there is no rule that promises be kept, the merchant is left guessing as to whether any amount will be paid or not. Credit disappears and with it both trade and such social intercourse as is on a higher level than play.

The question when, if ever, it is legitimate to break a promise has been touched upon in the previous chapter. Here it is only necessary to observe that the question does not arise within the life of business; promise-breaking in that sphere can never be justified from the point of view of that level. To ask if a business undertaking may be broken is like asking whether it be legitimate at a game of chess to upset the chess-board. Nevertheless, the economic justification of promise-keeping no doubt remains a utilitarian one; as I said before, questioned on the subject, economic man could reasonably reply, because honesty is the best policy. He is also entitled to carry his means and end outlook further, since the essence of economic life is its utility. Statements in the economic sphere must primarily be not pleasant as in the sphere of play or social convention (e.g. 'she is not at home', when the truth would better be expressed by saying, 'she will not see you'), or true, as in the sphere of a fuller morality, but useful. Commerce, however, is on a level more intellectually developed than that of play; we have seen that its rules are of a higher order; and hence commercial statements have more reference to truth than the euphemisms of playful social life. The assertions of advertisers cannot be taken at their face value, but they must not stray from truth altogether or otherwise they will fail of the utility which is their primary justification. Unless they have *some* truth, they will not be useful at all in getting or at least in keeping business. It is just this fact that in the economic sphere there is the clash, for those who reflect on it, between utility, its essence, and the presage or, as Hegel would say, the 'show' of higher rationality and higher ideals within it that this sphere becomes so unsatisfactory to many people in it and to many more outside. This is why attempts are made to moralize this sphere by slurring over its utilitarian essence through substituting a notion of 'service' for that of profits. This is also why, as men of higher education (and less business training) enter it, we find them thrusting utility into the background and taking an interest instead in administration for its own sake rather than for the sake of profit. Argument then arises about the best method of administration, and the essential purpose of the economic sphere, its utility, is overlooked. 'Whate'er is best administered is best', where 'best administered' does not necessarily mean 'most profitable'.

There is a similar reflection of the rational or moral in political life. While some laws are justified as effecting compromises between divergent interests, and others, like the rule of the road, are justified as contributing to the public peace, there are other laws which may be of a different character, such as the law of contract, and some features of constitutional law which may be regarded as not reversible, as the rule of the road is, or as compromises for the sake of peace may be, but inherently right as preserving the inalienable rights of civilized men. Laws of all these kinds may reach the statute-book through a political process but if laws of this third kind are actualities, then Plato and Hegel were not wrong in finding some non-utilitarian features in the state and in political activity.

Further evidence for the existence of such features may be found in instances where moral convictions sometimes enter the political sphere, and they need not upset the chess-board by making a revolution; instead they may produce political changes by political means, and yet the essence of their activity cannot be regarded as purely utilitarian. It is sometimes said by those who are anxious to preserve the essence of politics as utility, that in this sphere moral or religious questions are not political issues, and that when one arises with which for some reason Parliament has to deal, for instance the Prayer Book measures in the 1920s, then they are settled not as a party question but by free vote of the House. But this device to keep politics utilitarian is not always effective. Campbell-Bannerman won the 1906 election because his supporters thought that he was *morally* right about South Africa, just as *moral* indignation had previously been a great help to Gladstone. In 1935 the Hoare–Laval plan in connection with Abyssinia was greeted with such a wave of *moral* condemnation as to enforce Sir Samual Hoare's resignation; here the public was clearly ready to sacrifice a compromise arrangement for the sake of a moral principle.

The essence of politics is indeed the quest for utility—peace and security, just as the essence of economic life is the quest for utility as profit or power or the like. But just as there intrude into economic life certain features which demand a higher than utilitarian justification, so similar features enter political life too. In both of these spheres we find from time to time an attitude of mind and a form of action which recognizes ends higher than those which these spheres exist to obtain. The instability of promise-keeping, for example, i.e. of the law of commerce, is indicated by the inclusion in commercial documents of *caveats* in connection with *force majeure*, the act of God, and so forth. Such expressions are an admission that the rule of the economic sphere is not of ultimate validity, even though within that sphere there can be no good economic reason for breaking it, and therefore that the whole economic sphere is a subordinate one, not wholly autonomous, not wholly self-justifying; and this makes it reasonable to hold that this sphere is ultimately directed by higher ends lying outside and beyond its own strict boundaries.

CHAPTER 9

SCIENTIFIC AND PHILOSOPHICAL OBJECTIONS

Before proceeding to duty, in which moral experience and the forms of action and moral goodness culminate, it is necessary to deal with certain theories which run counter either to the method or the conclusions, or both, reached in the foregoing chapters. Most of these theories would bar the way to an advance beyond utility and would give less than its due to rightness. Some of these theories are old, but they have been assiduously propagated in this century and they cannot be ignored. They have been sponsored by some psychologists, anthropologists, Marxists, philosophers, and biologists,[1] and I proceed to deal with them in that order: I give psychology pride of place because its attack is the most formidable one.

1. FREUD'S ANALYSIS OF OBLIGATION

If I concentrate attention primarily on Freud, this is because he seems to me to have much the same position in psychology as Darwin in biology or Einstein in cosmology, although I am told by Professor Eysenck[2] that I am out of date and that Freud is only another Gall or another Spurzheim.

Freud recognizes that there is an experience of duty as that of being under an absolute obligation, and he does offer some explanation of it. In this experience, he holds, we are divided against ourselves, and Kant would say the same,[3] but he differs from Kant in holding that the moral law which we think we are constrained to obey is a construction of our own unconscious mental activity and therefore has no intrinsic validity. Freud analyses the self into *id*, *ego*, and *super-ego*. The *id* is the primary source of instinctive energy which supplies the driving force behind all our actions and is a basis on which all our life depends.

[1] Some of these attacks are conveniently summarized and shortly discussed in a still useful volume, *Science and Ethics*, London, 1942, by Professor C. H. Waddington and others, but I have tried to bring the discussion a little more up to date.   [2] *Op. cit.*, p 130.

[3] E.g. *Metaphysik der Sitten*, Part 2, Introduction, section ix.

The *ego* is the self of which we are consciously aware. The *super-ego* is the source of our moral control and is an unconscious agency within ourselves. It is a system of compulsions and prohibitions, and ethics is the consciously formulated part of these. The psycho-analyst has investigated the origin of this *super-ego* and discovered how it has been built up, especially by the infant's reaction to its environment. To begin with, we love ourselves as well as others, and this means that *id* impulses are directed inwards on ourselves, as well as outwards. But as we develop we become aware (through criticisms and punishments inflicted on us) of defects, physical, mental, and moral; and then if we refuse to face ourselves as we are, we build up an imaginary self, an *ego-ideal* to be the object of our self-love. This imaginary self then becomes an ideal to which the *ego* is constrained by the unconscious to try to correspond. This constraint is part of the system called the *super-ego*. Moral anxiety has as its forerunner anxiety arising from the influence of external critics and authorities. Thus in early youth we come up against rules and regulations laid down by parents and others in authority. Obedience is met with approval, and disobedience with disapproval. But these rules do not remain external to us; we tend to introject them, so that, as it were, we lay these rules on ourselves and so approve or disapprove of ourselves according as we obey them or not. Instead of being commands by parents they become, by unconscious process, the commands laid by the *super-ego* on the *ego*. Furthermore, in childhood our *id* impulses may be frustrated, and hence aggression is aroused. A child's aggression against its parents is futile, and hence aggression recoils against the self. The forbidding parents are introjected, or incorporated into the self, in the form of the *super-ego*. The latter is already aggressive enough, but it becomes still more aggressive when the child's aggression against itself is added to it. The *super-ego* becomes more stern and cruel than the parents.[1]

Thus the *super-ego* is a system of unconscious motives built up partly by introjection, partly by unconscious imagination, in order to help the growing child to master its problems and find satisfaction for some at least of its impulses. Notice, however, that the prohibitions and commands issued by the *super-ego* are of the most

[1] My summary of Freud is based on *The Ego and the Id*, Eng. tr., London, 1942.

varied kinds; the *super-ego* is used to explain not only compulsions to obey rules and customs but such compulsions as endless hand-washing or not stepping on lines between paving-stones, or touching lamp-posts. The compulsion of duty is an inner compulsion brought into existence by the self as the solution of a problem in early life. The fangs of duty are drawn by recognizing that it originates in childish and immature attempts to control one's life and environment. The psycho-analyst may be able to help to get rid of some compulsions in such a way as to produce that health of mind which consists in contriving to give *id* impulses an appropriate outlet.

2. IMPORTANCE OF FREUDIAN VIEW

There is a great deal of this which we may have to accept. Although Freud's whole procedure is now repudiated in some quarters, he was the prime mover of an era of psychological discovery which may rank as one of the great intellectual achievements in the history of science. Even the layman will have read how psychiatrists have been enabled to cure neurotics, and he has evidence of how Freud and his successors have helped the historian and the moralist by exposing clearly to view for the first time some of the recesses of men's minds. They have disposed of the view that *all* our conduct is within our conscious control, although they have enlarged the area of rational action by showing how many actions, formerly thought to be wholly irrational, are in fact actuated by reasons which the agent recognizes as such when he is introduced to them by psycho-analysis. To discover what has been the real, though unconscious, motivation of certain acts and thoughts, is to be free from determinacy by that motivation; it makes possible the substitution of self-control for repression and so enlarges the territory of human freedom. Nowhere is Freudian teaching more important for ethics than in the repeated proof that it is by consciousness that we are delivered from the dominion of complexes and enabled to control and modify them in the process. Thus there is psychological evidence for the view that mental health, as well as freedom, depends on enlarging the scope of self-consciousness. The precept of the Delphic oracle now finds scientific confirmation as the fundamental recipe for a healthy life.

3. OBJECTIONS

A. *General*

Nevertheless, psycho-analytic theory cannot be accepted as it stands. The gold must be sifted from the dross. The inference which I have just drawn about the power of consciousness to free us from compulsive drives is not prominent in the literature. On the contrary, much that is said about the *libido* seems to be a revival of one of the most prominent and least acceptable tenets of Schopenhauer, his doctrine of the will and its radical severance from intellect. Chapter xix of vol. 2 (edn. cit.) reads almost like a summary of parts of Freud.

It has often been pointed out that the case-material on which psycho-analytical theory was based consisted in the main of neurotics; it does not follow that we can generalize from them to the normal. We saw that Freud's own conception of the building up of an imaginary *ego-ideal* was conditional on the agent's refusal to face himself as he is. The consequences of repression may not be the same as the consequences of a consciously accepted discipline. It is also legitimate to examine the psycho-analyst's presuppositions; for example, is it not assumed, however illicitly, that there is an obligation to pursue health of mind and a belief in the rightness of rational control? It may also be suggested that the anti-religious strain in much psycho-analytical literature is not so much the fruit of psychological enquiry as a presupposition of the enterprise, a presupposition natural and proper enough in a scientist who studies nature. And the psycho-analytic account of moral obligation is not so much an explanation of it as an attempt to explain it away—and this springs again from the presupposition that the natural, the physical, the observable, the measurable, is all that exists, and that duty and obligation, not being measurable, must be false descriptions of some natural process which even if not measurable is clinically detectable and truly describable.

My main criticisms of the psycho-analytical theory of obligation are twofold: (i) It is necessary to distinguish between compulsions, and (ii) to discover a thing's origin is not necessarily to discover what it is now. And I must add something about the way in which psycho-analysis is being superseded in some quarters by what is called 'behaviour therapy'.

B. *Compulsions differ*

In order to show which compulsions the psycho-analyst's theory can explain and which it cannot, it is necessary to take a number of examples.

(*a*) *Dislikes*. Some are well-founded, others are hysterical. For both of them reasons may be given, but the reasons for the hysteria seem like excuses; the dislike has become a mania, and it is with mania that the psycho-analyst is at home. For example, I remember being much struck in the years following on the last war by the hysterical hatred that many people in my neighbourhood had for the Poles, and all sorts of rationalizations were given: they are Roman Catholics; they are reactionaries; they worked as labourers for the Germans; they have always been unpopular with neighbouring countries; they are too popular with Scotswomen. It seemed to me that the haters did protest too much, and that the hatred was really a sign of an uneasy conscience about Poland. It was harshly treated at the Yalta agreement and it then came under the heel of a totalitarian state which some of the haters were disposed to regard as a sort of Utopia. Instead of facing these facts and saying: 'Yes, the Poles have been badly treated', this admission is suppressed and our own sense of having somehow failed the Poles is projected on to them as *their* failure or *their* moral shortcoming; and the unconscious then generates this dislike, hysterical *because* unconsciously generated, as a means of supporting the view that it is the Poles, because of their hateful qualities, who are solely to blame. Yet the Poles were no more hateful than other men.

A man in high office once said to me: 'I wonder why x and y are so bitter in their opposition to me. They seem to be actuated by personal dislike, and yet it was I who got them appointed to their present posts, and they know it.' He forgot the remark of a nineteenth-century statesman: 'I wonder why x hates me so much: I never did him any favour.' To be benefited by another creates in some people who lack humility a sense of inferiority. This sense of inferiority they find intolerable; it is suppressed, and it takes its revenge in the form of an unreasoning hatred of the benefactor, for which all sorts of specious but fictitious reasons can be given.

In these examples I have used the psycho-analyst's concepts of projection and repression. But it would be a great mistake to try to explain all dislike in this way. If one man grievously injures another there is no need to look for any further explanation of the victim's dislike of the aggressor (though the aggression may possibly have been unconsciously motivated) than his consciousness of the injury. Moreover, in the hysterical cases which I have mentioned, the dislike might be assuaged or removed if the hater became aware of the projection and repression to which I have referred. But no necromancy will remove the dislike in the other case; reasoning may help, perhaps, if it can be shown that the injury was unintentional. Thus the cases are distinguishable: on the one hand the hatred is open to argument, persuasion, reason, because it had an intelligible and fully conscious basis; on the other hand reason is useless, because the hatred has its spring in something thrust out of consciousness and so inaccessible to argument. In the one case reconciliation is possible; in the other it is not, at any rate not until full self-consciousness is restored by lifting the barrier of repression.

(b) *Fears*. To them a similar analysis applies. Contrast an hysterical fear like claustrophobia in a railway carriage with the fear which a climber may reasonably feel if he slips on a mountain side. The hysterical fear is deaf to argument. The other can be controlled and perhaps even eliminated by consciousness and the effort to save oneself. There is a vital distinction between a pathological or neurotic fear and the one which arises from consciousness of a really hazardous situation.

(c) *Thoughts*. If we follow Euclid's argument to demonstrate the theorem of Pythagoras, we are indeed compelled to find the demonstration conclusive. If we think at all we must think in that way. But this is a different kind of compulsion from that exercised by a prejudice, especially an unconscious prejudice, which compels an individual to think in a certain way, or at least to ignore some facts and over-emphasise others. It is reasonable to distinguish between the dispassionate demeanour of the thinker who, 'in a cool hour', weighs the pros and cons with as open a mind as he can command, and the tensity of expression on the face of the prejudiced witness and the feverishness of his assertions. Here, however, the psychologist has rightly drawn attention to a danger. The man who protests that he is quite unprejudiced may nevertheless be a victim of a prejudice which he has not mastered. The road to sanity lies through being aware of the danger. And it is essential to remember that if some thinking were not prejudiced, we could never know that other thinking was.

(*d*) *Actions.* Consider dipsomania, a habit of tidiness, and a conviction of duty. There is something compulsive about all of them. The dipsomaniac, in his lucid intervals, does not *want* to drink; indeed he often wants not to. But the mania comes on and grips him and he cannot help himself; he is carried away irresistibly, as if by an avalanche. The tidy person cannot bear untidiness; he *must* clear up the mess on his desk before he can start work; he has to straighten the pictures before he can sit at ease by the fire. The moral man who hears the call of duty *must* obey. If you have felt the call of duty, ask yourself if this is the same kind of compulsion as that of any reputable habit that you may possess, and wonder if even the latter is comparable with the plight of the dipsomaniac. The plight is bad; the habit is good, because tidiness is an aid to the efficient doing of our proper job. Untidiness is not only aesthetically offensive but a waste of time. Both the plight and the habit, however, may have their source in the unconscious. Psycho-analysis might reveal the origin and the reason for both though the reason for the origin may not be the reason why the habit is maintained. Both may have started because of some emotional conflict and be solutions of that conflict. But an unconscious solution of a conflict may be either healthy like tidiness, or diseased like dipsomania. The danger of psycho-analysis is that it may create a neurosis if a man with a healthy habit goes to be psycho-analysed out of it. To destroy a valuable habit like tidiness by exploring its psychological origin may only rid the patient of a valuable means of organizing his life and so leave his mind swept and garnished and ready for occupation by devils instead. The unconscious can work for health as well as for disease, and we may be well advised to leave our minds alone and avoid psychiatrists until we are conscious of having become neurotics, or until our friends begin to recommend our certification.

We may admit that the bad temper which we ascribe to others is sometimes simply our own bad temper projected on to them—sometimes, but not always. Some people *are* bad tempered and are known to be so. So too we must admit that sometimes what is described by the agent as the call of duty is nothing of the kind but only some unconscious or neurotic compulsion of his own. For example, there are certain women who are greatly devoted to what they call public work; they say that it is their duty to serve others; but as they rush feverishly from committee to committee, punc-

tiliously attending every meeting and speaking every time, often
to the neglect of their unfortunate husbands, they display a lack of
sense of proportion; or, as we sometimes say, they take themselves
too seriously. There is a feverishness about their activities which is
a sure sign that the real drive behind them is their own self-
importance, their impulse to self-display, their failure humbly to
acknowledge the paramount claims of their own household.
Mrs Jellyby in *Bleak House* will serve as an example. On the other
hand, there are plenty of other devoted women whose service is
the spontaneous outflow of a humble and sympathetic character,
and whose sense of humour is not stifled by unconscious urges
productive of self-importance.

A man tells the truth in an awkward situation when prevarication
would make things easier for him. Why? Because he thinks it is his
duty. 'No,' says the psycho-analyst who wants to explain duty
away, 'that is only a rationalization. He tells it because he has
introjected a rule about truth telling which is socially useful and to
which the *super-ego* has given a sanctity that it does not itself
possess: or he tells it for self-display or self-immolation to satisfy
a sadistic impulse; or to satisfy claims of his *ego-ideal*.' Now it is
true that we obey convention before questioning it, but we can
question it. Moreover, our motives are often mixed; a man may
flatter himself that he is doing his duty for duty's sake, when if he
were more candid with himself he might discover some self-
interested motive there too. He may go further and say that he is a
miserable sinner and an unprofitable servant because the psychologist has analysed him aright and that he is not doing his duty but
only pursuing his interest or the interest of society: but he may
nevertheless think that he ought to liberate himself from unworthy
motives and do his duty, to tell the truth, no matter how awkward,
because that is what is morally required of him. He may on reflection hold that there is an ideal standard of conduct and way of life
with which he ought to conform, and this reflection may be
supported by reasons as good as the reasons he can allege for any
act or line of conduct or thought in his life. In such circumstances
reflection is asserting itself over impulse, and saying that whatever
a man's impulses or unconscious drives may be, still he ought to
conquer them by bringing them into the daylight of consciousness.
This is to distinguish a life of impulse or an animal life from a life
of principle and reflection or a human and moral life. When the

psychologist says that health consists in giving *id* impulses an appropriate outlet, he is forgetting the satisfaction due to mind. We do often fail to be minds; we are often at the mercy of unconscious forces because our self-consciousness has not been adequately developed; we often fall below the human to the animal level. But as we reflect on ourselves and on our power of reflection, we can see that these failures, though they may impair, do not destroy our potentialities or our duty to realize them. It is only for this reason that regression to the animal level is seen to be a failure. The compulsion of duty is not feverish or neurotic; it is self-conscious and rational; to attain it demands self-scrutiny and a development of self-consciousness sufficient to free us from the domination of the unconscious forces of impulse and prejudice.

A difference similar to that which, I have been arguing, exists between compulsions is to be found in the introjection which we saw was advanced as one of the sources of the *super-ego*. Introjection was said to be the process whereby rules laid down by parents and other persons in authority became interiorized as part of the *super-ego* which then lords it over the *ego*. What is being referred to here is the process of moral education. It is true that an education which is to enable a man to actualize his potentialities fully must be an education in *self*-control and *self*-discipline. Free political institutions are workable only for people who control themselves and have learnt to be law-abiding, i.e. to recognize the law not as an external *fiat* but as their own law, worthy of obedience as such. This is why such difficulties have arisen with the grant of independence to underdeveloped peoples in Africa, and why these have so quickly lapsed into dictatorships or anarchy. To educate a child in morality is not to coerce its obedience to rules whose justification, if any, it is too young to understand, but to induce it to adopt the rules as its own. In early life this cannot be done by argument, but an appeal can be made through a discipline as affectionate as it is firm. J. C. Flügel[1] quotes an interesting example: A child once refused to take the soup that its mother was offering on a spoon and pushed the spoon away rather violently. The mother persisted. The child suddenly altered its behaviour, seized the spoon with unnecessary violence, and poured the contents down its throat. Anger directed against the mother is directed against itself. Here the child's self-compulsion

[1] *Man, Morals and Society*, London, 1945, pp 36–7, 78.

L

is an instance of the first glimmering of self-discipline, but the fact that the child is angry, as the mother is not, is evidence that it is only a *first* glimmering. Nevertheless it is difficult to see why this process should be described as the beginning of a tyranny of the *super-ego* over the *ego*; this is to hypostasize abstractions and make schizophrenia a normality. The objection to describing it as Freud did, however, lies deeper. In talking of introjection he talks as if the child's mind were there, already existing, at the age of two. But a mind is something which is in process; it grows and develops. We have to *become* minds, i.e. self-conscious and reflective beings. It is not possible to throw external precepts into a mind that does not yet exist. We do subjectify external precepts in the course of moral education, but this process is part of the creation of mind and self-consciousness.

The process of moral education, however, may be ineffective; the child may be rebellious. The consequence is that impulse will not be adequately controlled. A clash arises between internal impulse and external command, and then, if self-awareness fails, rebellion may not be overt, but some inner compulsion may produce an outward and visible sign of rebellion; the girl who dresses as a perfect fright (in Flügel's example),[1] and we have plenty of them in our universities today, does not know why she does so, but the reason turns out to be that she suspects that her parents are in the right after all; she wants her own way, she represses her own suspicion, but it haunts her in the way that she compulsively dresses. I once reconciled a young man with his parents by getting him to shave off the beard which had been unconsciously motivated in the same way. The occurrence of neurosis, which is indeed a sort of unintelligible compulsion, describable if you like as the tyranny of the *super-ego*, ought not to be confused with the process of moral education. To use the same conception to explain both is to neglect the vital difference between the two. It is when self-knowledge fails, or when we hide the truth from ourselves, that moral education fails and neurosis supervenes.

Consequently, however successful the psycho-analytic theory may be with neurotic compulsions, it cannot properly be used as a weapon against a compulsion which is accepted deliberately, like a duty. A conscious resolve is a lock which the claustrophobia key

---

[1] *Op. cit.*, p 79.

will not fit. My emphasis on the difference created by consciousness is really derived from an acceptance of Freud's fundamental
insights.

C. *The argument from origins*

To discover how a thing originates is not necessarily to discern
what it is now. Even if moral conduct originated as a result of the
operation of unconscious mechanisms (and this is difficult to deny
since the process of training begins before the infant can speak for
itself), it would not follow that we continue to observe the compulsions and prohibitions because of some unconscious force. As I
have had occasion to point out before, we must not confuse the
beginning of a process with its end, or suppose that we can explain
the climax of a development by reference to its first term. The
development of mind is not simply the gradual assimilation of the
contents of an encyclopaedia. There is no development until there
is discrimination and the rejection of error. A boy may say 'thank
you', because his nurse always told him to. But he may later
continue doing it because he thinks his nurse was right. If we
accept the *id*, *ego*, and *super-ego* analysis, there is no consciousness
of *unity* of the self. Yet ability to be conscious of this unity is an
essential presupposition of psycho-analytic method. When the
repressed complex is discovered by analysis, the cure of the
patient depends on his recognizing the complex, the system of
repressions, as *his*. Cure depends on enlarging self-consciousness,
and so on consciousness of the self as a unity. Moral neurotics may
be dominated by repressed complexes or by *super-ego* compulsions;
they are indeed torn against themselves. But moral health is
different. Here the individual is practising self-control in virtue of
self-conscious and reflective thought.[1] He is consciously affirming
and accepting certain moral principles on rational grounds after
reflection. Where and how he acquired them is irrelevant. The
mechanism of inhibition is one thing; self-conscious control is
another. Awareness, and the possibility of control which depends
on awareness, is a different thing from the results of repression.
Contrast the feverish life of ritual purifications and observances
dominating every hour of a man's life, with the reflective con-

[1] This is what Kant saw in the passage cited in section 1 of this chapter.
The self constraint of virtue is not the constraint of one inclination by another,
but constraint by thought, i.e. by consciousness of duty.

sciousness of the man who devotes himself to ends for whose
validity he will argue and who finds his duty in being a certain kind
of person and acting accordingly. The one is dominated by
externals, in which the unconscious is properly included, the
latter enjoys the freedom of self-conscious reflection and of mind's
self-assertion against 'nature'.

The fear of the Lord is said to be the beginning of wisdom, but,
as Hegel said, only the beginning. In the early stages of the moral
life we may obey commands from fear or for reasons of self-
interest, for example to avoid punishment. But later on our reasons
may be purer. What an individual has been cajoled into doing by
his parents, he may later choose to do because it is his duty. It is a
mistake to try to find in childhood the key to adult life. While it is
true to some extent that the child is father of the man, it is necessary to remember that we only become men by putting away
childish things. Even if the state began in fear, it may not be
maintained for this reason. So far as the life of mind is concerned,
consciousness makes a difference to its object in a way that
psycho-analytic theory has sometimes too little recognized. To
become conscious of our complexes is to destroy their compulsive
character and to enable us to get rid of them or at least to master
them. Consciousness of fear modifies it and brings it under control.
Reason is not something just superadded to impulse; it changes its
character, at least from impulse to temptation. Dr Waddington
tells us that 'it is by no means impossible to observe the genesis
and thus the nature of an aim'.[1] If by 'genesis' he means birth or
beginning, he provides us with a palmary instance of the genetic
fallacy. The genesis of a thing is not its nature; if it were, morality
would be impossible. The stages of development would be mere
variations on the same underlying theme, like ice, water, and
steam. The 'nature' of science would be discoverable in the antics
of a witch-doctor. The power of mind to learn from its mistakes
would be denied. But if by 'genesis' Dr Waddington means the
coming-to-be of a thing, i.e. its whole history, then his statement
may be acceptable enough.

To all this an uncautious psychologist might reply as follows:
'Yes, from the point of view of your own consciousness, compulsions may differ as you say, and the process of moral education
will appear to be different from the building-up of neuroses. But

[1] *Op. cit.*, p 51 (my italics).

it is necessary to delve below consciousness and its deliverances. Introspection will not show the extent to which we are actuated by unconscious motives or the extent to which our thinking is distorted by prejudice. It is only when we carry analysis into the unconscious that we find that the differences to which you have referred are differences for consciousness only and not differences in reality'. We may reply to this that we can recognize hysteria in others, and why therefore can we not also recognize it in ourselves? If we do recognize it, we may not be able without psychoanalysis to discover what its unconscious spring is, but we can be confident that there is one and be on our guard accordingly. But this is only a superficial and inadequate reply to the argument. The real answer is to point out that if psycho-analysis did use this argument it would cut its own throat. If all compulsions were on the same level and had the same sort of origin, then science would be impossible.[1]

5. BEHAVIOUR THERAPY

A layman is hardly justified in entering into the controversy between psycho-analysts and the sponsors of behaviour-therapy. But it would be unscholarly to ignore the existence of this controversy and to pass over in silence the evidence accumulated by behaviour therapists. Here my authority is H. J. Eysenck, whom I have mentioned already. He is a scientist and not, so far as I can ascertain, a medical man. He studies 'behaviour'; if he finds that neurotic hatred of, e.g., cats and all furry animals, originated in some traumatic experience, he does not delve into what the experience was, he proceeds to treat this condition by providing something attractive along with the animals, which are gradually brought nearer and nearer to the patient, so that the animals are gradually associated in the patient's consciousness with something pleasant instead of with the unpleasant experience of long ago. Similarly he treats neurotic cravings by making the patient sick in the presence of what he has previously craved. Analysis and theories of, e.g., Oedipus complex and the like, are quite unnecessary. An habitual like or dislike can be neutralized by experimental treatment. But Professor Eysenck emphasizes more than once that some patients react better than others. Those who are intelligent,

[1] See Chapter 4, above, on determinism.

to whom the treatment is explained and who are then willing to try the experiment, react better than those of lower intelligence or those disposed to other forms of neurosis.

This recognition of the part that intelligence and conscious control has to play is given no emphasis. All the emphasis is on bodily structure, heredity, temperament, and environment; there is no emphasis on conscious reaction to these things. Statistics may show that fat men are more prone to coronary thrombosis than thin men, and so on. But what the collection of statistics will not show is the extent to which a man's mind may react to and surmount the handicaps of his physical frame, his heredity, and his environment. Professor Eysenck regards conscience as a 'conditioned reflex', as sometimes it is, but more than once he says that everyone must *make up his own mind* on moral issues involved in certain kinds of treatment. As a scientist, he properly concentrates on nature, i.e. on the external, i.e. on behaviour. But by leaving the influence of mind out of account, except in the asides that I have mentioned, he may fail to account for, or he may even distort, the individuality which he says the psychologist must regard as sacrosanct. This is why psychological theories, like Professor Eysenck's, about learning in rats cannot be applied without grave qualification to human individuals.

What Professor Eysenck does seem to me to have shown is that there are better ways of curing some neurotics than those based on some psycho-analytic theory. But he minimizes the importance of consciousness and mind, although that importance is there as an unacknowledged asset in his behaviour-therapy. Nevertheless, I admit that as a scientist committed to the study of behaviour he could do no other than he has done. Some of his attack on Freud seems to me to be excessive and to take too little account of the fact that, although medicine uses science today to an unprecedented extent, the physician is one thing and the scientist another. The former deals with individual patients. For science, individuals cannot *as such* enter the picture.

This excursus on psychology is justified by the importance of modern psychology and by the great contribution it has in fact made to the study of conduct. What I have been doing is, as I have said, clearing away the dross, so that the gold may shine the more brightly.

5. ANTHROPOLOGY

Secondly, anthropology. Here a much shorter treatment will suffice, mainly because its prime error, when it comes to reflect on moral conduct, is the genetic fallacy which has been sufficiently exposed already. Sir J. Frazer says 'To understand civilization study savagery'. This is the reverse of the truth. Ethical beliefs, it is alleged, can have no general or universal validity because they differ from culture to culture. This appears to imply that cultures differ but that there is no way of comparing their merits, presumably because each of them fits those who live under them. This relativism presupposes, but does not prove, that ethical beliefs are not amenable to judgments of truth or falsity. It is not only the moral beliefs but the scientific beliefs of the Ibo people which differ from our own, but the anthropologist is unlikely to apply his relativism to the latter. Moreover, even if all existing beliefs were a matter of local custom, as King Darius thought, according to the story in Herodotus, it still would not follow that truth or universal validity is impossible in this field. A discovery that existing beliefs and practices are only customs, without inherent validity, might well be the prelude to a quest of moral beliefs which were rationally and not merely customarily justified.

However, the anthropologist is really assuming that ethical beliefs cannot be known to be either true or false and that they are intellectually on a level with nonsense and morally on a level with the ritual of a dinner party. This is in sharp contrast to the attitude of moral and religious missionaries in the nineteenth century. They had no doubt that cusoms which they regarded as immoral, such as suttee, should be extirpated. On the other hand a distinguished lady authority on African affairs[1] draws attention to the fact that the Tiv people in Nigeria practise human sacrifice, and, though with a little hesitation, concludes that this practice ought not to be interfered with because it is part of a 'cultural system'. But whence comes this 'ought'? Those who take a view of this kind are asserting that it is *right* to leave those cultures alone, and *wrong* to proselytize. But this is an appeal to a standard of a kind, an appeal inconsistent with the moral relativism which is being upheld. To say that human sacrifice suits some peoples and not others is to run away from a problem. Why does it not suit us?

[1] Miss Perham: *Native Administration in Nigeria*, London, 1937, pp 152–9, 280.

Because, it may be said, it is at odds with our way of life. But in that case why is our way of life regarded as sacrosanct? Having discovered that our way of life is only one way of living, why do we not alter it for the better? If we say that to adopt human sacrifice would be altering it for the worse, then we are away from relativism and back to a moral standard. If we accept 'moral relativity', then differing moral ideals in different civilizations are just different facts, and there is no reason for preferring one to another. A choice, like that sometimes made by Europeans who go native in India or Arabia, for example, would on this view be due simply to emotionalism. Such a view suits dictators who know how to work on the emotions, but it does not explain why some people will go into concentration camps rather than fall in with a way of life which they think wrong. To say that they too do not think, but merely rationalize their feelings, is to make all thought emotionalism and so to destroy the theory at the very moment of its expression. What is sauce for the goose is sauce for the gander. If moral relativism is to be maintained, a scientific relativism must be maintained also, and this makes science impossible. Moral relativism is not a discovery by a science of anthropology: it is a presupposition with which some anthropologists begin and which therefore determines their conclusions. Professor R. M. Hare is not an anthropologist, but he seems to me to share what I regard as their error when he says that a moral system is a way of life and that we must just decide which system or way of life we are to adopt. The method by which our decision is to be reached is obscure, but apparently we decide by caprice or by a Kierkegaardian 'leap in the dark'. This is irrationalism, and it is not saved by Professor Hare's assertion that such a decision, far from being arbitrary, would be based on a consideration of everything on which it could possibly be founded.[1]

6. MARXISM

Thirdly, Marxism has joined in the attack on the absoluteness of moral obligation. Moral goodness cannot be seen through a microscope and so it must somehow be fictitious, perhaps a false description of something material or observable. In fact, an ethical system is an expression of class forces, brought into being by

[1] *The Language of Morals*, Oxford, 1952, p 69.

external social conditions which can and should be studied on the assumption that they are mechanisms. Now the Marxist is doubtless right to draw attention to the importance of external conditions (though he has a forerunner in Aristotle, for example), and to the way in which they do influence the shaping of moral ideals. But is he right to treat these conditions as mechanisms? The Marxist sees the influence which they exercise on us but may attend too little to our reaction to their influence. We may reject it and proceed to try to change the social order. In any event, social conditions have not existed from all eternity as they are now. They are what they are because of previous attempts to realize moral ideals of different kinds and they have often been modified in the interests of moral improvement. I have instanced slavery laws already. In his Theses on Feuerbach, Marx wrote: 'Philosophy has hitherto confined itself to interpreting the world; but the point is to change it.' If so, then philosophy, reflective thought, presumably will have some influence on social change and it must have some standard by reference to which the change is to be made. The content of a moral code might depend on conditions in the external world; but unless the notion of obligation itself is a reality (for example an obligation to make changes), the new world will never come. And this is admitted by Marxists who talk of the new 'virtues' which a new sort of society, the class-less society, will produce. The reference to 'virtues' and the whole programme imply that the new society and its virtues are worth pursuit. Why? On Marxist principles, or on any materialistic principles, there does not seem to be any answer. If conduct is a product, mechanically produced, of social conditions, it cannot be right or wrong, and there cannot be any motive for endeavouring to make social changes. If thinking is determined by social position or class, or if 'ideology' is only a rationalization of a man's social position, then all science, Marxist included, must cease to claim truth or to be worth pursuit. Why pursue what social conditions determine or will determine anyway? A materialistic system cannot give rise either to moral ideals or to truth as its product.

Some other Marxist propositions about morals seem to deserve a reply, especially since they are advanced by a distinguished Fellow of the Royal Society, Professor J. D. Bernal.[1] 'Moral conflict simply mirrors class conflict and will therefore disappear

[1] Summarized in *Science and Ethics*, pp 114 ff.

in the class-less society.' The moral conflict envisaged here is that
between different moral systems, not the conflict between inclinations or between inclination and duty of which an individual may
be conscious. For example, Jesus was poor and the Pharisees rich;
the legalism of the latter is supposed to represent their wealth and
Jesus' insistence on the spirit represents his poverty. The word
'represent' here is a metaphor, and there is no argument available
to prove this curious proposition. Those who talk of the class-war
are usually those who are anxious for their own reasons to produce
it, but in any event people of every kind of moral conviction are to
be found in all classes, in this country at any rate. As for inner
conflict, it is to disappear with class-less society too, because man is
naturally good and with the disappearance of class barriers all will
be well. Enough has been said already to indicate that it is only by
the negation of nature that the moral life is reached, and the notion
that goodness is natural can hardly survive a study of nature itself.
It is true that some things normally regarded as good, such as
prudence and abstinence, are regarded as things to be eliminated
in favour of socially induced motives. This presumably is an
endeavour to make men as near automata as possible, not controlling themselves, not being self-critical, but so indoctrinated
with Marxism from the cradle as to be clay in the dictator's hands.
Obsession with a class-less society in which there shall be no
conflict is to be satisfied only in a cemetery. Men cannot live
except by toil—they must wrest a living from nature; conflict
between persons is inevitable because some become lazy and
others industrious; conflict is inevitable unless thought is applied
to harmonizing human life through self-control and so through
compromise. Finally, we are to face the future instead of the past
—abandon traditional codes. This is a dream. Men have imagination, and this, together with choice, puts them in a position to bring
into existence what does not yet exist. But they also have memory;
their past is incorporated in the present, and so long as memory
exists, the present cannot be abolished. *Expelles furca tamen usque
recurret.* This is the history of revolutions.

7. LOGICAL POSITIVISM AND LINGUISTICS

Fourthly, logical positivism is now out of fashion, and it would be
a pity to waste time by flogging a dead horse, but some more

recent developments in what is still called moral philosophy in Oxford are hardly conceivable except as a *reductio ad absurdum* of positivism or an attempt to supply some sort of new content for a subject that positivism would seem to have destroyed. It is therefore necessary to say something about this whole movement and especially its presuppositions, for it is these that have really determined its conclusions. A stream will not rise higher than its source, and if a beginning is made by supposing that religion is a delusion or even a vice, and that an absolute moral obligation is a fiction, then the conclusion will not rise higher than some form of utilitarianism at best, or some form of scepticism.

In the last thirty years the most influential works on moral philosophy in these islands show that the study of the subject has gone through three main stages:

(i) Logical positivism, reviving Hume, asserted that if no observation could be relevant to determining a statement's truth or falsehood, then the statement was meaningless, where 'meaningless' signifies 'neither true nor false'. In this sense the poem about the Jabberwock, and all nonsense, is meaningless, and the same is true of exclamations. If a man says that it is his duty to help others, no observation can support either the truth or falsity of the statement, and therefore the statement is either just an exclamation: 'Helping others? Loud cheers!', or else a statement about a man's feelings of approval: 'I approve of helping others', and this is a statement of fact and so verifiable, at least in principle. This attempt by logical positivists to explain morality away is sufficiently rejected by the reflection that no observation is relevant to determining the truth or falsity of the verifiability principle itself, and therefore the principle by its very enunciation puts itself out of court. Now it is not difficult to see that the principle is advanced by those who believe in the omnicompetence of physical science and its methods; and it may be a good enough principle for scientific enquiries into nature. But while man makes natural science he does not make the scientist. Scientific method necessarily studies its object from without. But moral experience is something only to be understood from within. In trying to universalize an heuristic principle the scientist has forgotten himself and failed to see that he must be exempt from its operation. He ought to have remembered Leibniz's *nisi intellectus ipse*. He is like the advocates of the class-less society. They visualize themselves as its rulers and so in a class by themselves.

(ii) The second stage soon supervened on the first. Stevenson soon followed Ayer. If I say that I have a duty to help others, what I mean is that my attitude to helping others is a feeling of approval, and I invite you to share my attitude. And this invitation is conveyed in my use of the words like 'right' and 'duty' which are tinged with emotion and which help to prejudice others in my favour. Apparently, therefore an emotional attitude of approval, together with exhortation, is expressed in the conceptual language of moral obligation. How does this happen? It is rather like trying to show that altruism is at bottom a form of selfishness. Language is not an arbitrary symbolism but an expression of thought. To evaporate the notion of duty into the mist of approval and exhortation is to fail to explain how the notion of duty ever arose.

(iii) The transition to the third and latest stage is then simple. The ordinary usages of the English language must not be explained away: but they can be analysed and interpreted and cured of the ambiguities and inaccuracies which have been responsible for many of the puzzles which philosophers have tried to solve. Hence we must clear away a lot of rubbish before being able to discern what the genuine problems of philosophy are, and this we do by forsaking philosophy, *pro tem.*, for grammatical, philological, and lexicographical studies. Austin follows Stevenson. This quest is still continuing, but we have not yet been told what the philosophical problems will be (though there are said to be plenty of them) after we have settled 'if's' business and properly based 'can' and the like.[1]

All this is what comes of believing in the omnicompetence of science to give an account of nature and holding that man is part of nature and so, throughout his experiences, amenable to just the same methods of inquiry as those adapted to the study of the natural world. Once this belief is accepted great ingenuity must be used to explain away, or reduce to natural terms, all the higher reaches of man's endeavour, and we may well admit that great ingenuity has not been lacking. But no doubt similar ingenuity went to the weaving of Ocnus or to Piazzi Smyth's lucubrations on the Great Pyramid.

To attempt to deal in detail with all these theories would be

[1] The reference is to J. L. Austin's British Academy Lecture on *Ifs and Cans*.

tedious, and indeed beyond my competence because I cannot profess to have read all the endless permutations and combinations of these theories in the innumerable articles with which philosophical periodicals (in English) have been filled for so many years past. I emphasize the words 'in English' because the linguistic theories appear to be based on English alone as if it held the clue to the moral ideas of western civilization. A few general remarks, however, may be appropriate if only to illustrate by contrast the main thesis of these lectures.

If a moral judgment is only a statement of what I feel or an exclamatory expression of my feeling, then arguments about right and wrong are futile. This was readily admitted by Professor A. J. Ayer in his influential *Language, Truth and Logic*.[1] If they are futile, why do they continue? Professor Ayer would reply, I suppose, that this is because those who do argue are accepting in common a presupposition which is false, and a similar reason would be given, even by philosophers of a very different school from his, for calling many of the arguments of the medieval schoolmen futile, and these arguments are no longer pursued. Once the general public has accepted Professor Ayer's reduction of moral judgment to emotion and its expression, moral argument will cease. A good many other things, however, would cease at the same time. Freedom is one, because if emotionalism is at the root of conduct and moral distinctions are to be reduced to some sort of emotional background, it will be necessary to impose some control on a riot of emotionalism. No prospect would be more congenial to dictators; or indeed to advertisers who want us to feel approval and then to make a demand.

If I am told that the assertion 'freedom is a good' means no more than 'freedom, hurrah!' I wonder what sort of a world my interlocutor lives in. Minorities during the last few centuries have been ready to sacrifice their lives for freedom to worship God in their own way, for freedom from slavery, for freedom of speech. If all this is to be put down to mere emotional enthusiasm, then it is absurd to say that a state in which minorities are tolerated is any better than a slave state. Some libertarian movements may indeed be put down to agitators and mass hysteria, but not all of them. Here the conscious reflective conduct of the adult is being put on the same level as that of a baby crying for its rattle.

[1] P 112.

An analysis of moral judgment as feeling of approval plus an invitation to share my attitude is equally unacceptable. If I feel approval of a lady's toilette, what do I care whether anyone else approves or not? If I call it beautiful, I am still indifferent if someone disagrees with me. It is true that I am expecting other sensible men to agree with my judgment, but I am making a judgment and not merely expressing a preference. The same is true if I judge that Brahms' first symphony is better than his second. I am not just saying that it moves me more and that I hope you agree with me; I am making a judgment which I am prepared to defend, even if this defence be less logically rigorous than a reasoned defence of duty against philosophers who seek to explain it away.

On the view which we are considering, ethical disagreements are said to have their basis in a difference in 'attitude'. We refer to 'attitude' when we speak of matters on which we have not reflected, for example: 'I have not considered the merits and demerits of the nationalization of cement, but my attitude is at present against it.' And in this sense it is indeed purposeless to argue in favour of my attitude or against someone else's. But attitudes differ. My attitude to the nationalization of cement is different from my attitude to sugarless tea. For the former I may, if I study the subject and reflect on it, be able to find reasons; but the latter is, as we say, a matter of taste, and there can be no argument about it. Writers on ethics who specialize in 'attitudes' seem to regard our attitude to moral questions as all on a par with the sort of attitude, like Mr Robinson's, which prefers poker to bridge.[1] Moreover, attitudes are not unalterable; a favourable attitude to burgundy instead of claret can be altered by education; other attitudes with a basis, or potential basis, in reasoning can be altered if we reflect and discover either their rational basis or the fact that they are baseless and so can be changed. An uncriticized attitude may act like a prejudice as a determinant of thought, but the view which we are criticizing goes further than this. It appears to imply that we feel approval of toleration and then value it or take up a favourable attitude to it. The feeling is the ultimate determinant of the explicit valuation. Kant took precisely the opposite view when he argued that morality's value for us does not result from our interest in it; on the contrary, we become aware of its sublimity

[1] *Op. cit.*, p 43.

and then our subjective feeling follows.[1] It may be suggested, however, that when an experience has two sides, one subjective and one objective, it is a mistake to regard one as the cause of the other, even if one is logically prior to the other.

The linguistic philosophers were not wrong in finding unsatisfactory this combination of feeling and attitude and exhortation as an analysis of moral judgments, but instead of striking at the root of the theory on the ground that it is in essence naturalistic, explaining man's mental and spiritual life by man's natural origins, and so guilty of the genetic fallacy, they preferred to shelve moral questions altogether, for the present at any rate, and take refuge in considering the ways in which ordinary people talk in English about moral questions, i.e. in an analysis of common sense or of ordinary (i.e. non-technical) language. It is a mistake at this juncture, as they tell us, to ask what duty is; we must ask instead how the word is used. We must admit that this programme is compatible, as those other moral theories were not, with a belief in the absoluteness of the categorical obligation of duty, though it does nothing to explain what this obligation is or to justify a belief in it. In fact, to propose to study ordinary language is to enter what for philosophy is a blind alley.[2]

Ordinary language and common sense are an object of philosophic criticism and not its guiding stars. The reason for this is simple enough: common sense and the ordinary English in which it is expressed are a repository of former philosophies. A philosophy takes time to become part and parcel of the thinking of the man in the street: but it gets there eventually. Consequently it is not surprising if, when we begin to scrutinize the way that 'duty' is used in English, we discover that πολλαχῶς λέγεται. Ways of thinking change; they have to find expression in language, and the great writer moulds language to his purposes, thereby conferring on words new meanings and new nuances of meaning. To hope for results from analysing ordinary language is to treat language as if it were a corpse for dissection and not something which lives and changes because it is the expression of an ever-changing thought, or, I fear, of an ever-changing thoughtlessness. The word 'due' is now commonly used in a way which was described, rightly, as

[1] *Grundlegung*, Part III.
[2] With linguistic philosophy I have dealt at greater length in an article in *Philosophy*, October 1961.

'illiterate' by Fowler some forty years ago. Some of us are interested in the way in which 'duty' is used only in order to discover
whether the true conception of duty is being adequately expressed
or often enough, having regard to the history of the word, is not.
For a philosopher the interesting question is: what is duty? And
this is the important question for the layman too, because unless he
has some sort of answer to give he will be unable to answer the
further question: what is my duty here and now?

This last remark involves an implication on which I touched
in Chapter 5 and which the philosophers whom we have been
noticing would with one voice reject. It implies that the answer to a
philosophical question may help men to live better. Most philosophers hold up their hands in horror at the suggestion that philosophy might be useful: is it not a purely disinterested quest for
truth? It is not a philosopher's business to preach or to tell people
what to do. This last point may be granted. But if we do not study
logic in order to avoid logical errors or false inferences, and so to
think better, more clearly, more consistently, more effectively, does
the study not become indistinguishable from an amusement or a
game? It is not altogether insignificant that we have heard a good
deal in recent years about language games, or found our philosophers writing for one another instead of addressing the educated
public as so many of their great predecessors did. If we do not
study moral philosophy in the hope of thereby becoming better
men, and by teaching and writing assisting others to the same end,
we are simply in the position of a pure mathematician inventing
theorems and finding more and more ingenious, more and more
elegant proofs of them. We are retreating into an ivory tower and
professing to study human conduct without any hope or intention
of influencing it in any way. No wonder that those who take this
line confine themselves to the meaning and use of words and, as
philosophers, take no interest in the cave whence they have escaped
into the rarefied atmosphere of pure ingenuity.

If moral philosophy is to be valueless as a guide to practice,
where is any guide to be found? It has been asserted and it has
been as vigorously denied that the predominant sort of teaching of
moral philosophy in Oxford in the last thirty years has sent out to
influential positions a steady stream of men who have been made
into moral sceptics, with no ideals or principles of conduct to live
by, because these have all been pounded to smithereens in the

pestle of logical positivism, linguistic analysis, and so forth. They
have also been taught that religious faith is a vice[1] so that another
possible prop of conduct has been swept from under them. In these
circumstances the increase in undergraduate suicides, the need for
appointing psychiatric advisers for university students, and the
complaint of so many young people that they have nothing to live
for, are not altogether surprising. Destroy moral principle by
reducing it to the emotional level, and you create a generation with
no power to resist advertisers and dictators. One can only hope
that before Oxford moral philosophy reaches the common mass, it
will have been laughed off the stage. To try to refute it is useless;
all that can be done is to challenge its presuppositions and teach
better presuppositions in their place. It is some sort of positive
doctrine that is required as a moral guide, and this is what I am
trying to purvey.

8. BIOLOGY

There is, however, one alternative doctrine which has been propounded from some of the very quarters which I have been
criticizing, and some notice must be taken of it before a return can
be made to the main theme. At the beginning of this chapter I said
that there was a quintuple attack on the general trend of my
argument. I have dealt with four heads of this Hydra; I now come
to the fifth and last, well knowing that the heads will grow again
in one form or another, for I am no Heracles, but being fairly well
convinced that in any form they will be heads of the same serpent
which tempts man to forget his spiritual destiny, to revert to the
animalism from which he has risen, to ignore the imperative call of
duty and to guide his conduct by primeval urges instead.

The fifth and last attack I attributed to biologists. I am not sure
how much acceptance this theory has gained, but it has various
members of the Huxley family as its sponsors, and a recent defen-
der in Dr C. H. Waddington. It therefore deserves mention, but
the mention is brief because the objections to it are all too obvious.
This theory is at least a positive doctrine. It does indeed profess to
give some sort of guidance to those in perplexity. It does tell us, at
least in general terms, what we ought to do. It also provides the
anthropologist with a criterion by which different moral systems

[1] R. Robinson, *op. cit.*, p 221.

can be judged. The theory is simple: the purpose of morals is to
assist the course of biological evolution; moral codes do this more
or less effectively, and the code we should choose is the most
effective one; our duty is to abide by that code and so assist the
course of biological evolution as best we can.

It would be wrong to minimize the importance of evidence
which a biologist might allege to show how various species have
been enabled to survive by adaptation to their environment (or, as
I would prefer to say, by adapting their environment to themselves), or, I suppose, how some species have failed so to adapt
themselves and have perished and so ceased to hinder the evolutionary process. But as a moral theory this appeal to evolution is
very difficult to defend.

(i) In the first place, *why* are we to co-operate with evolutionary
development? The theory seems to suggest that we have some
choice in the matter. Dr Waddington tells us that his science can
show the sort of action which aids evolution and the sort that does
not, and we must believe him if he will modify his statement and
make it refer to the past. But even if science could foresee what
conduct is in the future to aid the evolutionary process, why should
we adopt this line of conduct? If the answer is that unless we do,
the human species will die out like the ichthyosaurus, the moralist
will still ask: why should we not let the species die? Individuals
have sacrificed themselves before now for a moral principle, and
have been praised and even beatified for so doing. It may be
argued that man as mind has intrinsic value because he is a moral
agent and a thinker. But in that event it is his moral convictions
that matter and it is his duty to follow them, regardless of what
happens to his biological species. If it is said that we have an
obligation to co-operate with evolutionary ends and not let the
species die, then some proof must be offered that this is an
obligation. Facts about what has contributed to evolution in the
past will not provide such a proof. On the other hand, if to escape
this the biologist says that we cannot help co-operating with
biological ends, and this may be plausible, the theory is irrelevant
to morality. We might as well talk about co-operating with a flood
and enough has been said already about a deterministic theory of
this kind.

(ii) Secondly, what are these evolutionary ends with which we
are to co-operate? Evolution has produced an interesting galaxy

of characters: the liver-fluke, beloved of those who deny the
operation of a benevolent Creator, the saint and the sinner, Hitler
and Albert Schweitzer, imbeciles, congenital idiots, and Dr
Waddington himself. He has the grace to admit that the end of
evolution is not yet known. But he thinks that science may discover it. Perhaps we had better wait on the discovery before giving
up our present moral convictions. But even after the discovery is
made, we shall still have to ask if the end of evolution is worth our
moral endeavour.

(iii) Even if the end were known and were found acceptable,
how can we decide what will help it? Perhaps science will tell us.
But even if it did, I would have to ask: Would humility help
evolutionary ends? I am sure that Nietzsche would have said, or
hoped, not. I do not know what the answer of others would be, but
is it relevant? I regard it as a great virtue, no matter what its
positive or negative contribution to evolution may be; and I think
I could produce reasons for my view, although they would depend
on believing that man as mind is far higher in the scale of importance, and of morality, than man as a member of a biological
species.

(iv) So far as I can see, there is only one way of making co-operation with evolutionary ends into a moral principle, namely by
assuming that these ends coincide with the design of the God and
Father of our Lord Jesus Christ. But this is an assumption unlikely
to commend itself to Dr Waddington and his fellow theorists of
evolutionary morals.

9. SUMMARY

The attacks on what I regard as the higher levels of moral experience, which have been considered here, are essentially
naturalistic. Right and wrong, good and evil, are supposed either
to be distinctions with a biological basis, e.g. what helps or hinders
the life of the *species*, or else to depend ultimately on feeling and
impulse and so to be based at last on the biological needs of the
individual. In addition to all the difficulties urged against this view
already, there is one other of some importance. If we ask a friend
why he did a certain action, the answer may be: 'Because I wanted
to', or again, 'Because I thought it right'. The second reply
implies that moral concepts like good, right, duty, all provide

reasons for acting. If we ask someone why he bought a certain book instead of borrowing it from the library, he may reply: 'Because it is Wednesday.' We assume that he is not joking and that therefore either the library was closed on Wednesday or else he made a habit of buying a book on that day. Similarly, in a society of English speakers, educated in the mores of English speaking people, the assertion: 'I did it because it was right' is intelligible only because in that society it is regarded as reasonable to act rightly and because the rightness of an act provides a reason, and a good reason, for doing it. In the same society, the fact that I wanted to do a certain action is *not* in itself a reason, or at any rate a good reason, for doing it. There are certain levels of experience, as we have seen, where mere wanting to do something is a sufficient reason for doing it. But the moral consciousness is aware of a clash between wanting to do something and having a duty to do something else, and in such a case the fact that a duty is present is a sufficient reason why we *ought*, at least, to prefer the duty to the want. Hence it does violence to common moral experience to reduce duty to wants, whether biological or other, or moral experience itself to feeling instead of seeing it as intrinsic to reflective thought. The naturalistic theories are not so much explanations of our moral experience as attempts to induce us to regard it as illusory; the moral experience of free men acting on reflective choice is being distorted into the experience of infants and of slaves acting on the impulses or passions or enthusiasms by which they are subdued and by which their moral life may be strangled at its birth.

The upshot of all this argument is that the naturalism of the theories considered conjures moral problems away instead of trying to answer them. It is essentially based on what I have repeatedly called the genetic fallacy of supposing that because man begins as a member of the kingdom of nature he ends there, and that his membership of this kingdom is all the truth there can be in an alleged kingdom of ends. The power and might of thought is denied, and man is made the creature of an emotion which really dominates him and on which his thinking is a mere epiphenomenon.

The essential defect of all these scientific theories is that they ignore human self-consciousness and reflective thinking. Knowledge of the stars does not affect the stars. But a study of human action does affect human action. The stars must just be observed from without, and the same is true of the rudiments of our mental life, the unconscious, the pre-conscious, and the like. But as our mind develops we become reflectively conscious of our conduct, and our knowledge of it puts us in a position to change it. Scientific method may serve to study conduct which is below the rational level, whether the conduct of neurotics or of crowds, but it is not adapted to a self-conscious subject matter. As I have said before, the scientist always leaves himself out; man does not make nature but he does make physical science. Finally, so far from being natural, so far from finding its obligations in co-operation with nature, morality is just as much a fight against nature as horticulture is a fight against weeds. In both these instances nature is not superseded, it is not destroyed in battle, but it is forced to do the will of the horticulturist or the good man.

Although, therefore, all these scientific theories of morality must be rejected in so far as they explain self-conscious and reasoned moral convictions in terms other than themselves, and especially in terms of experience at the natural level, nevertheless it must be admitted that they have a certain strength. They do call attention to the beginning of the moral life, and so to a factor which that life can never completely eliminate or transcend. This is a salutary warning against an intransigent rationalism or against any doctrine which forgets that men have feet of clay and that the perfection of a purely spiritual life is not to be had in this world.

CHAPTER 10

RETROSPECTIVE SUMMARY

At this point it may be well to take stock of the position now reached.

The process whereby we rise above the natural level on which our life begins, to choice, is one of self-transcendence, the gradual realization of an original potentiality. It is one through which reflection (the power of the negative) becomes explicit. The spur to every advance is negation, the rejection of what is, in order to bring into being what might be. With choice we arrive at the distinction between good and evil and so at moral experience. Good is the correlative of choice; evil is what we reject. It is the growth of mind from mere consciousness to self-consciousness and reflection that introduces us to moral experience.

The higher self which it is our duty to actualize so far as possible is inseparably bound up with reflection and self-consciousness. I would say with 'intelligence', if that did not call up an association with psychological tests. I prefer to speak of 'reason' although that may suggest the power of abstract argument which is the prerogative of the few. What I am arguing is that morality is bound up with the reflective thinking of which all men are capable unless they are congenital idiots or men who have had the misfortune, as we say, to have 'lost their reason'. The mental defective or the lunatic is one in whom the development of the higher self has been impossible or has atrophied, and because in these instances understanding and reflective thinking are limited, moral responsibility is diminished. This is what justifies me in speaking of the moral life as a rational life or as the life of reason.

Morality cannot arise until there is a mental development sufficient for speech and language, and for choice between truth and falsehood, or between choice and determination by impulse. Thus morality, like art, religion, and science, is at least an intellectual activity, but it is an activity in which man cannot help engaging if he is to realize his spiritual potentialities and lead the supra-natural life appropriate to a human being. Thus the aim of morality and its purpose, if to speak of purpose in this context be appropriate at all, is its own furtherance. Acting morally is not a means to living on the plane above nature; it is living on that plane.

This is denied. For example: (i) Mr R. Robinson says that the reason for morality is the alleviation of suffering.[1] In that event it is members of the medical profession who are moral, and the layman has a poor chance of a good life. (ii) Professor J. Kemp, who does discuss moral questions and not merely the meanings of words in his valuable study of *Reason, Action and Morality*[2] nevertheless tells us that the main function of moral rules and morality in general is to enable us to get on with our neighbours. I reply that law and convention may have this function, but not morality in general unless that is reduced to rule alone. (iii) Professor E. J. Furlong, in *Philosophy*,[3] thinks that we ought to obey the dictates of society because morality exists as a means to promote the end of society, the end being to further the welfare of the society's members. That, he thinks, is what morality is for. This is open to most of the objections urged above against utilitarianism.

What these philosophers seem to have in common is a view of morality as a shackle, something irksome, to be accepted only because some good cannot be had without it. But it is not a shackle; it is a liberation from nature to the life of spirit.

The different levels of experience on which choice is exercised and action is developed are all of them levels at which good is realized; pleasure, utility, rightness, are all goods. But they differ from one another in degree and therefore in kind as well. The degree of goodness in each of these experiences corresponds to the extent to which the ideal of the moral life is exemplified in each. From pleasure to duty *via* utility and rightness is an advance in mind, in rationality, in moral experience. The advance takes place because on the conscious experience of each stage reflection supervenes; and an advance is made to a higher stage by rejecting the one so far reached. Rejection is necessary because reflection discovers that what has so far been achieved is inadequate to the ideal. The driving force of the whole process is the end which was implicit at the beginning and which becomes more and more explicit at each succeeding stage. The Greeks held a view of this kind, but they placed the end outside and above man, Plato in the

[1] *Op. cit.*, p 137   [2] London, 1964   [3] 1966, p 276.

Form of Good, Aristotle in God as the unmoved mover of the stars. This led to an intellectualism which placed knowledge first, with the result that no proper place was left for action. Once Plato's cave-men had left the cave and discovered the Form of Good, they had no desire to do anything except continue to contemplate it. These chapters on the other hand have upheld the primacy of action; and the end is man's being as moral and spiritual. It is man's potentiality for the good life, and not just his origin as a natural life, that is gradually actualized through the processes that have been described. Even if the moral ideal is located outside us as well as within, we are still only moved by it because of its presence, potentially at least, within us. Even if to speak of 'being moved by' is a metaphor and sounds mechanical, it is not altogether misleading as metaphor. The magnet will not move glass but only iron filings or something else amenable by its constitution to movement by magnetic force.

It must not be forgotten that morality is exhibited in some degree in any choice. Play as a realm of capricious choice is the minimum realization of the moral life; economic life and political life are higher realizations. None of these is *per se* immoral; immorality at each level consists either in self-contradiction, i.e. in not living that level in accordance with its standards or rules but by some lower standard or by no rule, or else in adhering to that level when higher ground ought to be taken, e.g. by fiddling when Rome is burning. Furthermore every level has a necessary place in human experience. Those who cannot take higher ground than utility are in danger of lapsing into materialism; they are more conscious of man's natural origin than of his spiritual destiny. Those on the other hand who find morality only in duty and who lash out against the immorality of commerce or the lack of principles in politics are those who are so conscious of the spiritual life that they forget that the world they live in hovers between Heaven and Hell, and that although man is capable of controlling nature by self-transcendence, he cannot get rid of nature, so that the process of self-transcendence can in this world never be complete. As the Greeks put it, man's hard task in this world is ἕνα γένεσθαι ἐκ πολλῶν, in other words to unify himself, and so far as the moral life is concerned he does this by recognizing that in his diverse activities good of some kind is actualized, and that these diversities become linked together in an intelligible whole in so far as he realizes that it is one and the same good that glimmers, with different degrees of brightness in them, and gives them all, in the last resort, the light whereby they live. It is in this light alone that man can unify his diverse activities.

It may be asked: if good is correlative to choice, what is the moral ideal, what is goodness? A similar problem arises with truth, because truth is correlative to thought. Just as there are degrees of goodness, some goods being better than others, so there are degrees of truth corresponding to the different levels of thinking (sensation, perception, picture-thinking, ratiocination *et al.*, for which see, for example, Hegel's *Phenomenology*). It has been argued above that a tension between achievement and potentiality is the spur to action and the source of obligation; and this is true of thinking as well. The spirit of truth and goodness is present, however obscurely, within the finite individual, and his sensing of this gives him a guide to his thinking and choosing, and the realization of an obligation to follow this guide. He may reject or forsake this guidance and sink towards his origin instead of rising to his destiny, but his false thinking has some degree of truth just as his bad choice has some degree of goodness. It is because the ideal is really present and not merely transcendent that we struggle to realize it.[1]

From this general account of the development of the moral life, it follows that both goodness and rationality are realized to some extent at every stage. It is reasonable to seek pleasure, utility, and rightness within the spheres in which these goods are obtained; but although *dulce desipere*, we must remember that the poet added *in loco*. The pleasure of playing bridge must be sacrificed if it interferes with my work and becomes more than the occasional relaxation to which after work I am entitled. Utility must be sacrificed if it means seeking my interest at the expense of disobeying the law. And law too must be transcended if it frustrates individual welfare.

But if good is what we choose, and evil what we reject, how can pleasure be a good if it has to be rejected in favour of utility?

Good and evil are correlative to choice; we need not look for things that are good or evil in themselves whether anyone chooses them or not. It is part and parcel of the finitude which we can never wholly transcend that no choice is perfect. There will always

---

[1] This is further explained in the following chapter.

be some good in what we reject. Pleasure and utility are both goods, but utility is higher; if both pleasure and utility cannot be had simultaneously, the latter must be preferred. But this difference of higher and lower is also a difference in kind. By contrast with the higher good, the lower one, as rejected, is evil. Nothing is wholly and irremediably evil; evil is a negation; the only positive thing in what we reject and call evil is a low degree of goodness.[1] The law breaker is wrong and may be called evil, but he may be enjoying himself or achieving his own interest by feathering his own nest, and these are goods. His evil consists in what is *not* there; what *is* there is good, but a good chosen when a higher or more rational choice should have been made, and therefore too low a good in this situation. His evil consists in what he has *not* done.

If goodness and rationality appear at each of the levels that have been distinguished, the same is true of obligation. There are times when we ought to play, to seek our interest, to comply with the law. But the stringency of the obligation is relative to the height of the moral level of the experience. There is no obligation to play if we ought to be at work, but the contrary. It is this which makes it hard to expound the conception of duty clearly. It is at once the supreme moral experience and yet it does appear on the lower levels also, though sometimes disguised in some such form as: 'It is your duty to seek the welfare of others because it is in your interest to do so.'

There is one further point about pleasure, utility, and rightness which needs to be mentioned before an attempt can be made to expound the concept of duty, namely that as we move up the scale of moral experiences we find that the characteristic value of each includes the lower ones incidentally; and this is why it is easy to identify one with another. Consider play and enjoyment on the one hand and craftsmanship and efficiency on the other. In a game we may be foiled of the enjoyment expected, and reflection on this experience reveals that what inhibited enjoyment was inefficiency, or lack of skill; similarly, we soon discover that there is no enjoyment in playing the piano until some degree at least of efficiency or manual dexterity is acquired. Even if the enjoyment we seek is mere basking in the sunshine, we have to choose carefully and efficiently the place to bask. As soon as we set ourselves to play or

[1] Cf. above, pp 64–6.

to seek enjoyment deliberately, we find that we seek efficiency too. Thus the quest for enjoyment develops into the quest for efficiency. Efficiency is only a means after all, and yet, once discovered by reflection to be necessary, it becomes an end. Here we have two goods, enjoyment and efficiency, related to one another like two stages in growth. One is higher or more developed than the other; the first grows into the other as reflection develops, but the second is the negative of the first; the acquisition of a skill may well be irksome and not enjoyable at all; music lessons can be very tiresome. As goods the two differ in kind, because one negates the other: and they differ in degree because one is higher than the other. Triangles do not differ in degree but only in kind and therefore you can define them. Temperatures do not differ in kind but only in degree and therefore you can measure them. But this simultaneous difference between goods in both kind and degree makes it impossible either to measure them in degree or quantitatively, or to define them by reference to their kind. This is why good, like other moral realities, is not amenable to study by the methods of physical science.

Rightness, as we have seen, is universal. The law is no respecter of persons. But pure universality without subjective satisfaction is given the bad name of Pharisaism and legalism; and it therefore invites negation by its polar opposite. If the universal claims to be everything, while the individual is nothing, the individual will rise up in protest and fling off the shackles of the universal. If right is abstracted from good or benefit, as in legalism, or in the moral philosophy which claims that right and good have no necessary interconnection with one another, then good or benefit can come on the scene only as the opposite of right, as something which the individual demands for himself in defiance of the rigour of universal law. The development of human society, actuated by the development of mind which is its inner principle, and which continually demands more and more adequate expression in institutions, makes legal codes obsolete and outruns the attempts of casuists to subsume new cases under old laws, as well as the attempts of lawyers to preserve the old bottles by legal fictions.

Good, however, abstracted from right and thus set in opposition to it, degenerates into mere self-assertion and the satisfaction of desire: or into some notion of welfare, where what is in question is material welfare, the welfare of man as nature rather than the spiritual welfare of man as a moral being. Thus when right and good are isolated from one another, the moral life is 'sundered into its extremes and lost'. Nevertheless there is something to be said for the primacy of good as that which we choose. Even if an act accords with a rule, the rule will not produce it; without action the law is a dead letter. It is action, and so choice, which is required; will, that supposed faculty, can never suffice. 'The laurels of mere willing'—or of mere setting ourselves to do something—'are dry leaves which never were green.'

Reflection makes us dissatisfied with appetite and leads us to choice. It is reflection again which makes us dissatisfied with cravings and the pleasure which their satisfaction produces. Utility leaves us asking useful for what and why? And rightness leaves us in perplexity if rules conflict and in exasperation if the universality of law oppresses the individual. All these have had their place in one sector or at one level of our experience but they all turn out to be unsatisfactory. But why are they unsatisfactory?

At all these levels, as we have seen, we encounter both good and obligation. Playing a game affords enjoyment and we ought to play by the rules; economic action affords benefit and utility, and just as at the former level we can see that we ought to play a game according to the rules, so we see that we ought in the economic sphere to seek the good which it affords; law-abidingness is an obligation, for the very notion of law is of something which ought to be obeyed, and we have seen that it is a recognizable good itself. What then is it which drives us on from one of these experiences to another?

'Power may compel: interest may bribe: pleasure only seduce: but reason alone can oblige or command.' So Richard Price quotes Dr Adams.[1] It is our own reflective self-consciousness that, by rejecting each of these goods and obligations in turn, discovers the criterion by which they are all to be judged unsatisfactory; the criterion is the ideal of truth and goodness present in man as mind, or reflective self-consciousness, or as reason itself (when reason is used, as before, in a wide sense and not as meaning mere ratiocination) or, as Hegel preferred to say, as spirit.

It is one and the same person who is conscious of the various levels of life to which I have referred; in each of them he accepts

---

[1] *Review*, Oxford, 1948, p 117 fn. I have modified the quotation. Dr Adams wrote 'persuade', not 'seduce'.

and enjoys the good which it affords and he lives in each according to the rules or standards prevailing in each. But, in so far as his self-consciousness is reflective, he cannot live his life in watertight compartments, and therefore he has to make a unity of his life if he is not to be the victim of repression or neurosis. And the only way of doing this is to make it a unity under the guidance of what I have called reason.

The process of self-transcendence which is the growth of mind and the development of its potentialities has introduced us to higher and higher levels of moral experience and corresponding to these, higher and higher types of good, and more and more developed types of action. The most rudimentary type of action which we considered was simply the body's occupancy of space: it was followed by reflex action, to which we might add an activity like snoring which is something I do but am not conscious of doing and for which I therefore disclaim responsibility. *My* action proper begins with choice and therefore with choice in embryo as caprice. The development of mind, however, and especially the development of reflection, produces a demand for rational choice, and action proper is action for which a reason can be given. For a capricious choice no reason can be given; it may have an unconscious cause, which psycho-analysis might discover, but the very fact that such a cause is unconscious is proof that for the caprice there is no reason.

Two reasons for choosing have been considered, namely 'because this is useful' and 'because this is right'. Neither is wholly satisfactory, because each is only a partially rational explanation of our choice. We are left asking 'useful for what?', and we find that the end is simply taken for granted in any form of utilitarianism, or, if not taken for granted, then chosen capriciously. And 'because this is right' is equally unsatisfactory, because the choice may not be the only thing that is right in the situation. More than one rule may be applicable, and 'because it is right' does not explain why we choose to abide by one rule and not another, nor does it explain why we choose this method of abiding by the rule and not another one.

This is why the claims of mind or rational choice are not satisfied at any of the levels so far considered, and why the concept of action, as mind's self-creativity, has not yet been fully actualized.

It is for reason that the other levels are each in their own way unsatisfactory, and it is the gradual development of reason which makes it possible for us to mount from one to the other. And reason's claim is that we should do our duty. It is reason which lays down the limits of our participation in each level and our acceptance of its standards. It is unreasonable to play all the time; unreasonable to seek profit or utility all the time, for what shall it profit a mortal man if he gain the world and lose his own soul; unreasonable to hold to every jot and tittle of the law to the exclusion of subjective satisfactions. It is by the conception of duty alone that the moral life can be unified in a way which reason can accept, and in dutiful action alone that action is with full adequacy exemplified.

CHAPTER 11

ACTION AS DUTY

1. THE EXPERIENCE OF DUTY

We have come to the parting of the ways.

The touchstone of a moral theory is whether it regards moral rules or principles as merely useful, and justified in so far as they are useful, or whether it holds that there are obligations intrinsically binding of themselves. They may be useful, but that is incidental. It is not their utility which makes them obligatory. In other words, the real difference is between those who believe in duty as an absolute obligation and those who believe that, if there are duties, then what makes them duties is their utility or their effectiveness in producing some result.

It is to Immanuel Kant that we owe the first clear account of the consciousness of duty, although we ought to give credit also to Richard Price.[1] The great division between moralists who are utilitarians and those who are not might equally well be expressed as a division between those who are Kantians and those who are not. Kant was aware of the distinction between right and duty, or between law and morality, as the division of his *Metaphysics of Ethics* into two parts shows. For him, moral worth is to be found in the doing of one's duty for duty's sake, and duty is a compulsion laid by our higher self on the lower; the law of duty is a law of reason recognized and reverenced by us as reasonable beings so that we command ourselves to obey it; in obeying it we are free, free from domination by impulse or by any end arising from our original nature. Nothing is good without qualification, i.e. nothing is morally good, except a good will; every other good can be put to bad use and so is never good *simpliciter*. Here at last the moral life reaches its culmination.

The moral life of duty is its own reward; it is the realization of man's potentialities, the triumph of his spiritual being over nature. It is self-justifying in the sense that it is reason living its own life, now explicitly enjoying itself instead of existing only implicitly in various degrees in the lower levels of action or moral experience.

[1] *Op. cit.*, pp 109 ff.

It is also experienced as an absolute and unconditional demand. The utilitarian bids us do this if it is in our own interest or in the general interest, and so forth. But the command of duty is *do this*. It is an absolute and not a conditional obligation. The command is issued by mind to itself, and not by x to y.

This is simply a description of what the experience of duty is. We have seen that some psychologists try to explain the experience away and would invite us to rid ourselves of this compulsion which has in their view no rational basis. Utilitarians explain it away too, by holding that no obligation can be unconditional; all must depend, in their view, on whether what we take to be a duty does or does not contribute to the diminution of suffering or to peaceful social relations and so forth. And yet if the experience which I have described is illusory, it is a curiously persistent illusion. What perhaps leads some to try to explain the experience away is a nest of difficulties which have commonly been raised against the conception, especially as it is expounded by Kant. His categorical imperative is a universal law, and it is particularized into maxims which must accord with that law. This leads to a description of duties in terms of rules which admit of no exceptions. Kant's insistence on the duty of telling the truth in all circumstances, no matter how fantastic, has come in for special criticism. Again, it is said that ought implies can, and therefore in any situation there is an act which is my duty and one which I can perform because I ought to do my duty. But how do we ascertain what our duty is? It may not be so easy to answer this question as Kant sometimes suggests.

I am not concerned to expound or to defend Kant, or to enquire how far these common criticisms of him rest on misunderstandings and insufficient knowledge of Kant's writings. That task has been discharged by Professor H. J. Paton. But the difficulties which some have found in the conception of duty can, I think, be removed.

2. MORAL GOODNESS AND THE SENSE OF DUTY

Goodness is correlative to choice and therefore is always related in some way to action. We do confer some kind of goodness on *things* that we choose, for we talk of a pleasant party, a useful tool, and the right card to play. But *moral* goodness belongs to the agent alone; it cannot be ascribed to things at all. This is because moral goodness at its highest consists in doing my duty, and doing my duty is being a moral being, i.e. one which endeavours to give to moral principle a dominion over impulse, etc. Nor can moral goodness be ascribed to an action *if* by action we mean only its outer moment, i.e. something occurring in the world and not in ourselves. If a man heads the list of subscriptions to a charity because he hopes thereby to be well thought of by his neighbours, there is no moral worth in the subscribing by itself. Moral goodness at its highest is present only when we do our duty because it is our duty.

This is attacked by those who say that motives cannot be commanded and that while it is sensible to tell a man to do his duty, it is futile to tell him to do it from a sense of duty. This, however, is to confuse right with duty and motive with feeling, and it sunders a concrete action into two extremes: the thing done and the motive. But in separation from one another, neither has any moral value. There is no moral value in subjective feeling or 'attitude' as such, regardless of what it achieves, and no moral value in an act which is in essence not charitable but self-interested. If motives were feelings of course they could not be commanded, but it is sensible to tell us to cultivate the virtue of charity, recognizing it to be a specification of conscientiousness, or to cultivate the recognition that we are moral agents, bound as such to develop our moral agency, and to obey the law of our being as rational, or as self-consciously reflective. Even if an ungrateful man cannot sensibly be bidden to feel grateful, it is still sensible to say that he ought to be grateful. The virtue of gratitude is not a feeling. Ingratitude has not been acquired in a day: it results from a long history of selfishness. Even so, a man can improve if he recognizes the claims of duty; he can master his ingratitude, as a man may master his irascibility, if he sets himself to do so. 'Motives' then are outside our control only so long as they are supposed to be feelings given by nature and so to remain unaltered by reflection and choice. In particular the 'sense of duty' can be commanded in the sense that a man ought to rise to this level, because a sense of duty is nothing but the consciousness of duty itself.

A man conscious of duty, and so of the compulsion of lower by higher, knows that duty must be done for duty's sake; i.e. moral agency, or the development of our mental and spiritual personali-

N

ties, is its own end, just as beauty, or rather the apprehension of beauty, is. The moral life is a growth, a process, and a development; the compulsive power of duty is discovered in this process; the moral ideal has been there all the time, implicitly, as the spur to the process; Pascal's phrase puts the point when he says: 'Thou wouldst not have sought me if thou hadst not already found me'. Our duty is to choose, i.e. to be minds, to triumph over our natural beginnings; what we ought to do is, having risen to the level of choice, *to choose to choose*: this is the formal character of our duty, and it may be called conscientiousness, and the fact that this word and consciousness have the same root is not accidental.

No external force can produce conscientiousness. We must achieve this ourselves, and we achieve it by the constant endeavour to be minds and to develop them. If we were wholly minds, then there would be no obligation to be minds; if we were not minds at all, then obligation would be impossible. Life would simply be a matter of gratifying natural impulses and desires. Obligation[1] exists as the consciousness that we have got some distance on the road which leads from what we have so far become to our becoming what we implicitly are. We are conscious of the distinction between a higher and a lower self; we recognize the worth of the higher self, and it obliges us to cultivate it and develop it more and more, and this respect or reverence for the higher carries with it an obligation to live more and more on the higher instead of on the natural plane. The highest fulfilment of this obligation is to do our duty; we fulfil it by choosing (this is the formal side of duty) and to choose is to act (this is the content or material side of duty). The act is in the first place the choice of choice itself, and in the second place the thing I have chosen to do or the alternative I have chosen to accept.

3. OUGHT AND CAN

If a man's duty is supposed to be no more than to make some specific change in the external world, e.g., to use one of the examples beloved by some Oxford philosophers,[2] to return a

---

[1] This was touched upon in Chapter 7.

[2] This curious fondness for trivial examples is parallel with the use of the 'red patch' in essays on perception, as if the truth of the complex were discoverable in the simple or of the higher in the lower.

borrowed book, then it is pointed out that this may be impossible of fulfilment—I may have a stroke of paralysis for example,
and therefore it cannot be my duty to do this act, because it is
senseless to say that I ought to do something which I cannot do.
But why is it senseless? 'Ought' implies 'can' at the initial stage of
duty, i.e. at the stage when I must choose, when I must be mind
and not body, when I choose to cultivate my moral agency. This
is an achievement, the achievement of the essential moral require-
ment: become what you are. But it may indeed be impossible for
me to go further and carry out my choice into the external world.
This, as I have said before, is the human lot, the sign that our
natural beginnings and our natural environment can never be
transcended. Balzac may not appear among the moralists but he
hit the nail on the head when he wrote: 'He saw life sanely,
realizing that its universal law obliges us to put up with imperfections in everything.'[2] The spirit of morality and duty can never
be perfectly realized in this world. We are all miserable sinners and
unprofitable servants; what we ought to do we cannot always
completely do. This is sometimes due to our inability to eliminate
natural obstacles. but it is sometimes our own fault. The dipsomaniac simply cannot choose—he is driven by his mania—but his
past actions have made it possible for him to succumb to mania.
Even on the rack or on the bed of sickness, I can fulfil my duty to
be dutiful, to exercise compulsion on impulse and desire, to
develop mind and the moral spirit, instead of reverting to animalism.

4. WHAT MY DUTY IS

Ought I to do what is right or what I think is right? Ought I to do
the act which is objectively my duty whether I know it or not, or
what I think is my duty in this situation, having got the facts of the
situation right, or what I think is my duty in this situation, even
though I have got the facts wrong or have misinterpreted them?
These are questions which arise at the level of right, not at the
level of duty; in these questions right and duty are being confused.
They also imply an abstract objectivism because they presuppose
that (a) there is an act which is objectively my duty, whether I
know it or not, and (b) there is one act which ought to be done to

[2] *Cousine Bette*, Eng. tr., London, 1948, p 389.

fit the facts of the situation, whatever they are and whether I know it or not. Those who propound these conundrums, having started with objective presuppositions, produce, naturally enough, subjective conclusions. What I ought to do, they say, is to set myself to do the best I can, so that moral worth becomes wholly subjective and it accrues to me whether I succeed in doing my objective duty or not.

My duty in fact is the one act which I can choose when I reflect on my whole situation and especially on the level on which my act is to be done; it is subjective in being chosen by me, but objective in that it accords with the universal law that duty be done, that I make myself a choosing person, and not an automaton. If I say of someone else that he does not know where his duty lies, I am saying that he has not reflected, that his conscientiousness is blind or ill-educated or superficial. Since judgment of others is hazardous, the blindness and superficiality may be in me. But duty is a matter of reason and rationality, of thought, and it is therefore not to be assessed by reference to the external world or the facts of a situation, but by thinking alone. It is to manufacture fictions to suppose that there is an objective duty which may be unknown to me. This is like Kant's *thing in itself*, a needless hypothesis. To postulate the existence of the unknown is to claim knowledge of it.

5. DUTY AND RULE

The beginning of duty, as we have seen, is conscientiousness, and a sense of duty is part and parcel of this, i.e. of my consciousness of having a duty, and so of being under self-compulsion to perform it. But the other factor in this conscientiousness is that of acting on principle. We have seen that duty arises with the development of mind or reason, and thinking proceeds by distinguishing and uniting universal and particular. This individual act which I choose has universal and particular elements. It accords with rule and applies the rule to a particular case. To triumph over the hindrances to the moral life is to be guided by a universal, by a rule, by a principle, instead of being determined by a series of disparate and chaotic impulses and desires. Political life is impossible without rules to produce harmonious action by the citizens, and rules are equally inescapable in the moral life for the same reason; we can become one instead of many only by ordering our life on principle. 'A man will not take duty seriously who does not take rules seriously. Grammar is not style, but there is no getting to the latter except *via* the rules of the former.'[1] This is why the experience of rightness, as the negative of expediency, is a vital stage on the way to duty. Kant is not wrong in seeing that there is something in the experience of duty which justifies associating it with obedience to a universal law. This law may be variously expounded: Be a man. Respect yourself. Command yourself. Respect others as persons. Act on the principle of acting on principle. But however it be expressed, the law is issued by our own reason to ourselves. And it is the same law which all men, in so far as they are rational or are reflective self-consciousnesses, issue to themselves, because it is what reason commands. Act on principle means act thoughtfully and do not try to make exceptions in your own favour. This is vital, and it must always be urged against those who would have us act on sentiment, i.e. on feeling. Feelings differ, but we cannot have one morality for ourselves and another for someone else. Even Hitler paid lip service to this when he demanded 'justice'. Impulses and desires vary from man to man, but in reason men meet on common ground. And as Kant goes on to point out, the principles into which this universal law is specified ought to harmonize with one another, both in the individual and in society. Only thus can a moral order be created or a moral life be lived. Although it is we who lay on ourselves the command to obey this universal law, it is not a law which we choose; on the contrary, the existence of the law is what makes the development to choice possible. It is the law inherent in the moral life in much the same way as the laws of thought are intrinsic to thinking itself; they are not imposed on thinking, because thinking is and must be free; they are the ways in which, and in which only, we think clearly. The moral law is the way in which and in which only we choose, in so far as our choice is rationally or ideally guided and is not drawn down by selfish aims or by our animal nature. The presence of rule in rational life is inescapable. The man who repudiates all rules is making a far more comprehensive rule, namely a rule to ignore all rules. The man who says he will accept only rules which tend to diminish misery is making to that effect a new rule which has no utilitarian justification.

Nevertheless, rule cannot be the whole of duty. The principles

[1] R. G. Collingwood, in an unpublished note.

on which duty requires us to act are all general; they cannot be comprised in a legal code. Duty transcends rightness. There is something determinate about the dutiful act which is chosen in circumstances of difficulty or crisis. 'This one thing I do.' When Oates walked out into the snow in the hope of saving his companions if he went to his death, his act was as determinate as possible. But if we think in terms of rule, we find that there may be several alternative ways of abiding by it, all of them right; whether we return a book by hand or by post may not matter, and there is nothing wrong in leaving to caprice the choice between different right ways of abiding by a rule. But caprice is a recessive element as we mount from lower to higher levels of moral experience. If my duty were simply to abide by a specific rule, then if I adopted one way of complying with it, I would fail in the duty of adopting the other way, since every way of abiding by the rule would have to be a duty. This is why the fulfilment of a duty to seek benefit in the economic sphere or rightness in the sphere of law is less morally valuable than the fulfilment of a moral duty at the level of personal relationships. The latter is more determinate than the others. But once again because of the imperfections of our world, even that act is not wholly determinate, and our duty is to that extent incompletely fulfilled. But it is more nearly fulfilled than in any utilitarian or regularian action. There are always alternative ways to the end, alternative ways of keeping a rule and the choice will be by convenience or caprice. On the other hand, duty at its height is the experience that '*Ich kann nicht anders*'. This is not intuition, since intuitions differ, and intuition is only another name for subjective inclination or caprice. On the contrary it is the result of making up my mind. The act is laid on me by myself as a rational being, and I shall be false to my moral nature and the law of my higher self, if I fail to act accordingly. Although my self-mastery is never complete, my subjection to duty and my choice of this individual act is the measure of my command of myself and my situation. Service is perfect freedom. The choice of duty is a rational choice, and for it there is no external criterion whatever. The same is true of knowledge. Facts, evidence, etc., are no criterion; because knowledge is my reaction to these, my conception of them, my criticism of them; and there is no criterion for this criticism save that of mind itself.

6. DUTY AND FREEDOM

In subjecting itself to duty, mind is fulfilling itself and being itself, abiding by its own true nature and destiny. It is therefore free in this subjection, and this is the only true liberty. It is no limitation on this freedom that we cannot square the circle or speak Chinese. We find ourselves in the world, in a specific situation, and this with its limitations we must accept. It is no use lamenting that we cannot leap over Rhodes, to take Hegel's example.[1] But the situation does not determine our action. It is we who act. Our action is based on the facts of the situation, but our recognition of the facts deprives them of their mechanical character. Our action is our response to a known environment, not the product of that environment. Hence there is no freedom in refusing to do our duty. On the contrary that refusal is to put mind in bondage to something not itself, or to frustrate its development and therefore its freedom.

7. MORAL EVIL

Choice is the first step to moral responsibility, to full moral agency, because it is the vindication of the agent's freedom from psychological stimuli. But the choice has ultimate moral worth only if the agent in choosing is reverencing moral goodness, fulfilling his duty, and determining himself in the pursuit of moral ends, i.e. in the pursuit of the fuller realization of his own moral agency or spiritual potentiality. If this is moral goodness, what is evil? Kant is sometimes interpreted as meaning that *either* a man wills or chooses, *or* else he is swept away by impulses, etc. If this were true, then all evil would be done under the influence of some uncontrolled craving or desire. Such a view suits those who believe that man is naturally good, and that evil is due to some abnormality curable in the psychological clinic or by some alteration in social conditions. Enough has been said already to dispose of a theory of 'natural' goodness, and experience in our own lifetime has provided us with examples enough of the difference between the sins of the flesh, or the murder committed in a passion, and cold calculating cruelty, like the Moors murders for example. The villain chooses to choose—his act is to that

[1] *Ph. d. Rechts*, Preface, edn. cit., p 11.

extent deliberate—and therefore he has risen to the moral plane and entered the sphere of judgment. But he reverences nothing, and he identifies his choice not with the moral ends implicit in the fact that it is a choice, but with his own selfish ends. He sins against the light and this is both irrational and immoral. His evil is the distortion of choice. *Corruptio optimi pessima.* This is why calculating villainy is so much worse than the sins of the flesh; the latter are at least not fully chosen. The curious thing therefore is that there must be some good in a man before he can be judged evil. He must rise to the moral plane in choice. If you judge a picture aesthetically and call it bad or ugly, you are attributing to it some aesthetic merit, as you are not when you judge it by its size and consider its suitability for filling a blank space on the wall. If you call a judgment irrational, you are still treating it as rational to some extent, as you are not if you call it meaningless or nonsensical. Similarly to call a man evil is to regard him as within the moral sphere and entitled to be assessed by a standard of moral judgment. He makes himself evil because he at once establishes his moral agency and spurns it. And his evil is in his spurning and not in what he effects in the world around him. There may be evil in what he effects, but not moral evil; that resides in the agent alone. The evil man gets to the threshold of duty and then turns his back on it. His evil is in what he does *not* do, as we have seen already.

8. CONFLICT OF DUTIES

It is when duty is made a matter of abiding by certain rules which admit of no exceptions that we are confronted with the problem of a 'conflict of duties'. In a given situation there may be two rules both of which it will be impossible to obey, and yet obedience to both is said to be a duty. The stock example is that of Antigone. It is her duty to bury her brother but also her duty to obey her sovereign who has forbidden the burial. Those described as deontologists have spent a long time trying to discover on what principle, compatible with their belief in rules of duty without exceptions, conflicts of this kind can be resolved. One suggested principle is that of regarding the two duties by which Antigone is faced as only *prima facie* obligations. This is not helpful. Either these are obligations, in which case the conflict remains, or they are not, in which case the conflict is explained away instead of being resolved. Those who uphold this view are disposed to say that the agent sees which of the *prima facie* obligations is the real obligation: this relapse into intuition, a characteristically feminine solution, transports us out of the realm of duty, choice, reflection, self-consciousness, back to sentiment and feeling and caprice. Alternatively, it is suggested that these conflicting obligations differ in stringency or gravity, and the more stringent or the weightier is the one which really is a duty. But what is the criterion? How is gravity or stringency to be assessed? The difficulty is much the same as that which confronted Mill when he wished to assess pleasures qualitatively. I have indeed already suggested a criterion of stringency, though it depends on a doctrine of levels of moral experience which deontologists do not seem to expound.

If instead of regarding this conflict as a conflict of duties we look on it as a conflict of rules, the problem then is to decide by which rule, if by either, it is our duty to abide. The answer may not be difficult so long as the two conflicting rules are rules appropriate to different levels of our experience as they were in Antigone's experience, and this is the answer I suggested long ago when in dealing with rightness I asked about the circumstances in which a promise could be broken. Duty will require us to subordinate pleasure to utility, for example, or political ties to moral ones, at any rate on certain occasions; because we are morally required to prefer the higher, and so more nearly moral good, to the lower. But suppose that the rules conflict within one level of experience? A doctor is bound by the Hippocratic oath, or by the rules of his profession, to cure his patient if he can. He is also bound by the rules of his profession not to call in an unqualified man. And yet there have been eminent unqualified men who have cured or helped patients when orthodox medicine has been powerless, the late Sir Henry Barker may be an example. Now this is a genuine conflict of rules which cannot be solved at the level of rules, nor can it be solved by regressing to benefit; for those who regard benefit as the sole justification of rules, both the rules which confront the doctor are beneficial. In such a case there is nothing for it but for the doctor to ask himself where his *duty* lies, or at any rate that is his only recourse as a rational being, under the moral law. He must rise above the sphere of rules and rightness to the sphere of duty. He may try to put the responsibility on someone else whom he consults, but that only throws the decision, the same decision, on someone else.

In the nineteen-forties, an enemy airman flew low and machine-gunned the Leuchars children as they were coming out of school; the aeroplane crashed and the pilot landed injured. The same doctor, called to help the injured school children, tended the airman and saved his life. He told me so. He abided by the rules of his profession. But ought he to have let a scoundrel die instead of abiding by the Hippocratic oath? Even if someone is prepared to argue that letting the man die was a greater benefit than keeping the oath, on the ground that if the man recovered he might do wicked harm again, he is still only making a rule that doctors may let scoundrels die instead of trying to cure them. Had the doctor a duty to ignore the rule and let the man die? Should he have risen above the regularian sphere to the dutiful, above specific rules to the general principle implicit in an ideal which is rationally grasped?

A decision here is the agent's own choice. It is his moral responsibility which is at stake. In what sense can his choice, whatever it is, be wrong? He may after the event, and on further reflection, conclude that it was wrong. The choice, however, and his reflection has then revealed to him more and more of what the claims of morality are. These, as I have urged, we discover only in choosing and in reflecting on our choices. Our moral potentiality, or our moral destiny, is made plain to us only gradually in so far as we advance in the self-creativity of mind or choice or will or practical reason. To discover the act which we must do is also to discover, because we are thinkers, the general principle under which it falls. Some guidance can always be given. We must reverence our higher nature, that spur to our moral development. We must reverence it in others so that we must act in a way which is to actualize not only our own moral personality but the moral order of society. We ought to direct our lives towards the rational end of moral self-realization in a society to whose moral order we contribute by making rules for ourselves which harmonize with the moral personalities of others. Our choice of what principle to obey here and now is a deliberate and thoughtful choice, and it implies a principle which is a specification of the moral principle to become what we are, to choose to choose, to guide ourselves by the moral ideal incarnate in us to some extent and revealed to us increasingly and gradually in our moral choices. There is no way out of a conflict of rules save by going on to the moral universal principle or spirit which all rules which we lay on ourselves are struggling to express in different ways. The spirit must always have forms through which alone it can work, and the general principle of abiding by the universal law of choosing to act on principle instead of allowing ourselves to be determined by impulse or desire is a general principle which we have to particularize. How to particularize it in a given case is a matter of our reflective choice in the light of such considerations as I have mentioned. This is why 'judge not' is such an important precept. It is easy to condemn someone whose problem has not been ours and which therefore we have not been able fully to appreciate.

9. CONTENT OF DUTY

Fortunately for us, however, these conflicts are exceptional in our experience, in so far as that experience is in the main ordered and regular. Most of our duties are associated with and arise out of our station in life, or rather stations, for our life is lived on different levels. It may seem paradoxical, but the fact is that we acquire moral goodness not by seeking it but by dutifully seeking goods of other kinds.[1] We ought to do our duty all the time and do it for duty's sake, but this abstract universal principle needs to be particularized or given content. It gains its content when we realize that we have to choose to pursue faithfully and well whatever activity is involved in the level of experience on which we are living, and seek the good appropriate to that level. (This matter was touched upon above in Chapter 4, section 3.) The aim of economic life is utility or benefit or profit, and in living on that level of life it is our duty to adopt this aim.

Another example of how duty gains its content may be found in work. To some people, work is a necessary evil and they would think that Aristotle was right in holding that we work only in order to attain leisure. Work, however, is one way in which the potentialities of mind are realized. In one sense it is a means to an end; it is the externalization and the realization of mind. Work is the price at which the gods sell their blessings to men, but it is not

[1] See a remarkable article by A. Macbeath in *Mind*, April, 1948. It does not seem to have had from moralists the attention it deserved.

just a means to those blessings—as the objectification of our minds it is a blessing in itself. Morality is the living of a rational life, but rationality is nothing unless it has an objective expression in language and in act. Work is thus an intrinsic part of the moral life. This is why unemployment is a tragedy. If it were only an economic evil, then it could be counteracted by raising the dole. But this is to relieve the economic hardship and to leave the moral evil untouched.

To hold that work is a moral duty is to invite the question: what work? The answer is: today's work. It is a pity when morality is regarded as something exceptional, and duty as something forced on us only in a moment of crisis. Morality is displayed not in extraordinary exertions only but in the dutiful performance of one's daily tasks. Morality is normality, which includes both senses of the word 'norm'. Young people especially are tempted to say: If only I had noble work to do then my whole heart would be in the doing of it, but what I have to do is so trivial, contributing so little good to the world that it cannot call up the enthusiasm I would give to nuclear disarmament or abolishing a colour-bar. This, however, is just an insidious temptation. It is the man careful in small things who wins his way to promotion and the care of larger things. Most of us occupy only a very small position in the world; the range of our influence is trivial; but the sooner we recognize the fact, the sooner will we cure ourselves of pride, and the readier we shall be to be faithful in the small vineyard entrusted to our care. We are committed to certain tasks by reason of the situation into which our choices have brought us, and our first duty is to fulfil these. Puzzled about our duties, the first thing we have to realize is that we must do those under our own nose, and do them dutifully, not regarding them as irksome but as the opportunity given to us to actualize and develop our own moral agency.

10. SELF-RESPECT

This development is the gradual actualization of our potentialities as minds. Will or choice is a self-creative activity. We choose to choose and thus discover more of what mind and its practical law is. There is no faculty of will lying dormant in our nature waiting to be used on occasion. Will is simply my conscious and reflective choice. When we say 'no' to desire and so choose, we bring will or choice into existence for the first time, and we keep it in existence and develop it the more we continue to master nature and make self-determined choices. Similarly, intelligence or reason exists only in the act of thinking and is brought into existence when we reflect on sensation. To hold that intelligence or will is something latent and inactive until used, neither clear nor confused, neither good nor evil, is to multiply entities unnecessarily and to advocate occult entities like the 'soporific virtue' of opium. In thinking, an ideal of truth is implicit, guiding thought and becoming more clearly known as thought proceeds. Choosing, similarly, is guided by an ideal of moral perfection discovered in choice and increasingly known as choices are made.

The nature of duty, and what it requires of us, is discovered to us by our several experiences of obeying its command, the command laid on us by ourselves. In this sense a moral order, in which all men have their part to play, may be a presupposition of moral experience. Reason does not, as Kant suggests, frame the ideal of perfection *a priori*; it discovers it within itself as its own guiding star whether in the form of perfect truth or moral perfection. Empiricists have never been able to explain how we come by a concept of perfection. We discover the ideal within ourselves, and it is the spur to our endeavour. We cannot derive it from the external world. The Kingdom of God is within you.

This is the foundation of self-respect. This is a paradox like self-control or self-command. But these paradoxical expressions persist only because they are true descriptions of our experience. If the first essential in a rational life is 'know thyself', because to neglect this is to fall a victim to unconscious complexes, to self-deception, and so to hypocrisy, with the inevitable result of snuffing the candle of moral experience, then the second essential precept is 'respect yourself', i.e. remember that you are a moral being and respect yourself accordingly. We can, however, preserve our self-respect only by fulfilling our duties. Habitual vice is always accompanied by a loss of self-respect and the sense of shame. The gambler reduced to penury cadges shamelessly from all and sundry. We can respect ourselves only because of our consciousness of a higher self which somehow embodies an ideal which so far we have partially, but only partially, actualized.

II. CONSCIENCE

Instead of saying that we make up our minds what our duty is or what our higher self prescribes that we must do, some would say that our duty is simply to do what our conscience tells us. Conscience has already above been connected with consciousness, and it must not be regarded as a faculty which, persisting unchanged, can be brought into action at any appropriate opportunity. Conscience is often exempted from rational criticism as if its voice could never be wrong. But why should we suppose that a man's views on the Pyramids or the flatness of the earth may be mistaken, but not his views on moral conduct? While it is true in a sense that a man ought to follow his conscience, it is his prior duty to see that his conscience is educated. An uncriticized conscience may be the expression of some unconscious and irrational complex; it may be mere moral prejudice; it may be what its possessor has been taught about conduct; it may be the representative in a man of the moral judgments of his own set, and these may be fallible; an uncriticized conscience may not be as some suppose the voice of God directing its possessor's conscience, but the very reverse—a temptation to or an expression of spiritual pride. Conscience is not a faculty at all. If it is said to be an intuition, that is only another word for caprice, and this would deprive it of all claims to respect. On the contrary, it does deserve respect because a man's conscience is simply his own power of moral judgment. It is therefore not infallible. Subsequent reflection may satisfy him that he chose wrongly, that his 'conscience' was unenlightened or inadequately trained. No doubt it is my duty to follow conscience, i.e. my own moral judgment, just as a scientist must abide by his judgment of the evidence, even if later he finds his judgment mistaken. The moral agent has personal responsibility for his choice, and he cannot excuse himself by suggesting that his 'conscience' is determined for him by Bible or priest or psycho-analyst. What these may tell him he must consider and then either accept or reject for himself. We cannot find out what our duties are by turning up an encyclopaedia or a manual of casuistry: we must make up our minds for ourselves. It is interesting to notice that Kant saw this when he wrote his *Metaphysic of Ethics* and included in it a number of 'casuistical questions' to most of which he did not supply the answers, although in the earlier *Critique of Practical*

Reason[1] he had suggested that a decision on where duty lay was always simple.

12. KINGDOM OF ENDS

To say: 'Be a man'. 'Respect yourself', or: 'Act reflectively and self-consciously on the principle of acting on principle', is still a long way from telling us what to do. It is to Kant that it is natural to turn when we consider the content of moral action. When we act we have some sort of end in view. Now in craftsmanship the end may be the production of a table to order; the end is given to us and we use the appropriate means, and we shall or shall not attain the end according to whether we have skill enough or not. It is possible to analyse a dutiful act into means and end too, but the relation of means and end differs here. The end of moral action is not outside it but intrinsic to it, and the means to it, moral action, is not one which can fail of its effect. I do my duty in order to be a moral being, a rational agent, and so an end in myself. To say that morality is the supreme end and that the moral agent is an end in himself is tautologous, because moral goodness has no existence except in the moral agent. In so far as a man lives on the moral plane he is an end in himself and is respected as such. Thus 'respect yourself as an end' and 'respect other rational beings as ends in themselves' are maxims which provide part of the content of duty.

What does it mean to treat ourselves and others as ends in themselves? Kant gives an interesting answer: we are to seek our own perfection and do what we can to make others happy. At first sight this looks like advocating one morality for ourselves and a different one for others. But Kant explains[2] that the individual seeks his own happiness by nature; it is purposeless to make this a matter of obligation, because a man need not be compelled to do what he will do anyway. On the other hand, perfection is what an individual must seek for himself; no one can give it to him; he must reach after it, however asymptotically, by doing his duty and making himself mind and a moral being. Moral responsibility must be his own—it cannot be conferred on him—and it is only by accepting and discharging this responsibility that any advance

---

[1] Tr. Abbott, p 126.
[2] See, e.g., *Metaphysic of Ethics*, Introduction to the Doctrine of Virtue, Section 4.

towards perfection can be made. This is true, and yet although we cannot promote the perfection of others, we must be careful not to put obstacles in the way of their achieving it, or as we commonly say, we must not put temptation in others' way.

This leads to a final attempt to visualize what the notion of duty implies, namely to Kant's conception of the Kingdom of Ends. We are to respect ourselves and the law of our own practical reason. This means acting on principle so that the individual chosen act does fall under a rule, even if it be a new rule made in this situation and abrogating an old rule. Now if others are to be respected as ends, if we are to forward their happiness, then the rules we make for our own actions must be such as will cohere with the rules made by others. This is a reasonable 'must', because others are moral agents and therefore rational beings, like ourselves. Thus we must make for our own conduct only those rules which will contribute to a harmonious moral order, i.e. rules compatible with and not obstructions to the moral development of others, and they must equally treat me similarly. The moral order is one in which all the members respect and issue and abide by the same rules.

One difficulty in this conception arises from the special obligations which have come before us more than once; consider for example the special obligations which arise for husband and wife from their marriage vows. We also have special obligations to our circle of friends; we cannot generalize and say that all mankind are legislating members of the Kingdom of Ends and forget the *special* obligations laid on us by the conditions of human life. Marriage is the institution which has enabled civilized man to control and sublimate the natural cravings of sex. Our circle of friends is of necessity limited and small. It is not possible for us to love our casual acquaintance as much as our *fidus Achates*. Consequently it is not surprising that Kant describes the Kingdom of Ends as only an ideal, and it is unfortunate that he expounds it, in part, in such legalistic terms. It is more like an ideal of Heaven where we are told there is no marrying or giving in marriage; and we are also enjoined to believe that 'if any man come unto me and hate not his father and mother and wife and children . . . he cannot be my disciple' (Luke xiv. 26) or that 'he that loveth father or mother more than me is not worthy of me' (Matthew x. 37). However, although we must fulfil our special obligations, we must keep in sight the ideal of respecting all men as ends in themselves and the necessity of adjusting our maxims so far as possible accordingly. We must not build the special obligations of marriage into an *egoisme à deux* or make our circle of friends into a closed coterie (often with a contempt for those outside it).

The Kingdom of Ends is an ideal. And when we try to act in accordance with it we must avoid two opposite errors: one is that of concentrating so much on the ideal that we forget or ignore certain conditions and rules inescapable in our actual life, i.e. the spheres of utility and right; the other is to concentrate so much on the actual that we forget the ideal and then easily relapse to a level below that of duty. The ideal is something partially realized already; it is only for this reason that we discover it, and it can be further actualized only by being given a concrete shape in those subordinate spheres of utility and right in which, as we have seen, it glimmers or shines. To dispense with these is to invite moral and social chaos. But we must always be ready to revise moral and legal codes as our moral insight develops with the deepening of our knowledge of the ideal. Furthermore, men are finite—they are bodies as well as minds. Consequently the material side of life can never be conjured away. The existence of material goods, however distributed, inevitably leads to a clash of human purposes. By processes of law we reduce and check these clashes as much as possible, but they cannot be eliminated. It follows that life must be lived at times on the utilitarian level and at other times on the regularian. But the essential thing is to make the ideal, the spirit of morality in a society of moral agents linked by a devotion to rational or spiritual ends, the criterion of judging the worth of our rules and obligations, and the ultimate court of appeal when crucial moral decisions have to be made.

Kant's Kingdom of Ends provides us with a goal for moral effort and also with a general guide to the choice which is our duty; no more specific guide can be given. Moral responsibility cannot be conferred on anyone but neither is anyone to be deprived of it or exempted from shouldering it himself. This ideal is not purely transcendent; it transcends our achievement, but it is immanent within us none the less as the law of our practical reason. In self-respect or in respecting others as moral agents we clearly distinguish between a higher and a lower self, but the higher self is constantly growing and developing its potentialities, or rather it

o

should be; for this development is precisely what it is our duty to promote.

13. DUTY NOT A MEANS TO AN END

The imperative of duty, we saw, is simply 'do this'. May we not reinterpret this and say 'do this if you want to be moral'? This suggests a means and end relationship all over again, and the suggestion is false. Doing your duty is being moral; it is a means to the building up of our moral life only because it is at the same time that building. Efficiency and prudence are goods of a kind; but not the highest moral goods. The efficiency which is reasonable and which in certain circumstances it is a duty to pursue, ceases to be reasonable or a duty if the end is abandoned, and it may be. Prudence is a duty in some circumstances but in others it is but a cloak for self-interest, and our duty may be to take an imprudent risk. But the highest moral end, unlike efficiency and its end, or prudence and its end, cannot be abandoned or altered without immorality. There is laid on man as mind, as reflective self-consciousness, an absolute and unconditional obligation to do his duty. To fail here is to fail absolutely. Inefficiency and imprudence are venial faults. Immorality is not.

There is no explaining away the absoluteness, the unconditionality of duty. In war thousands heard this call and obeyed it, despite the sacrifice of home, friends, comfort, and even life. No consideration of custom, social pressure, or calculation of interest can explain away this experience of an absolutely imperative call. This is an indispensable ingredient in what duty means. Those who would explain it away are those who have not had the experience or who, having had it, have found it so uncomfortable that they desire to exhibit it as an illusion or as misunderstanding or as misinterpretation of our human condition. It is this absoluteness of duty which has led to the view that duty is too harsh a guide for our actions, to the view that duty is not freedom as has been argued here, and to the view that if duty is a *stern* daughter of the voice of God, so much the worse for duty.

14. SUMMARY

The main characteristics of duty, if I may now gather together the threads of this discussion, are: (i) My duty is chosen; it is therefore a possible experience only for reflective or rational beings. (ii) Although I choose it, it is the only thing that I can deliberately choose. My duty is what I absolutely must do; it is a categorical imperative, but this compulsion comes from within, just as our being compelled to accept Euclid's proof is the compulsion of thinking itself and not a compulsion imposed on it. (iii) In spite of the compulsion, I am never more free than when I am doing my duty. I am free from the domination of nature both within and without. By determining myself in accordance with practical reason, I am freely building up my moral life, making myself more and more of a mind, i.e. a moral agent. And this is the only true freedom, and the only freedom within my power. All other kinds of freedom are limited by the physical world or by social or political institutions. (iv) Duty involves pleasure, because it is a choice made wholeheartedly with the whole of my real self; it will involve rejection of some demands of a lower self, but this is a liberation. Kant was not wrong in seeing that duty had to work against some at least of our inclinations. (v) Duty involves utility; the doing of one's duty contributes to the building of one's moral character while at the same time it is the expression of that character in action. Means and end coalesce. Moreover duty, as we have seen, is not mere rightness, but includes a subjective side too, a subjective satisfaction. There is no duty to do something futile. (vi) Duty accords with law or principle, first with the universal law of acting on principle, and secondly with general principles, such as 'respect others as persons', which our choice affirms. If our choice abrogates a law, it does so only by making another. We give the law to ourselves, and as law-makers we are also law abrogators, not law-breakers. But as rational beings, as thinkers, we always discern in our act its universal and particular elements. The act is a particular application of some principle or other. If this were not so, the act would be due to impulse alone. Right and good are thus simultaneously actualized in the doing of one's duty. (vii) At the highest level, where duty is the choice to be a moral agent, ought implies can. (viii) But at lower levels we must do our duty by dutifully seeking goods of kinds other than the highest moral goodness. It is our duty to play the game according to the rules, and so to gain the pleasure which playing the game properly and at the right times provides. And the same is true of other levels. Our duty is to seek the good which that level provides. That good will therefore be one level of moral good, but the highest moral good is attained only at the highest moral level when our duty is done for duty's sake, at the expense, as so often, of rejecting the goods of lower levels of moral experience. It will be a duty *not* to seek the good of play when we ought to be at work, *not* to seek economic good at the expense of failing in a duty to put principle above gain. (ix) We have to act on principle. Our duty must include rightness to the extent of trying to make our rules cohere with those of other moral agents. This is what Kant called the Kingdom of Ends. It is an ideal, as he said; it is like the Kingdom of Heaven. But it ought to be our ideal all the same.

CHAPTER 12

MORALITY AND RELIGION

In the previous chapter I tried to expound the conception of duty as an absolute and unconditional obligation, and I pointed out that this characteristic of duty was so difficult to explain that it was not surprising that attempts were made to explain it away as a product, for example, of unconscious complexes. Against such attempts I have argued in previous chapters.

1. DUTY AND RELIGIOUS BELIEF

Is an explanation possible by associating duty with religion? Can the unconditional command 'do this' stand on its own feet, or in other words is it explicable by pure reason alone, or does it need some religious basis or support? If it needs no such basis or support, does it presuppose, if it is to be fully intelligible, some sort of religious belief? It may be urged that all knowledge rests ultimately on premises or presuppositions which cannot be proved and must just be believed, but the question still presses, does the moral experience of duty imply or require any *religious* belief?

We must first look again at the fact that nowadays many who accept moral obligations and duties would deny that they are absolute or categorical obligations, and our duty to fulfil them, they would say, results from and has its origins in social needs and social pressures. People have to live in societies, and therefore they must submit to certain restrictions on their freedom. Thus, it is argued, we ought to accept these restrictions for the sake of our peace or our happiness. Hence their claim on us is hypothetical: do this if you want to be happy; do this if you want to be sensible enough to live at peace with your neighbours. Here the 'if' is vital. It is true that, brought up in a moral and law-abiding society, most people *do* want to live at peace with others; they do not want to revert to Hobbes's state of nature where the weakest goes to the wall. But there are others, the Napoleons or the Hitlers who want power, and who are prepared to send the weaker to the wall.

As soon as it said that moral rules are devised for peace and security or for the preservation of harmonious relations, the imperative of morality becomes hypothetical. There can be no reverence for a moral law if it is a law devised for the convenience or comfort of men. But Kant's categorical imperative was accompanied by his conviction that the moral law was to be *reverenced*. There can be no absolute claim and no categorical imperative unless the call of duty is something which calls forth our *reverence*.

We have seen that utilitarianism must always take an end for granted. The end could be other than it is. Its selection rests on caprice or, on what is the same thing, intuition. This is why utilitarian action cannot satisfy the claims of mind as reflective or rational choice.

When we come to the categorical imperative of duty, however, there is only one possible end. The doing of one's duty is obedience to the supreme categorical imperative, namely *become what you are*. In choosing to choose, mind is being itself, becoming more and more what it has it in it to be, and so actualizing further the spirit implicit within it from the start. Here mind recognizes itself as mind and determines itself by the ideal which dwells within it. It recognizes that it *ought* to determine itself by the ideal, because it has got a deeper inkling of what the ideal is, and because the ideal then calls forth what Kant rightly calls *reverence*.[1]

This is why I think that those who accept Kant's categorical imperative have already crossed a boundary and entered a realm where morality and religion join hands. Moral and religious experience are bound up together in the sense that the latter must influence the former and then that the former influences the latter. The influence seems to be reciprocal. This statement does not deny that moral experience is one thing and religious experience another. In the name of religion usages have been prescribed from which moral conviction has recoiled. And many recognize that they ought to do this or that, while at the same time they assert that they have no religion at all and are in fact its bitter opponents.

The difficulty here is to discover whether the opponents of religion have or have not one of their own. Is there *nothing* which they reverence? Today we do find around us some who reverence nothing, least of all themselves. But their moral life, if relics of it

---

[1] Cf. Hegel: It is from the recognition of a higher power that there arises the recognition of absolute duties, duties without rights; what we receive for fulfilling them is not reward but grace. *Ph. d. Rel.*, Lasson, vol. i, p 14.

persist, is moral nihilism. As soon as there are moral convictions, a recognition that there are things we ought to do, even if the ought is only an hypothetical imperative, there is present, so far as my experience goes, a reverence for something, it may be for personal integrity, or for men as sufferers, or even for animals.

Morality and religion seem to me to be bound together as closely as the concavity and the convexity of a curve. One may be described without the other, but one cannot be had without the other. Many utilitarians in ethics turn their backs on the Christian religion, or on any religion, but I am inclined to think that they have an unrecognized religion of their own. They worship what I take to be idols—like the greatest happiness of the greatest number or the well-being of mankind or men as sufferers. I say 'worship'. They would repudiate the word, but they give us no reason for accepting the end which they advocate as the goal of all beneficial means. Still less can they give any reason for supposing that respect for men as sufferers (to quote Mr Robinson's guiding principle) is a categorical imperative. Indeed Mr Robinson maintains that no rule can have a categorical justification.

And thus I come back to the justification of the categorical imperative which Kant and his followers have taken duty to be. Can it be justified on purely rational grounds as Kant thought it could?

2. DUTY NOT EXPLICABLE ON PURELY RATIONAL GROUNDS

An argument to the contrary, which I cannot but support, is advanced by Mr J. R. Silber in his introduction to a translation of Kant's *Religion within the Bounds of Reason alone*.[1]

Kant held that even the most wicked man does not repudiate the moral law, because this would be to deny his own personality, and so to lose freedom, and this is irrational. To repudiate the law is to be free, but the power to reject anything is derived from the law. Freedom is the *ratio essendi* of the obligation to obey the moral law; but respect for the law and duty to obey it is the *ratio cognoscendi* of freedom. Therefore to reject the moral law is to reject moral personality and therefore to be irrational. The unfortunate thing, however, is that strong personalities have

[1] New York, 1960

indeed rejected the moral law, without detriment to the strength of their personality and their freedom—Napoleon and Hitler can be cited as examples. The cold and calculating villain is possible; his freedom depends no doubt on his rationality, on his power to think and choose between alternatives. 'Personal fulfilment is possible for the irrational will so long as it uses the theoretical and prudential capacities of rationality to its perverse ends.' Sinning against the light is a possibility too often actualized.

We cannot show that the categorical imperative can be explained on rational grounds alone. A man may guide his life by the quest for power after power or wealth after wealth and claim that this is what he *ought* to do because this is the way to gain his end, personal satisfaction. But the 'ought' here is hypothetical. He adopts an end arbitrarily, and only if he adopts it is the choice of means obligatory. He will be a person and indeed a 'strong personality' and his quest may be conducted with the highest intelligence. Even if moral personality atrophies in this process, a demonic personality may remain, and it was this possibility that Kant denied.

It is possible to reply that this sort of quest is nevertheless irrational. On what ground is the end chosen? We can easily argue that some rules must be kept if you want goods like power or wealth. Power may be gained, but not retained, by the untrustworthy; nor is there a royal road to wealth without keeping commercial contracts.

But on what principle are the goods of any utilitarian doctrine to be selected or classified? If you fall back on fulfilment of human needs you are either back in a crude naturalism, and moral experience is thrown out of the window, or else you are forced to classify the needs of the body and distinguish them from those of the spirit, and you are at once in a realm where utilitarianism has nothing to say, and in a realm above nature where, under whatever name, religion holds sway.

We are told that man must love the highest when he sees it. This is very doubtful. Men may have seen the highest and rejected it as silly in favour of wealth or power. This is irrational if man is spirit as well as nature. It is irrational for anyone who asks *quo tendimus?*

When we read the writings of many moral philosophers, not least those of our own day, we cannot but be struck by the absence of reference to our human condition. The only certain thing in human life is that we all die. Consequently it matters not whether we die early or become centenarians; even the latter are short-lived in comparison with the time-span of our western civilization, to name no other. Surely it is a grave problem how we are to live our lives in the short time appointed to us.

'Let us eat, drink, and be merry, for tomorrow we die.' This prescription has been rejected by countless thousands. Perhaps it is less unpopular in some quarters now.

Why should it not be accepted? St Paul would have apparently accepted it but for his belief that the dead would rise again. It is not necessary to share his belief. A sufficient ground for rejection is that we are moral and spiritual beings. The aphorism suits animals but not men.

Like the animals we are doomed to an early death; but if that were the whole truth about us, it would be reasonable to make our life as comfortable as possible and to be selfish individualists, to diminish our misery but without having any reason for bothering about the lot of others.

If, being all in the same boat, we then try to diminish the misery of others, we are either back at mere feeling, a blind guide, or we are taking a different view of human life, conscious of an obligation to help others. This is reasonable only if we are not 'as the beasts that perish'.

Consciousness of obligation, or that we ought not just to eat, drink, and be merry, lifts us above the beasts, to what? To the consciousness that man is between the beasts and God and that he is the temple of the Holy Spirit. Religion will 'keep breaking in'.

Man's rise in the moral life to the conception of duty for duty's sake has gone hand in hand with his higher and higher conception of God. Moral and religious experience, though different, have been as closely interconnected as the concave and the convex in the curve.

This is still disputed. It may be argued that a scientist or a scholar has an unconditional obligation to seek the truth, and that he would be not only false to his vocation if he compromised with the truth but also he would be contradicting himself.

This is true. But a man may give up being a scientist or a philosopher. The obligation is unconditional only *if* the specific vocation is accepted and pursued. No doubt man as mind has an unconditional obligation to seek truth as well as goodness, and if a man says that he has sought truth and not found it and that he will now seek pleasure instead, he fails in his duty. But the duty derives from the fact that man is mind and not nature, that his spirit is the candle of the Lord; and this is to go beyond the sphere of nature and enter that of the supra-natural, and is this not the sphere of religion?

An ingenious attempt to preserve a categorical imperative on a basis essentially naturalistic has been made by my friend Professor Blanshard. In his *Reason and Goodness*[1] he carries me with him through his criticisms of those old and new moral philosophies which are chiefly current today, but I find it hard to follow him when he comes to construct. 'The command of duty,' he says, 'is really categorical. . . . Nature has determined that we should seek certain forms of self-fulfilment. It is only through the seeking of these ends that we have become what we are.' Thus human nature addresses to itself the categorical command: 'If you are to be what you want to be, and what you cannot help wanting to be, do this'. Some of us would say: 'Our hearts are restless till they find rest in thee.' But is this what 'we cannot help wanting'? On the contrary, if we consider only the natural desire for the thing we cannot help wanting, then we are of all men most miserable for we are just as the beasts that perish. It is only with the advance of mind that we come to say no to natural desires and discover the needs of mind itself; and on the latter it is all too easy for us to turn our back. Professor Blanshard's desires come *a tergo*, whereas what the moral life introduces us to are desires *a fronte*. He does indeed intercalate an 'if' when he writes 'if you are to be what you want to be', and this introduces an ambiguity, because it does look forward, and not just backward to 'nature'; and I wish I could interpret his reference to 'nature' as meaning not the origin but the destiny of mind; but his argument precludes this interpretation. If we are just to follow natural desires determined by nature's decree that we should seek forms of self-fulfilment, there is no acute moral problem. Morality indeed arises at that level where men see that there are things they ought to do *if* they are to be happy or to live an harmonious natural life. But the categorical imperative can come only later when conscious tension is created by an awareness at once of man's natural origin and his spiritual destiny. At that point, however, we have gone beyond nature and science into the sphere of religion.

The imperative of duty has been recognized as categorical, without any religious support by, for example, George Eliot: 'God, Duty, Immortality—how inconceivable the first, how unbelievable the third, and yet how peremptory and absolute the second.'[1] Unfortunately we are not told how this conversation proceeded or what reason she had for thinking thus of duty. Recently, however, there has been an ingenious attempt to uphold the categorical imperative on purely secular grounds.[2] Duty, we are told, is to abide by the usages of the society to which we belong. Here the imperative is categorical in the sense that it is utterly regardless of one's pleasure or advantage, of inclination or propensity, whether the usage in question is trivial, when transgression makes one a bounder; or serious, when transgression is scoundrelism. If we claim to belong to some community, its usages are a standard for us and therefore imperative. Rebels against the usages of their society rely on its protection for their other activities, and thus their mode of life is self-contradictory and indefensible.

This, however attractive, is a defence of legalism, or of Kant's association of duty with *law*. And to take account of usage as well as law may be reasonable. But, as I have argued, duty is on a level above right, and therefore above law and usage.

Mr Armstrong begins his article by quoting the story (to which I referred in Chapter 9) of Darius and the Callatiae in Herodotus, and he proceeds to accept what appears to me to be the moral scepticism of the King. Usages differ from culture to culture; are they all to be accepted as valid within the culture in question? Can they not be compared and criticized? If usage is to dictate duty, then moral reformers are wicked; their departure from usage is on the same level as that of the criminal who disregards it. Is it wrong to be unconventional?

To these questions Mr Armstrong has a reply. Moral reformers who reject a given usage do so in reliance on some more fundamental usage; for example, the prophet Micah advocates substituting

---

[1] Quoted in C. C. J. Webb: *Kant's Philosophy of Religion*, Oxford, 1926, p 85.
[2] A. MacC. Armstrong: *Usage and Duty* in *American Philosophical Quarterly*, January, 1965. I have been helped by correspondence with Mr Armstrong in which he has explained and elaborated his view.

justice for burnt offerings as the sacrifice which God requires;
he takes for granted the usage of rendering certain honours to
God and merely reinterprets the form which this usage should
take.

But, if so, then existing usage is being judged by some standard
higher than that of usage itself, and this brings us once more to the
difference of level between the right and the dutiful, the legal or
the customary and the absolutely obligatory or the sacred. The
sacred that is not also moral is only what abases us or is necessary;
while the moral which is only usage or law and not also sacred is
merely the prudent. Moral experience at its height is only one side
of the curve of which the other is religion.

3. VIRTUE AND RATIONALITY

As this is often denied it may be as well, in considering what
relation, if any, there is between morality and religion, to ask how
far, in describing our moral experience at its highest, we can get
without having recourse to religion at all.

It is necessary to emphasise the words 'at its highest' because it
is obvious, e.g. from recent writings by humanists, that they have
strong moral convictions, while they have no explicit religious
belief. It is only necessary to cite their plea for abolishing religious
instruction in schools and to acknowledge that their plea has moral
and not political grounds. Nevertheless, their moral convictions
seem to rise no higher than some form of utilitarianism, and they
may pay too little attention to the way in which, throughout history,
morality has been bound up with, though not necessarily dependent on, the ultimate beliefs which different societies at different
times have had about the nature and destiny of man.

My thesis in this chapter is that while the categorical imperative
of duty is intelligible only as an accompaniment of religious belief,
belief of some sort accompanies also those moral theories for which
moral imperatives are only hypothetical.

I take moral experience to reach its zenith in personal relations,
because it is here that we can get nearest to treating others as ends.
In the economic and political spheres we are bound by the practice
and rules and aims within them. Many relationships are on a
business footing, as we say, and so, if not wholly impersonal, still
not on the personal footing of love or friendship. If a managing

director gets too friendly with his subordinates, or with some of them, he may find himself forced to fail in his official duties. This is why those who carry responsibility are often lonely and why they are accused of being aloof by those who do not understand what carrying responsibility involves.

Now the virtues of charity, meekness, and humility are generally associated with Christian ethics, and, indeed, to some who repudiate Christianity, they may not appear as virtues at all. But can they be exhibited as required by reason, i.e. as part and parcel of moral experience as such, independently of any connection whatever with religion?

If the body, or this individual in his finite character, is the most important thing, then there is no place for meekness or humility. These are mere folly. It will be for the fittest to survive. Charity, or love of one's neighbour, will on this basis be confined to care for his material well-being. However, we have seen that the whole development of the moral life is an attempt to subdue body and become mind, to cultivate not the finite side of a man but the potential infinite, his mind and his choice. Morality bids us pursue not finite satisfactions but rational ends, to pursue morality itself and to treat men as ends and so as moral beings.

Envy, hatred, malice, selfishness, jealousy, ingratitude, the evils against which the law of the land does not operate and in which moral weakness is above all exposed, are bad personal relationships, due to ignoring the infinite and thinking in terms of finite advantage. They poison the moral order by substituting greed for charity or humility; breaking a rule is far more venial than sinning against the spirit of morality which all its rules attempt to enshrine. Escape from these evils is dependent on living life *sub specie aeternitatis*, on contrasting the poverty of our achievement with the infinite whose indwelling in us at once humiliates us and exalts us above nature, and on regarding others as minds and not bodies alone, as sharers in a common purposive rational life with a common end, the development of moral personality.

The idea of a college is that of a society of scholars pursuing learning in common and treating each other on that footing, each respecting the other's work, and not acting so as to obstruct it. But when learning is pursued as only a useful professional training or a means to professional advancement, when one man begins to regard his subject as more important or more respectable than his colleague's, then envy and the rest enter to corrupt the society, and its most striking feature is a scramble of one man against another for posts of administrative responsibility. Similarly, if marriage ceases to be a partnership for moral ends, it becomes voidable on terms, like other commercial contracts. It is when we think of our fellows as persons, with a moral life of their own, with which our own must be reconciled—for reason is at the basis of it in both cases—that charity, meekness, and humility fall into place. Morality consists in moulding the finite in accordance with the claims of the infinite. So long as the claims of reason as the infinite, as the moving spirit of our whole moral development, are ignored or set aside, some form of utilitarianism will serve as a means of organizing the mechanical side of living. But it is when we get beyond utility that morality proper begins, and *sentimus experimurque nos aeternos esse* is a possible inference from moral experience at its highest and the charter of the moral philosopher.

The moral ideal of the Kingdom of Ends is a society of moral beings devoted to moral ends, pursued through choosing to do specific duties arising out of the varying relationships in which they stand to one another. In this process the moral consciousness grows and develops and the habit of virtue, charity, humility, and so forth is cultivated. These virtues are what are expressed in a morally ordered society of moral agents. Now these virtues, as I have suggested, may be Christian. It certainly took mankind a long while to learn them. In the Old Testament the Jews are represented as being actuated by material gain; they did what they were told, because they were promised a land of milk and honey. Later their motive for keeping to their law was their pride in being an exclusive and chosen people under a special covenant with their God. They then rose to the notion of rightness and became almost enslaved to a rigorous law determining almost every feature of their life. In the East the golden rule occurs, but it does not necessarily imply humility or even charity. Plato and Aristotle, devoted to intellectual life as they were, could not get beyond a morality for a leisured class of the highly privileged Greek peoples; slaves and barbarians were outside the pale. It was Jesus who explicitly preached the virtues to which I have referred, but here I have tried to show how they are implicitly involved in the account hitherto given of moral experience. Nevertheless, whether this account extricates morality altogether from religion may be doubtful, as some of the language which I have had to adopt makes plain.

4. MR ROBINSON'S MORALITY WITHOUT RELIGION

A recent attempt to disentangle morality from religion altogether deserves mention. This is Mr Richard Robinson's book, to which I have referred several times already, *An Atheist's Values*. This is as good a defence of humanist ethics as I know. I have learnt too much from it not to treat it seriously and to explain why it has not convinced me.

Mr Robinson's ethics has the virtue of simplicity. All rules are restrictions on freedom and their only justification is that their reign will tend to alleviate misery. Human beings and the higher animals deserve respect because they all are sufferers. Morality is far from presupposing or implying religion, because religion is an evil and religious faith a vice.

'Alleviate misery', like 'seek the greatest happiness of the greatest number', may be a helpful slogan for a social reformer or a politician, and it is significant that when Mr Robinson comes to write about political goods most of what he says is sound common sense. He might decline to draw any distinction between political action and moral action, because alleviation of misery is his criterion for both. But does a theory which would assimilate moral action to political action do justice to moral experience?

Political action in a free country entails compromise. It is the pursuit of what is practicable, not of the ideal. But moral action is different. Mr Robinson does in fact sometimes recognize this himself: (*a*) he rejects a morality based on rewards and punishments on the ground that to act for a reward or in order to avoid a punishment is 'prudence and not morality' and prudence is a great virtue in a statesman; and (*b*) although he is most reluctant to elevate anything above the alleviation of misery and although he usually insists that any course of action is to be judged by its consequences, i.e. by its contribution to the alleviation of misery, he does finally say that the pursuit of knowledge and truth must override any consideration of the consequences. This would seem to imply that the pursuit of knowledge and truth is a categorical imperative for which his principle of alleviating misery provides **no** grounds.

But for that principle itself he provides no grounds either. Consequently his readers must infer that he just *sees* that his principle is valid or that he *believes* it to be valid. I would prefer to accept the second of these alternatives, because a belief can be rational, whereas mere sight or intuition is purely subjective. But Mr Robinson's diatribes against faith and belief are so strong and so frequent that it may be on intuition that he relies.

However all this may be, the pressing question is: What is this 'misery' which we are all to alleviate? If toothache be an example, then a dentist is fulfilling a moral obligation in the course of his professional work; and the politician ought perhaps not only to provide a national dental service but pass a law compelling everyone to see a dentist every few months. I suspect that Mr Robinson's love of free institutions may be at odds with his fundamental moral principle.

When the first Lord Leverhulme set out to alleviate what he regarded as the misery of the Hebrideans, he discovered that his conception of misery did not always coincide with theirs. Sorrow and pain are inevitable in human life; misery, however, is a sort of attitude to our lot. It may be alleviated by personal contact and affection, but it is hard to see how rules can be laid down for its alleviation. And yet Mr Robinson does say that 'the lessening of misery demands rules . . . rules whose reign lessens misery'.[1] He instances 'rules of good faith and sincerity and respect for others'; but even if keeping these rules did as a matter of fact lessen misery, is that the reason for keeping them? The reason may be that others *deserve* respect, and that insincerity is incompatible with self-respect, or with human dignity. Mr Robinson refers many times to human dignity and its 'demands'; and he tells us that reason commands that we love truth.[2] This seems to take us back to morality and a categorical imperative once more, but we are then told[3] that 'the dignity in every man which demands our respect seems to be mainly his capacity to suffer'. Why this capacity demands respect is not made clear, but Mr Robinson does not shirk the obvious consequence: 'all vertebrates ought equally to be respected by all men as fellow sufferers'. What remains mysterious is why this respect is to be given not to all living things (as Schweitzer has taught) but, among animals, to vertebrates or 'higher animals' only.[4]

[1] P 112.   [2] P 13.   [3] P 186.   [4] P 154.

Mr Robinson's attack on religion is violent, but instead of offering a reply I am tempted to wonder why he has not considered the extent to which religion has alleviated misery. He points out the difficulty of getting evidence to settle the question whether, with the decline of religious faith in the last two centuries, there has been a decline in morality too. But he recites evils done in the name of religion without making any enquiry into the other side of the picture. This is because he is obsessed with the idea that faith is irrational, a forcing of ourselves to believe against the evidence, and so a vice. He can quote some theologians in his defence (Luther, for example, who said in his *Table Talk*[1] that Reason is the greatest enemy that faith has), and he says, quite reasonably, that he cannot read everybody, but I could wish that instead of being a devoted fellow of Oriel and taking his quotations from Newman, he had read John Oman.

Mr Robinson discards religion because, in his view, it is an affront to reason. He never considers its contribution to the alleviation of misery, and yet, evidence might suggest that nothing has done more to alleviate human misery than the 'consolations of religion', although we must grant it to him that these have not been available to the 'higher animals'.

One of the most interesting things in Mr Robinson's book is his remark that much of the moral teaching in St Matthew's gospel is commended on the ground that those who follow it will be rewarded while those who reject it will be punished, and that therefore to accept this moral teaching is not morality but prudence. This difficulty I feel as keenly as he does. But he does not stop to expound the difference between morality and prudence or to tell us whether he is accepting Kant's distinction between counsels of prudence and the categorical imperative of morality. Even if his humanitarianism can be expressed in hypothetical imperatives, such as 'do this (or obey this rule) if you want to diminish suffering', much that he writes suggests that he thinks that we *ought* to diminish suffering; and his devotion to the pursuit of knowledge and truth has the ring of an absolute or categorical devotion. But the question then presses: How on his principles is this categorical imperative, this *ought*, to be explained? He thinks that we *ought* to pursue knowledge and truth be the consequences what they may, though he certainly hopes that the consequences

[1] Eng. tr. London, 1875, p 164.

P

will diminish suffering in the long run. But *why* ought we to take this line?

5. PROFESSOR MACLAGAN'S FRONTIER

Professor Maclagan in his *Theological Frontier of Ethics* offers an answer. He argues that morality cannot be dependent on religion and that our consciousness of absolute obligation is not, for example, a consciousness of God's command, but arises from our awareness of a group of 'objective values'. 'A genuine sense of duty cannot possibly be totally disengaged from a sense of the values that are the source of the duty: and on the other hand the sense of these values cannot be totally divorced from a sense of duty— were they so divorced they would at the same time lapse from being *desideranda* to being *desiderata* simply.'[1] Our obligation is always to do something specific, to do this rather than that; and if our preference is even to seem to ourselves to have the constrained and authoritative character that belongs to *judgment*, there is the assumption of . . . an objective 'order of values'.[2] Of these values, however, we have no 'intuitive apprehension'; we have only an 'inkling' of their existence. It is important to distinguish ideals from values. What gives the ideal a mandatory character which a 'project' does not have is the fact that ideals picture or are thought to picture a situation that somehow incarnates in the living tissue of historical process certain values. . . . Our power to create ideals implies an order of values, and only so do the ideals that we create become authoritative for us. But the values which give ideals their substance are not 'grounded in the nature of God'; they are independent of all actual purposes, though they are the objective control and standard for those purposes.[3]

This theory seems to me to be, in essence, Platonism, as Professor Maclagan seems to admit,[4] although he says that Platonic idioms are inadequate at the end. I wish I could understand it better.[5] My friend admits in his Preface[6] that certain difficult problems about the epistemology and ontology of 'value'

---

[1] *Op. cit.*, London, 1961, p 168.   [2] P 54.   [3] Pp 84–7.   [4] P 85.

[5] N. Hartmann's *Ethics*, a work that had a vogue in its day, does not further enlighten me. In his view, ethical values are not to be discovered in the conduct of man (Eng. tr., i. 99) but must first be known before conduct can be judged as good or bad. Against the objectivism of this pure transcendence I may have said enough already (see above, Chapter 6).   [6] P 10.

are indicated but not enlarged upon in his book. Although he may be right, but I do not think he is, not to be perturbed by an assertion that to use 'value' as a noun is a 'pernicious barbarism',[1] I wish he could have at least explained why it is legitimate so to extend the normal meaning of the noun (the value of a share is what a buyer will pay for it on the Stock Exchange) as to describe as a 'value' something which is 'authoritative', *desiderandum*', and the objective source of our duties. 'Value' is an expression derived from economics. Its use in ethics seems to me to be unfortunate, especially since these curious entities, objective values, are supposed to be the norm of our ideals. However, it is possible that in the last resort this is a quarrel about words, because while I know that Mr Robinson is an enemy, much of what Professor Maclagan says encourages me to think that he is an ally, despite his terminology and despite my failure to have even an inkling of a group of objective values as the authoritative source of my duties.

6. DUTY NON-NATURAL

The categorical imperative of duty, explicitly accepted by Professor Maclagan and accepted implicitly here and there, if I interpret him correctly, by Mr Robinson, is so difficult to explain that (if I may recapitulate my previous contentions) it is not surprising that attempts are made to explain it away as a delusion, the product of bad psychological training. No doubt this line of argument gains some plausibility in the light of the curious things which have been regarded as duties by fanatics, but any attempt to explain the categorical imperative away results in substituting prudence for morality, and so in making morality rest on the hypothetical imperative of utilitarianism or the like, together with an assumption that an end such as happiness or the alleviation of misery, is the natural one to seek, having regard to human beings and their condition as parts of the finite natural order. This is no solution. The natural order is something that exists *for* the mind. It is an object for mind, an object which implies a subject. Mind does come to knowledge of itself through its knowledge of the object and through reflection on that knowledge. Nature however is always the realm of externality—everything in it is outside its

[1] P 54 fn.

neighbour—while mind is just what triumphs over this externality in that it attains to self-knowledge, though only after a process through which, after leaving the innocence of the Garden of Eden, or after self-alienation, it develops its self-reflective capacities. Only so does it create natural science, which is not and cannot be itself natural; as an attempt to understand nature it does not stand outside it, because as external it could only be natural all over again; on the contrary, as the truth of nature it is part and parcel of mind. Consequently, an end supposed to be 'natural' is one that mind can only reject. On these terms the categorical imperative cannot be explained away. It is an essential ingredient of a morality developed by the advance of reflection, and so reasonable and not natural.

7. LOVE AS TRANSCENDING DUTY

A quite different method of dealing with the categorical imperative of duty is to deny its ultimate validity and to urge that duty must go the way of pleasure, right, and utility. It is alleged that there is a higher moral level still. The sternness of duty, its fight against impulse, must be superseded by the spontaneity of love.

This, in effect, is an invitation to go beyond morality to religion, or beyond the morality of duty to a morality whose ultimate sanction lies in the love of God and submission to the divine will. The difficulty here is that morality seems to be absorbed into religion altogether. The contention is that the good life is the one which gives full scope to generous impulse and not the one which is hag-ridden by observance of an irrefragable law. But the contention is to be saved from sentimentality only on the assumption that the love on which it relies is love not only, or even primarily, love of our neighbour, but love of God who is love.

This contrast between love and duty has never been expressed more powerfully than by Hegel in his essay on *The Spirit of Christianity*. Kant had pointed out that between a life morally ordered by the priests of Siberian tribes in the East and by Bishops and Puritans in the West there was a great difference in manner but none in principle; the laity took their orders; they were not obeying the law of their own reason and therefore were not free. This, Hegel implies, is just like the Pharisees; they obeyed every jot and tittle of the law. But, as Hegel goes on to say, the man who is free in Kant's sense is free only because his reason masters his appetites. He is a man who lords it over himself: '... the man who listens to the command of duty carries his lord in himself, yet at the same time is his own slave'. 'One who wished to restore humanity in its entirety [to harmonize inclination with reason] could not have followed Kant in saying "act out of respect for duty and contradict inclinations" because this 'would tack on to man's distraction of mind an obdurate conceit'. Consequently Jesus seeks to fulfil the law. This fulfilment is an inclination to act as the law commands, i.e. the law loses its form as law. The opposition of duty to inclination has found its unification in the modifications of love, i.e. in the virtues.'[1] The implication of this seems to be that the virtuous man acts in accordance with the law of duty without any constraint. Love fulfils the law automatically and does not abrogate it.

But in any case, what love is this? *Dilige et fac quod vis*, said St Augustine. But this is, in his mouth, a *religious* precept. If you love God, then 'do what you will', because your love of God will automatically produce compliance with his will; loving him, you will not choose to will otherwise than in accordance with his commands. Thus the proposal to supersede Kant with the teaching of Jesus is an invitation to go beyond the morality of pure reason alone, to a morality suffused by religion, an invitation which, in later years, Hegel seems to have declined.

It may indeed be argued that parents who love their children make sacrifices for them with no thought of law or duty, and that the sacrifices would not be virtuous if they were the product of a sense of duty alone and not of a warm and loving heart as well. And a similar argument may be used of a relationship of husband and wife, or even of a man and his friends. Love, however, in itself may be self-indulgent or over-indulgent. Love without the guidance and the background of moral principle never held a marriage together or secured the moral welfare of children.

Lady Oppenheimer in her persuasive *Law and Love*[2] argues that although some rules are necessary in family life, especially for children's education, it is love and not rule or the thought of duty which holds the family together and is the source of the conduct of its members. The fundamental idea of justice must be firmly established; only on this basis can the love which transcends

---

[1] Eng. tr., Chicago, 1948, pp 211–25.   [2] London, 1962.

justice be properly built. But while rules help family life to run
smoothly, the motive power must be supplied by love. Lady
Oppenheimer is concerned with Christian ethics and she is using
the family as an helpful analogy. Her real point is that love is what
God requires; that rules are only a *praeparatio evangelica*; that we
should love our neighbour and be prepared for the exceptions to
rules which love will demand. If mankind were united in love as
God's children, that would be the Kingdom of Heaven. It is clear
that this transcendence of rigorism is basically religious. Without
moral principle or the religion which Lady Oppenheimer professes, love is a blind guide.

A devotion to duty need not lack the spontaneity of affection,
and a constant thought of duty easily declines into moral Pharisaism. This is the answer to those who say that the quest for moral
goodness, like the quest for pleasure or happiness, is self-defeating.
D. M. Baillie believed that the attempt to be moral leads to
Pharisaism instead of to real goodness.[1] But this would be true only
if morality itself required us to be thinking of it all the time, or to
be patting ourselves on the back and saying 'what a good boy am
I.' But it does not. On the contrary, the curious thing is that what
the moral man is conscious of is failing in his duty. To put the
point on a lower level, a man who is paid a salary for doing his
professional work does not, if he is a reasonable and moral man,
ask himself every night whether he has earned his salary, or
whether, having succeeded that day in some special endeavour, he
should be paid more; what does trouble him is a *failure* which may
make him ask himself whether his salary has been earned.

8. RELIGIOUS AND MORAL BELIEFS

How can a religious man who believes in God as Truth and
Goodness and a loving Heavenly Father help having his moral life
determined by this belief? I do not know how Professor Maclagan
would answer this question. He writes about moral experience as
if it could be 'divided at the joints' from religion. He seems to
think that you can have a morality dictated by objective values
without religion at all, although religious faith may in various ways
help a man to abide by such a morality. This may be his retort to
Mr Robinson, and if so they will dispute with one another *ad*

[1] *God was in Christ*, London, 1948, p 121.

infinitum. In this situation, I have two things to urge: first, any moral system rests on or implies belief of some kind; secondly, if a morality of the categorical imperative does not actually rest on a religious belief, it coheres with it and is perhaps intelligible only in association with it.

9. CONTENT OF MORAL SYSTEMS

In speaking of a 'moral system', it is necessary to distinguish between its form and its content. Three different forms have already come before us: hypothetical imperatives, categorical imperatives, and love. By content I mean the actions enjoined by or issuing from these forms. Whichever form be adopted, acceptance of faith of some kind is implied, and the content is determined by faith too. It is possible, however, for agreement on form to be accompanied by disagreement on content, and *vice versa*.

If we study the writings of moralists whose work has been chiefly influential in moulding opinion in this country during the last two or three centuries, we cannot but be struck by the fact that despite all their differences about the form of morality, they are substantially in agreement about its content. They all state or imply that certain actions, as for example lying and murder, are wrong and certain other actions, as for example promise-keeping and justice, are right. Controversies have arisen not about the rightness of promise-keeping (to abide by a single example, by now all too familiar) but only about the reasons for supposing it to be right, or about the kind of obligation it is, or about how far the rule that promises ought to be kept permits of exceptions. Interest in these controversies may have led us to overlook the underlying agreement and to neglect to scrutinize the reasons for its existence.

In recent years, however, this agreement, at least in certain spheres of moral experience, appears to be diminishing. Eminent ecclesiastics in South London have argued, for example, that extra-marital sexual intercourse is not necessarily wrong, and they have been accused of attacking *morality*. This charge they repudiate. It is only part of the content of a moral system that they are attacking. Similarly when young people today are accused by their elders of immoral conduct or of lacking moral standards, their defenders are quick to point out that even if the young reject some of the content of the moral system of their elders they are neither immoral nor amoral; they believe passionately in loyalty and frankness and they despise hypocrisy (though they do not tell us or ask themselves why). Their belief is not reasoned but passionate. What this new morality (if it be rightly so called) denies is not the difference between right and wrong; it denies the rightness of certain specific actions which our moral teachers in this country have believed, though for different reasons, to be right. What is being challenged is not morality so much as the morality of our nineteenth century; and the challenge forces us to look behind the differences between Kant and Mill, Paley and Sir David Ross, and to examine the reasons for their basic agreement about the content of morality.

The system of moral conduct now thus challenged has been built up on two main foundations. The first is theological; divines have taught that the moral law is the law of God. Certain actions have been enjoined and others banned by God's decree and men have been persuaded to obedience by the fear of eternal punishment or the hope of eternal reward, and since he is changless from and to all eternity, so is his will and his decree. It follows that the moral law is one and unalterable throughout history. The second foundation is the attempt to apply scientific methods to conduct and therefore the attempt to discover a moral almanac as certain and as little liable to historical change as the nautical almanac. If the theological foundation enters philosophy through Butler and Paley, the scientific one is already present in Locke who alleged that a science of morals could be constructed as unassailable as the science of geometry, and it appears again in Hume's attempt to construct a science of human nature. Blended with theological elements, it appears once more in Kant's belief that ethics must be constructed absolutely *a priori* and be valid not for any specific age or nation but for all rational beings.

Both theology and classical physics have sought to expound the character of something eternally unalterable. It is this theologico-scientific background of our moral system which has led us to take for granted the immutability of that system, and to see in a revolt against *our* morality a revolt against morality itself. In other words, we have forgotten that ethics is a theory of conduct or of action and therefore a theory of historical events, and by our exclusion of history from the moral sphere we have distorted the picture and so left ourselves helpless against the defiance of what we take to be morality. We are committed, it would seem, to a non-historical moral system, and history takes vengeance upon us for our neglect by producing the modern challenge to our moral principles and beliefs. The challenge is not to be met by arguments about whether promise-keeping is right because it is God's will or because it is productive of the interest of mankind, for these beg the question at issue; nor is it to be met by an analysis of the concepts of right and good, for such an analysis concentrates attention once more on concepts not actions, on science not history. The historical challenge itself implies that these concepts have a history and a growth, and the attempt to analyse them as if they were static entities like a tetrahedron is inevitably to look asquint upon them and so to fail in any attempt by such a scrutiny to save 'morality' once it is denied.

The destruction of 'morality' or to give this historical phenomenon a less misleading name, the death of one moral system and the birth of another, is no new phenomenon; and we might have little difficulty in seeing that it is this phenomenon which now confronts us, if we had attended more carefully to similar phenomena in the past and so not made the mistake of supposing that, e.g., promise-keeping was one of the 'Foundations of Ethics' instead of one integral moment of a specific economic or social or moral system. In fact, as a closer examination will show, the foundation of any ethical system is not the concept of good or the idea of duty or the quest for pleasure; these are all part of the superstructure. The foundation is always a faith, and an ethical system dies when the faith on which it rests or with which it coheres is no longer believed. Faith here includes not only a religious belief but also belief in the principles which underlie the whole social order or 'culture'. Loss of faith at any given time will befall some believers but not others, and those who still cling to the dying faith will accuse the unbelievers of immorality. The Pharisees saw in the teaching of Jesus the defiance of God's law, the destruction of the established moral code, and the conflict between Jesus and the Pharisees is not like the conflict e.g. between Kant and Mill where there is agreement on the content of morality and a dispute only on its form (however important that be); it is not a conflict which might arise between two Jewish rabbis about what the will of God is on some specific issue. On the contrary, it is a conflict between two different conceptions of God and therefore a conflict of both form and content of morality. On the one hand we have a belief in Jehovah, the jealous God of a chosen people, a God who exacts sacrifices and requires implicit obedience to every jot and tittle of his commands. The result is an ethics of convention and external observance, coupled with a legitimate pride in being a Jew and in fulfilling the law. On the other hand there is a belief in a God of love, in whose eyes all men are equal, a God to be approached with contrition of heart and whose laws are made for man. From such a belief is derived an ethics of love for which motive is more important than externals and in which humility is substituted for pride. If all men are equal in God's eyes, pride is sin, and if God is love and goodness, sinful man is in duty bound to humble himself.

In both these cases the moral system, however it may be supported by arguments drawn from revelation, or the welfare of man, or the conception of a good society, or the adaptation of moral precepts to man's nature and so forth, rests ultimately upon a religious belief about the nature of God and of man's relation to him. And Christianity conquered Europe as Judaism did not, simply because the Christian God was accepted and Jehovah was rejected. To this day the Jew, in so far as he remains true to his traditional faith and has not been assimilated to the traditions of the Christian peoples among whom he lives, is apt to be a stranger and an alien, misunderstood or feared or distrusted if not persecuted, because the basic presuppositions of his life differ from those of the Christians among whom he has made his home. Beneath all superficial differences, there is more kinship between the ethics of Moses and that of Islam than between that of either of them and Christianity, because the God of Mahomet too is a jealous God, the God of a chosen people, a unity and not a trinity; and the ethical principles consequential upon a belief in Allah are therefore similar in form to those derived from the faith in Jehovah even if they are accompanied by a different content.

Two further examples may be quoted in order to indicate that fundamental moral changes are rooted in changes of belief. (a) To an advocate of the mediaeval church and state, the destroyers of those institutions appeared to be immoralists, flouting not any one moral principle, but the whole of established morality. It could not be otherwise; if certain institutions are believed to be sacrosanct, any attempt to reform them must seem to be sacrilege. Hence it is not surprising that Machiavelli urges his Prince to break all the laws of God and man and has in consequence incurred for himself the charge of immorality. And yet Machiavelli is an enemy not of morality but only of that system which based morality on service to Church and State and not on the welfare of the people. For it is to save the people that the Prince is to act; mediaeval institutions had ossified until they resembled Plato's *Republic* rather than the City of God; and Machiavelli sounds the keynote of the modern world in insisting on the satisfaction and freedom of the private individual instead of his enslavement to an objective institution. Here again, the ethical consequences flow from a change in belief; in religious belief, from the Reformation; in beliefs about man and society, from the Renaissance. To make claims for the sanctity of the individual, to abolish the hierarchical distinction between priest and layman, appeared to the Reformers to be to enter at last into the fullness of the Christian inheritance, while the Renaissance brought back into Europe the inheritance of Greece.

(*b*) It was a common complaint on the West Coast of Africa when I worked there that the least trustworthy employee was a native clerk educated in a Christian Mission school. Why? It is easier to produce doubt than to implant a new faith; and mission teaching always runs the risk of being a solvent of the old faith before producing an understanding of the new. With the death of the old faith goes the loss of the ethics which accompanied it and the result is that the native boy has forsaken the moral life of his own people without yet having won his way either into the religious beliefs or the ethical tradition of his English employer. And for a time at least the boy is an ethical nihilist, a renegade in the eyes of his own people, a rascal to his employer, and it is no wonder that under the disfavour of his associates, black and white alike, he becomes a political agitator or the editor of a subversive newspaper. The immoralism of the Christian educated clerk is not, like Machiavelli's, the result of the substitution of a new faith for an old; it is rather the rejection of an old faith, the failure to assimilate the new one despite its responsibility for that rejection, and consequently the adoption of the Mephistophelean spirit of denial. This may be the plight of some young people today, and we cannot forget the sad history of some African states which have won independence in recent years.

For a clear instance of the unacknowledged debt of ethics to religious faith, we may turn to the pages of Mill's *Utilitarianism*.

Mill himself was a 'rationalist', avowedly a disbeliever in revealed religion, and it is therefore natural to expect that in *his* ethics, if anywhere, we might find a moral philosophy built on a purely philosophical or argumentative foundation. But it is notorious that the transition in his book from the selfish pursuit of personal pleasure to the altruistic quest of the greatest happiness of the greatest number depends on an illogicality which ought not to have deceived even an elementary class in logic. To the questions: Why be unselfish? Why seek the good of others?, Mill has no answer. He takes it for granted that the general interest is the moral end and that all will agree with him that the pursuit of this end is obviously right. He remarks that the teaching of Utilitarianism here is in harmony with the precept of Jesus: love thy neighbour as thyself; but it does not seem to occur to him that it is from the teaching of Jesus that the utilitarian end is derived. Mill was educated as an agnostic; but his father, a Scotsman, had been brought up in a Calvinist atmosphere and been early indoctrinated with the precepts and practice of Christian ethics. He was in fact trained for the ministry. The son's character was educated on the same lines except that the religious principles, on which rested his life of self-discipline and self-sacrifice for social ends, were ignored. And it is for this reason that Utilitarianism requires us to aim at an end which its author is powerless to justify. He takes its validity for granted without realizing the fact; and he is still further from realizing that by his rejection of the Christian religion he is rejecting the matrix from which his altruistic morality and his liberal politics grew, without trying to provide some other matrix instead.

Kant is in no better case. He claims that the foundations of ethics must be wholly *a priori* and derived purely and simply from the nature of a rational being. But the rational being, he holds, is an end in itself, and yet if we inspect his reasons for this view, we find that they are no reasons at all. He believes that every individual soul is of unique value, and he believes this because it is the teaching of the New Testament, transmitted to him through his upbringing in German Pietism. Again, it is a commonplace of Kantian criticism that he is only enabled to show that certain actions are self-contradictory and therefore, on his principles, wrong, by first of all assuming as valid a certain system of nature with which such actions conflict. Theft for instance is doubtless wrong if private property is presupposed to be right, but there is no logical contradiction in a conception of a kingdom of ends from which private property is absent. Or to take a different instance, self-love, he holds, impels us to the improvement of life; hence if self-love impels us to suicide because life has become miserable, self-love is in this instance opposing itself to itself, and therefore suicide is self-contradictory and wrong. The argument has been criticized but it may be not unfair to say that Kant believes that suicide is wrong because he has been taught so by the church. In fact, suicide is an excellent example of the difficulty of deriving ethical principles from 'pure reason alone'. By this method the Stoics reach one conclusion, Kant another. The different position recently of suicide in the legal systems of England and Scotland is also instructive. It is hard to see what reason can be alleged for believing suicide to be wrong except a reason based on the religious belief that God alone, the giver of a person's life, may take it away. To be one's own executioner is to deny one's dependence on God and to usurp his function.

Contemporary ethics has been equally unable to escape from dependence on religion, although it has become customary to use language which obscures this fact. We have often read of a goodness whose character we simply intuit, of *prima facie* obligations which we simply see to be obligations if we reflect. In the writings of Professor Moore and Sir David Ross—whose influence on English moral philosophy has not yet been wholly superseded by the work of linguistic analysts—we read nothing whatever of the debt of ethics to religion, though much of its debt to common sense or 'the moral consciousness'. We are reminded of Mill's 'verdict of competent judges', i.e. of reflective men who can discriminate between higher and lower pleasures. There is no hint here of any realization that 'common sense' is a repository of beliefs derived it may be from religion or it may be from the philosophy of the past, and that these dictates of the moral consciousness may be those of the writer but perhaps may not be universally shared. In fact we are here again confronted by a background of belief masquerading as 'intuition' and so given a veneer of authority and exempted from examination. On the inadequacy of intuitionist theories of conduct I had something to say earlier. But I add one further consideration here.

If we examine the writings of intuitionists and observe the list of

obligations which they see to be *prima facie* binding, we are sure to
be struck by the fact that, although they profess to be intuitions of
objective realities as universal and necessary as those of mathematics, they are in fact conditioned throughout by their historical
setting. The lists of goods are those which we should expect to find
in the cloistered life of a university: the obligations are those
arising from e.g. a Christian upbringing or from the belief in social
responsibilities characteristic of nineteenth-century radicalism.
What is strikingly absent from the work of intuitionists is the
strain and stress of moral doubts, the experience of being harried
by temptation, the conception of action as creative initiative
instead of as the choice between alternatives fixed from the start.
In short, the intuitions are not insights into objective truths, but
the assertion in a dogmatic form of the beliefs in which the
intuitionist has been educated and which have now become part
and parcel of his life. In that sense they are indeed for him objective
realities, for they are the texture of the world as he knows it. But
they cannot claim exemption from the criticism of others who live
in a different world; they cannot claim like the objects of mathematical study to be outside the historical series; they cannot claim
to be infallible certainties. They are matters of faith, and if they
are to be upheld against those whose intuitions are different, that
fact must be recognized.

10. MORAL AND RELIGIOUS BELIEFS CHIME IN WITH ONE ANOTHER

It is the same man who is moral and religious (or irreligious).
Moral and religious beliefs chime in with one another. I think this
is so because while religions inculcate a morality (and sometimes a
queer one), moral systems imply religious beliefs (sometimes odd
beliefs). But if, as I think, a moral system rests on or implies belief,
what is the belief in question? Need it be *religious* belief? It is
necessary to consider separately beliefs underlying the content of
morality, and beliefs underlying the three forms which I have
distinguished.

For some people the content of morality is simply what God
wills or commands, for others it depends on a belief in certain
objective and authoritative values. This belief is not obviously
religious, and Professor Maclagan for example, in some moods,

would strongly hold that it was not religious at all, but he also avers that genuine moral commitment is religious in quality, because religion means, at least, the supreme development of the moral will.[1] A moral content derived from the authority of objective values thus seems to be inseparable from a religious belief. On the other hand those who, like Professor Kemp, regard the purpose of morality as securing an harmonious social life, will derive the content of morality from a study of fact. But then the question of what we ought to do will again be a question of fact, because on any given occasion we will have to do what as a matter of fact will contribute to an harmonious social life. This we must repudiate, following Professor Paton in his Gifford Lectures: 'What does not remain open is the possibility that knowledge of what I do or you do, of what bees, ants or robins do . . . can be, or be a substitute for, any kind of moral judgment.'[2]

This I take Professor Kemp to reject, because, on his view, actions, rules, principles, will be morally justified if in fact they contribute to social harmony, or, as Mr Robinson would say, to the alleviation of suffering. Here there is a denial of all transcendence. Human beings are part of an order of nature. A belief in human dignity or in the individual as deserving of respect is legitimate if it helps to secure harmony, and so forth, but can have no other justification. The belief that the purpose of morality is to promote harmony is still just a belief; to call it a religious belief may seem to be extravagant, and yet a belief which is the negation of religion turns out to be but faith in a different religion, perhaps in the worship of humanity. Without such a worship Mr Robinson's ethics becomes unintelligible. He believes in human dignity because we are all sufferers, but a consciousness that we are all in the same boat doomed to the same destruction is no ground for respecting our companions. It may suggest to us that to fight one another is futile and not sensible, but this falls far short of respecting one another or believing in one another's dignity. In reading *The Last Chronicle of Barset* we may pity the Perpetual Curate of Hogglestock, but we have no reason to *respect* him unless we have a faith that all men are equally children of God. Finally, to derive the content of morality from love leaves us asking love of whom? The answers can only be: (i) our families and friends, but this leads to the moral chaos of sacrificing to the

[1] *Op. cit.*, pp 183–4.　　[2] *The Modern Predicament*, London, 1955, p 316.

interests of our few loved ones the interests of everyone else; or (ii) the love of God, and this is religious belief; or (iii) love of our fellow men, which takes us once more to the religion of humanitarianism.

11. FORM OF MORAL SYSTEMS

Consideration of the form of morality leads to a similar result. The three forms are: the spontaneity of love, the hypothetical imperative, and the categorical imperative. If the first be not the love of God, then its implications are the same as those of the hypothetical imperative. The latter implies a morality of prudence: if you wish to be happy or at peace with your neighbours, do so and so, or alternatively develop your own nature. Mr Rhymes[1] defends this sort of attitude on religious grounds: 'I believe that the whole idea of the higher and lower in man is misleading; it denies the validity of Christ's Incarnation'. Others defend it on grounds that are not obviously religious at all. But if all imperatives were hypothetical it would be more important for science to be useful than true; and on what can be based the belief that there are no valid categorical imperatives? The basis can only be a conception of what human life is and of what man's place in the universe is. The 'Free Man's Worship' with its defiance of man's wretched fate, is a worship after all, even if it be only the Free Man's worship of his own mind or unconquerable soul. And with the notion of worship we are back at religion. Even Mr Robinson cannot dispense altogether with religion because he wants 'ceremonies' as a support to his non-religious ethics.[2]

12. THE CATEGORICAL IMPERATIVE

The categorical imperative is an absolute *thou shalt*; it implies absolute devotion. And the realm of nature will not provide us with any absolute. It can provide the finite alone, for nature is the realm of finitude. The experience of duty as something with an absolute claim upon us implies a belief in the infinite. I appeal to the experience; the defence of the categorical imperative as the summit of morality, propounded by Kant, has never been so effectively upheld as by Professor Paton whose *Categorical Imperative* has never been answered, let alone refuted. But,

[1] *Sunday Telegraph*, January 5, 1964.   [2] *Op. cit.*, p 157.

assuming the experience of this imperative, and its moral worth, what does it involve and imply? In the first place it is reasonable; we would not be ourselves if we did not hear and obey the call which is binding on us, not as creatures of nature or as sufferers, but as thinkers. Secondly, it would be foolish to seek knowledge if it were not to be had or to be scientists if the universe were not intelligible. Our quest for truth implies that we believe in the intelligibility of nature, so that, as I have urged earlier, the universals are implicit within it waiting to be actualized by becoming known. And the same is true of morality. Either we are deluded or else we live in a moral world, a world not alien to a moral quest. And we cannot reasonably say that we are deluded here, because if we were deluded here we would be deluded everywhere. Truth would be as unattainable as moral worth. The quest for truth and the call of duty both involve absolute claims, and the absoluteness is there, faintly, in ourselves as the call of ourselves, as self-conscious agents and thinkers, to realize more completely this presence of the infinite within our finitude. Moral advance, like the advance of knowledge, is the discovery of reality.

Confronted with a duty we are confronted with something absolute which we are constrained to obey, although in obeying we find ourselves perfectly free, free from nature, free in the life of reason, free in the service of the ideal. Mere knowledge of the ideal will not produce action but only contemplation. I have tried to describe how we rise from desires for we know not what, to rational choice. We do not leave desire behind, but it becomes a desire for the fulfilment of the higher self. We are conscious of a tension between what we are and what we might be, and this produces the desire to make ourselves different and better. But this happens only because the ideal is not purely transcendent; it is partly realized in us already. My admiration of medical skill leads to no action on my part, for I have no such skill of my own. But a man's ability to play the piano to some extent will encourage him to try hard to play it better. In politics too, the effective ideals are those which have been partially realized already; utopianism merely produces the fanaticism which is the very opposite of effective political action. Being good to some extent, to however slender an extent, we discipline our desires towards becoming better, towards realizing less inadequately what we already have it in ourselves to become.

Q

I have spoken of an ideal to which duty implies an absolute devotion. What is this ideal? It is very differently conceived by people of diverse beliefs. For some it is themselves, or self-culture; for others it is humanity, with a consequent humanitarianism and efforts to alleviate suffering or increase happiness. Others again make the ends of evolution their ideal, and others still give all their devotion to animals.

But it is difficult to find rational grounds for an absolute devotion to self, to animals, to other human beings, or the ends of evolution. It might be said that it was reasonable enough to devote ourselves to what we love, and love of self or animals or humanity or science may be a powerful enough director of action. But love can never be a ruler of a moral life, unless indeed it be the love of God. No one has put this more plainly or more persuasively than Professor Paton.[1] Between a good man and a good-natured man there is a significant difference. Generous emotions may not accord with what an objective situation demands.

An absolute devotion to finite objects or to an unknown God, like the ends of evolution, or even to objective 'values', is to worship idols and so is a superstition which indeed is the implication of some moral systems. But the absolute devotion which duty involves implies the conception of an ideal by which we ought to orientate our lives and which is partially realized in our own moral life already. This chimes in with—I do not say rests on or even implies—devotion to a God conceived as good and true, as a loving Heavenly Father.

That any moral system must chime in with religious belief (or with that belief which overtly negates what it calls religion, but only implies another one) is obvious enough in history. For example, we have seen in our own time in this country a growth in material prosperity and a decline in the hold which organized religion has on the people. The growth in material prosperity has been aided by the teachings of certain moralists and certain psychologists who have denied transcendence and urged us to concentrate on ways of alleviating human misery; the categorical imperative has been denied, by theologians as well as by others. The curious thing is that prudence has been taught from the pulpit, with many quotations from St Matthew's Gospel about obtaining reward and avoiding punishment, while this is repudiated by humanists like

[1] *Categorical Imperative*, London, 1946, pp 52-5.

Mr Robinson who yet believe in a categorical imperative to pursue knowledge and truth. At the same time this stern element in Mr Robinson's doctrine is set aside by other humanists who concentrate on fulfilling our nature or seeking happiness and so on moral rules which are all hypothetical—do this if you want that. Once this Gospel is preached, it is no wonder if material prosperity becomes the aim, if a true moral endeavour is set aside, and the worship of an idol, wealth or ease or the like, is substituted for the worship of God. A culture is never wholly homogeneous; it will contain progressive and recessive elements; but it will always have a central core of which its religion and its morality are mutually supporting facets. It is less irrational to worship God than to worship abstractions like the goal of evolution or a Platonic form or finite ends such as types of human welfare, because in the last resort it may be to a person alone that a reasonable man can give his whole devotion and reverence. This is not to give reason a regulator outside itself, because it means that our reason is regulating itself by the infinite in which it shares and which it so imperfectly enshrines. The finite is the infinite's self-limitation. Moreover the wisdom and goodness of man is but the flickering light in him of the wisdom and goodness of God himself.

Without this use of religious language I cannot make intelligible and rational the unconditional character of duty. John Laird may not have been wrong to suggest that 'consistent Kantians must bring divinity into their ethics'.[1]

[1] *Op. cit.*, p 106.

INDEX

GEORGE ALLEN & UNWIN LTD
London: 40 Museum Street, WC1

Auckland: PO Box 36013, Northcote Central, N4
Barbados: PO Box 222, Bridgetown
Beirut: Deeb Building, Jeanne d'Arc Street
Bombay: 15 Graham Road, Ballard Estate, Bombay 1
Buenos Aires: Escritorio 454-459, Florida 165
Calcutta: 17 Chittaranjan Avenue, Calcutta 13
Cape Town: 68 Shortmarket Street
Hong Kong: 105 Wing On Mansion, 26 Hancow Road, Kowloon
Ibadan: PO Box 62
Karachi: Karachi Chambers, McLeod Road
Madras: Mohan Mansions, 38c Mount Road, Madras 6
Mexico: Villalongin 32, Mexico 5, DF
Nairobi: PO Box 30583
New Delhi: 13-14 Asaf Ali Road, New Delhi 1
Ontario: 81 Curlew Drive, Don Mills
Philippines: PO Box 4322, Manila
Rio de Janeiro: Caixa Postal 2537-Zc-00
Singapore: 36c Prinsep Street, Singapore 7
Sydney: NSW: Bradbury House, 55 York Street
Tokyo: PO Box 26, Kamata

PHILOSOPHY OF SPACE AND TIME

MICHAEL WHITEMAN

A mathematician who is also a mystic is exceptionally well qualified to survey the mysterious subject of space and time. Dr Whiteman, Associate Professor of Applied Mathematics at Cape Town University and author of *The Mystical Life*, brings the mathematician's detachment and the mystic's insight to this book and presents the most thorough treatment of space and time yet seen. For the expert he provides an indispensable textbook likely to stand unchallenged for many years; for the intelligent layman, an opening into an absorbing field of knowledge, in a world where religious beliefs about the nature of the universe have lost their authority, but interest in the infinite is at its greatest.

PHILOSOPHY OF WHITEHEAD

W. MAYS

Whitehead stands out among modern philosophers by his depth of vision and wide range of interests. This book effectively demonstrates that his thought has a much greater consistency and precision than is usually assumed. The author convincingly argues that the key to the understanding of Whitehead's philosophical system is to be found rather in his earlier philosophy of science than in traditional philosophy. He contends that logical, mathematical and physical ideas, as well as descriptions of direct experience, play an essential role in Whitehead's later thought. On the one hand, this book gives a critical exposition of the main concepts of Whitehead's philosophy as seen in their scientific perspective. On the other, it clarifies his treatment of specific philosophical problems, such as the nature of sense-perception. causality, free-will and the body-mind problem. In this way the author throws a new light on those features of Whitehead's system which have puzzled philosophers for three decades.

HEGEL: A RE-EXAMINATION
J. N. FINDLAY

This book attempts a critical reinterpretation of Hegel's idealism and his dialectical method, and stresses their connection with many contemporary philosophical ideas and methods. It also seeks to give a comprehensive statement of Hegel's system, with sufficient clearness to be of some use to the layman, and enough detail to assist the student of Hegel's difficult writings. After three introductory chapters, dealing mainly with Hegel's notion of *Geist* (Spirit) and his notion and use of Dialectic, it covers the contents of the *Phenomenology of Spirit*, the *Science of Logic*, the *Philosophy of Nature*, and then deals with Hegel's Psychology, his theory of Law, Morals, the State and History, and finally with his treatment of "Absolute Spirit" i.e. Art, Religion and Philosophy.

PHILOSOPHY AND RELIGION
ALEX HÄGERSTRÖM

During the first half of the twentieth century an anti-metaphysical philosophy grew up at Uppsala University in Sweden. The founder of the movement was Alex Hägerström, although the development of its distinctive ideas was the composite achievement of a number of extremely capable philosophers, not the least of whom was Adolf Phalen.

The Uppsala philosophy had a profound impact on Swedish thought, which has become almost universally anti-metaphysical in the twentieth century. American and British positivism, however, was all but oblivious to the Scandinavian movement. This failure of communication was especially unfortunate from the Anglo-American side, for the approach of the Swedish positivists was much more judicious than that of the Vienna circle. The Swedish philosophers might have shown how positivism could avoid the mistakes which have brought it into general disrepute.

Philosophical discussion has been returning to the problem of metaphysics, albeit now with more of a historical interest. The present volume represents a perhaps belated attempt to introduce into this discussion the distinctive ideas and approaches of the Swedish school, the consideration of which is so long overdue.

PHILOSOPHY AND ILLUSION
MORRIS LAZEROWITZ

The main object of this book of essays, as of its two predecessors, is to improve our understanding of technical philosophy. The central enigma of philosophy, which has caused deep disquiet in many thinking people, is that nothing in it ever gets settled; rival philosophical views and their arguments remain suspended in thin air, without finding a secure resting place. The essays may be considered as contributions towards answering a question raised by Hans Reichenbach: 'Why must philosophers forego a generally accepted philosophy?' The explanatory hypothesis that the author puts forward about the peculiar linguistic character of philosophical views and arguments, will be recognized as having its roots in Ludwig Wittgenstein's later thought. Some readers of Wittgenstein distinguish between the 'false philosophy, in his work and other parts of it which they find more congenial to their own thinking. Wittgenstein's 'false philosophy' falls into what Professor Lazerowitz calls 'Metaphilosophy' and it holds out promise of an enlightening answer to Reichenbach's question. The essays of this book have the unity of a single orientation, the development of a hypothesis which will give us insight into the workings of philosophy.

NEW SHAPES OF REALITY
MARTIN JORDAN

A. N. Whitehead was a major philosopher of great originality. His work touches all our preoccupations, from the nature of society to the destiny of man. On the subject of God it reads sometimes like a technical commentary on the books of Pierre Teilhard de Chardin, although there is no evidence that Whitehead had any knowledge of the latter, Unfortunately Whitehead was obscure—too obscure even for his one-time collaborator, Lord Russell, who confesses as much in his recent Autobiography. Also Whitehead fared poorly in academic circles because his work looked too much like old-fashioned metaphysics to be congenial in the twentieth-century climate.

Now there are signs of a Whitehead revival. The author, who has been fascinated by Whitehead for a quarter of a century, has written this book to encourage the trend.

THE PHILOSOPHERS OF GREECE
ROBERT S. BRUMBAUGH

This brilliant survey of the key ideas of Greek Philosophy covers a period and scene unmatched by any other. It was a time when the germinal forces of Western culture were formulated by the world's great classical thinkers. It was the age of Thales, Anaximenes, Empedocles, Heraclitus, Parmenides, Zeno, Anaxagoras, the Sophists, Plato and Aristotle. It produced the great philosophical writings of metaphysics, cosmology, politics and logic—a unique record of man's use of reason to explain the world about him.

As Dr Brumbaugh traces the evolution of Greek Philosophy, the reader sees his own familiar world emerge from the mist of myth which surrounded the ancients. "What is real?" asked Thales, the great inventor and engineer, who sparked the systematic development of natural science. Following Anaximander, who extended the law to the physical world, came Pythagoras and his followers with the discovery of pure mathematics.

It was Socrates who was to introduce the second major question into Western Philosophy: 'What am I?'

His question led to a new phase of inquiry and inspired new approaches to politics and education. Endeavouring to answer both Thales and Socrates, Plato and Aristotle brought together all the earlier insights into two great speculative systems.

THE RELEVANCE OF WHITEHEAD
I. LECLERC

This collection of essays marks the centenary of the birth of Alfred North Whitehead. The continuing influence and significance of Whitehead's thought is exemplified in the way in which the various writers, who do not constitute a particular school, approach their chosen topic of enquiry. While a few devote themselves specifically to the assessment or criticism of aspects of Whitehead's work, others develop Whiteheadian themes and suggestions and still others follow their own lines of thought to which Whitehead has been relevant.

THE DISCIPLINE OF THE CAVE
J. N. FINDLAY

These lectures are the First Series of a course of Gifford Lectures whose Second Series was given in December 1965–January, 1966 and is entitled *The Transcendence of the Cave*. The Second Series will continue the theme of the First Series and will be essential to its complete understanding.

The lectures make use of the Paltonic image of the Cave to emphasize the fact that men feel their familiar experience to be full of many and strange restrictions, and to involve puzzles and discrepancies which they do not even see the possibility of solving and removing. Deep-set philosophical perplexities of this sort can be seen as arising out of the misunderstanding and meaningless abuse of ordinary ways of thinking and speaking. But they can equally be seen, in the Platonic phrase, as 'drawing us towards being', providing an apagogical proof of the 'absurdity' of ordinary thought, speech and experience except as modified and supplemented in ways which may point altogether beyond it. What may be called a mystical and otherworldly element, and a graded series of experiences in which it is enjoyed, may therefore need to be introduced into or rendered explicit in all our experience action and diction, not as some gratuitous modification or addition, but in order to give a viable sense to the most commonplace human utterances and activities. The presuppositions of such a manner of reasoning of course involve much fundamental criticisn and revision of contemporary conceptions of language, logic and meaning and of their relation to experience and to the teaching of the use of words.

ESSAYS IN ANALYSIS
ALICE AMBROSE

The essays in this book are addressed to problems in logic and foundations of mathematics, metaphysics and epistemology. The problems are all root-problems in their fields, and range from questions concerning our knowledge of the external world to questions about logical entailment, mathematical proof, induction.

GEORGE ALLEN & UNWIN LTD